UNIX® System V

User's Reference Manual

UNIX® System V

User's Reference Manual

AT&T

Prentice-Hall, Inc., Englewood Cliffs, NJ 07632

Library of Congress Catalog Card Number: 87-60148

Editorial/production supervision: Karen S. Fortgang
Cover illustration: Jim Kinstry
Manufacturing buyer: S. Gordon Osbourne

Printed in the United States of America

10 9 8 7 6 5 4 3 2 1

ISBN 0-13-940487-2 025

Prentice-Hall International (UK) Limited, *London*
Prentice-Hall of Australia Pty. Limited, *Sydney*
Editora Prentice-Hall do Brasil, Ltda., *Rio de Janeiro*
Prentice-Hall of Canada Inc., *Toronto*
Prentice-Hall Hispanoamericana, S.A., *Mexico*
Prentice-Hall of India Private Limited, *New Delhi*
Prentice-Hall of Japan, Inc., *Tokyo*
Prentice-Hall of Southeast Asia Pte. Ltd., *Singapore*

Table of Contents

UNIX® System V

User's Reference Manual

Introduction

This *User's Reference Manual* describes the commands that constitute the basic software running on the AT&T 3B2 Computer.

Several other documents contain other valuable information:

- The *User's Guide* (P-H) presents an overview of the UNIX system and tutorials on how to use text editors, automate repetitive jobs, and send information to others.
- The *Programmer's Guide* (P-H) presents an overview of the UNIX system programming environment and tutorials on various programming tools.
- The *Programmer's Reference Manual* (P-H) describes commands, system calls, subroutines, libraries, and file formats needed by programmers.
- The *System Administrator's Guide* (AT&T) provides both procedures for and explanations of administrative tasks.
- The *System Administrator's Reference Manual* (AT&T) describes the commands used by system administrators.

While the commands are each part of a specific utility, they appear, in alphabetical order, in a single section of this document called "Commands." The various utilities represented in this section are as follows:

1. AT&T Windowing Utilities
2. Basic Networking Utilities
3. Cartridge Tape Controller Utilities
4. Directory and File Management Utilities
5. Editing Utilities
6. Essential Utilities
7. Graphics Utilities
8. Help Utilities
9. Inter-process Communications
10. Line Printer Spooling Utilities
11. Performance Measurement Utilities
12. Security Administration Utilities
13. Spell Utilities
14. Terminal Filters Utilities
15. Terminal Information Utilities
16. User Environment Utilities

Security Administration Utilities are expressly provided for U. S. customers.

Section 1: Commands

The entries in Section 1 describe programs intended to be invoked directly by the user or by command language procedures, as opposed to subroutines, which are called by the user's programs. Commands generally reside in the directory **/bin** (for **bin**ary programs). In addition, some programs reside in **/usr/bin**. These directories are searched automatically by the command interpreter called the *shell*. UNIX systems running on the 3B2 Computer also have a directory called **/usr/lbin**, containing local commands.

The numbers following the command are intended for easy cross-reference. A command followed by a **(1)**, **(1C)**, or **(1G)** usually means that it is contained in this manual. (Section 1 commands appropriate for use by programmers are located in the *Programmer's Reference Manual* (P-H).) A command with a **(1M)**, **(7)**, or **(8)** following it means that the command is in the appropriate section of the *System Administrator's Reference Manual* (AT&T). A command with a **(2)**, **(3)**, **(4)**, or **(5)** following it means that the command is in the appropriate section of the *Programmer's Reference Manual* (P-H).

Each entry in the Commands section appears under a single name shown at the upper corners of its page(s). Entries are alphabetized, with the exception of the *intro*(1) entry, which is first. Some entries may describe several commands. In such cases, the entry appears only once, alphabetized under its "primary" name, the name that appears at the upper corners of the page. The "secondary" commands are listed directly below their associated primary command.

All entries are presented using the following format (though some of these headings might not appear in every entry):

- **NAME** gives the primary name (and secondary name(s), as the case may be) and briefly states its purpose.
- **SYNOPSIS** summarizes the usage of the program being described. A few explanatory conventions are used, particularly in the **SYNOPSIS**:
  - **Boldface** strings are literals and are to be typed just as they appear.

- *Italic* strings usually represent substitutable argument prototypes and command names found elsewhere in the manual.
- Square brackets **[ ]** around an argument prototype indicate that the argument is optional. When an argument prototype is given as "name" or "file," it always refers to a *file* name.
- Ellipses **...** are used to show that the previous argument prototype may be repeated.
- A final convention is used by the commands themselves. An argument beginning with a minus **(–)**, plus **(+)**, or an equal sign **(=)** is often taken to be some sort of flag argument, even if it appears in a position where a file name could appear. Therefore, it is unwise to have files whose names begin with –, +, or =.

- **DESCRIPTION** discusses how to use these commands.
- **EXAMPLE(S)** gives example(s) of usage, where appropriate.
- **FILES** contains the file names that are referenced by the program.
- **EXIT CODES** discusses values set when the command terminates. The value set is available in the shell environment variable '?' (see sh(1)).
- **NOTES** gives information that may be helpful under the particular circumstances described.
- **SEE ALSO** offers pointers to related information.
- **DIAGNOSTICS** discusses the error messages that may be produced. Messages that are intended to be self-explanatory are not listed.
- **WARNINGS** discusses the limits or boundaries of the respective commands.
- **BUGS** lists known faults in software that have not been rectified. Occasionally, a suggested short-term remedy is also described.

Preceding Section 1 is a "Table of Contents" (listing both primary and secondary command entries). Each line of the "Table of Contents" lists an abstract of the command.

How to Get Started

This discussion provides the basic information you need to get started on the UNIX system: how to log in and log out, how to communicate through your terminal, and how to run a program. (See the *User's Guide* (P-H) for a more complete introduction to the system.)

Logging In

You must connect to the UNIX system from a full-duplex ASCII terminal. You must also have a valid login id, which may be obtained (together with how to access your UNIX system) from the administrator of your system. Common terminal speeds are 120, 240, 480, and 960 characters per second (1200, 2400, 4800, and 9600 baud). Some UNIX systems have different ways of accessing each available terminal speed, while other systems offer several speeds through a common access method. In the latter case, there is one "preferred" speed; if you access it from a terminal set to a different speed, you will be greeted by a string of meaningless characters (the **login:** message at the wrong speed). Keep hitting the "break," "interrupt," or "attention" key until the **login:** message appears.

Most terminals have a speed switch that should be set to the appropriate speed and a half-/full-duplex switch that should be set to full-duplex. When a connection has been established, the system types **login:**. You respond by typing your login id followed by the "return" key. If you have a password, the system asks for it but will not print, or "echo," it on the terminal. After you have logged in, the "return," "new-line," and "line-feed" keys all have equivalent meanings.

Make sure you type your login name in lower-case letters. Typing upper-case letters causes the UNIX system to assume that your terminal can generate only upper-case letters and will treat all letters as upper-case for the remainder of your login session. The shell will print a **$** on your screen when you have logged in successfully.

When you log in, a message-of-the-day may greet you before you receive your prompt. For more information, consult *login*(1), which discusses the login sequence in more detail, and *stty*(1), which tells you how to describe your terminal to the system. *profile*(4) (in the *Programmer's Reference Manual* (P-H)) explains how to accomplish this last task automatically every time you log in.

Logging Out

There are two ways to log out:

- If you've dialed in, you can simply hang up the phone.
- You can log out by typing an end-of-file indication (ASCII **EOT** character, usually typed as "**CONTROL-D**") to the shell. The shell will terminate, and the **login:** message will appear again.

How to Communicate Through Your Terminal

When you type to the UNIX system, your individual characters are being gathered and temporarily saved. Although they are echoed back to you, these characters will not be given to a program until you type a "return" (or "newline") as described above in "Logging In."

UNIX system terminal input/output is full duplex. It has full read-ahead, which means that you can type at any time, even while a program is typing at you. Of course, if you type during output, your input characters will have output characters interspersed among them. In any case, whatever you type will be saved and interpreted in the correct sequence. There is a limit to the amount of read-ahead, but it is generous and not likely to be exceeded.

The character **@** cancels all the characters typed before it on a line, effectively deleting the line. (**@** is called the line kill character.) The character **#** erases the last character typed. Successive uses of **#** will erase characters back to, but not beyond, the beginning of the line; **@** and **#** can be typed as themselves by preceding them with \ (thus, to erase a \, you need two **#**s). These default erase and line kill characters can be changed; see *stty*(1).

CONTROL-S (also known as the ASCII **DC3** character) is typed by pressing the control key and the alphabetic **s** simultaneously and is used to stop output temporarily. It is useful with CRT terminals to prevent output from disappearing before it can be read. Output is resumed when a **CONTROL-Q** (also known as **DC1**) is typed. Thus, if you had typed **cat yourfile** and the contents of **yourfile** were passing by on the screen more rapidly than you could read it, you would type **CONTROL-S** to freeze the output for a moment. Typing **CONTROL-Q** would allow the output to resume its rapid pace. The **CONTROL-S** and **CONTROL-Q** characters are not passed to any other program when used in this manner.

The ASCII **DEL** (a.k.a. "rubout") character is not passed to programs but instead generates an *interrupt signal,* just like the "break," "interrupt," or "attention" signal. This signal generally causes whatever program you are running to terminate. It is typically used to stop a long printout that you do not want. Programs, however, can arrange either to ignore this signal altogether or to be notified and take a specific action when it happens (instead of being terminated). The editor *ed*(1), for example, catches interrupts and stops what *it* is doing, instead of terminating, so an interrupt can be used to halt an editor printout without losing the file being edited.

Besides adapting to the speed of the terminal, the UNIX system tries to be intelligent as to whether you have a terminal with the "new-line" function, or whether it must be simulated with a "carriage-return" and "line-feed" pair. In the latter case, all *input* "carriage-return" characters are changed to "line-feed" characters (the standard line delimiter), and a "carriage-return" and "line-feed" pair is echoed to the terminal. If you get into the wrong mode, the *stty*(1) command will rescue you.

Tab characters are used freely in UNIX system source programs. If your terminal does not have the tab function, you can arrange to have tab characters changed into spaces during output, and echoed as spaces during input. Again, the *stty*(1) command will set or reset this mode. The system assumes that tabs are set every eight character positions. The *tabs*(1) command will set tab stops on your terminal, if that is possible.

How to Run a Program

When you have successfully logged into the UNIX system, a program called the shell is communicating with your terminal. The shell reads each line you type, splits the line into a command name and its arguments, and executes the command. A command is simply an executable program. Normally, the shell looks first in your current directory (see "The Current Directory" below) for the named program and, if none is there, then in system directories, such as **/bin** and **/usr/bin**. There is nothing special about system-provided commands except that they are kept in directories where the shell can find them. You can also keep commands in your own directories and instruct the shell to find them there. See the manual entry for *sh*(1), under the sub-heading "Parameter Substitution," for the discussion of the **$PATH** shell environment variable.

The command name is the first word on an input line to the shell; the command and its arguments are separated from one another by space or tab characters.

When a program terminates, the shell will ordinarily regain control and give you back your prompt to indicate that it is ready for another command. The shell has many other capabilities, which are described in detail in *sh*(1).

The Current Directory

The UNIX system has a file system arranged in a hierarchy of directories. When you received your login id, the system administrator also created a directory for you (ordinarily with the same name as your login id, and known as your *login* or *home* directory). When you log in, that directory becomes your *current* or *working* directory, and any file name you type is, by default, assumed to be in that directory. Because you are the owner of this directory, you have full permissions to read, write, alter, or remove its contents. Permissions to enter or modify other directories and files will have been granted or denied to you by their respective owners or by the system administrator. To change the current directory, use *cd*(1).

Pathnames

To refer to files or directories not in the current directory, you must use a pathname. Full pathnames begin with /, which is the name of the *root* directory of the whole file system. After the slash comes the name of each directory containing the next sub-directory (followed by a /), until finally the file or directory name is reached (e.g., **/usr/ae/filex** refers to file **filex** in directory **ae**, while **ae** is itself a subdirectory of **usr**, and **usr** is a subdirectory of the root directory). Use *pwd*(1) to print the full pathname of the directory you are working in. See *intro*(2) in the *Programmer's Reference Manual* (P-H) for a formal definition of *pathname*.

If your current directory contains subdirectories, the pathnames of their respective files begin with the name of the corresponding subdirectory (*without* a prefixed /). A pathname may be used anywhere a file name is required.

Important commands that affect files are *cp*(1), *mv* (see *cp*(1)), and *rm*(1), which respectively copy, move (i.e., rename), and remove files. To find out the status of files or directories, use *ls*(1). Use *mkdir*(1) for making directories and *rmdir* (see *rm*(1)) for removing them.

Text Entry and Display

Almost all text is entered through an editor. Common examples of UNIX system editors are *ed*(1) and *vi*(1). The commands most often used to print text on a terminal are *cat*(1), *pr*(1), and *pg*(1). The *cat*(1) command displays the contents of ASCII text files on the terminal, with no processing at all. The *pr*(1) command paginates the text, supplies headings, and has a facility for multi-column output. The *pg*(1) command displays text in successive portions no larger than your terminal screen.

Writing a Program

Once you have entered the text of your program into a file with an editor, you are ready to give the file to the appropriate language processor. The processor will accept only files observing the correct naming conventions: all C programs must end with the suffix **.c**, and Fortran programs must end with **.f**. The output of the language processor will be left in a file named **a.out** in the current directory, unless you have invoked an option to save it in another file. (Use *mv*(1) to rename **a.out**.) If the program is written in assembly language, you will probably need to load library subroutines with it (see *ld*(1) in the *Programmer's Reference Manual* (P-H)).

When you have completed this process without provoking any diagnostics, you may run the program by giving its name to the shell in response to the **$** prompt. Your programs can receive arguments from the command line just as system programs do; see *exec*(2) in the *Programmer's Reference Manual* (P-H). For more information on writing and running programs, see the *Programmer's Guide* (P-H).

Communicating with Others

Certain commands provide *inter-user* communication. Even if you do not plan to use them, it would be well to learn something about them because someone else may try to contact you. *mail*(1) or *mailx*(1) will leave a message whose presence will be announced to another user when he or she next logs in and at periodic intervals during the session. To communicate with another user currently logged in, *write*(1) is used. The corresponding entries in this manual also suggest how to respond to these two commands if you are their target.

See the tutorials in Chapter 8 of the *User's Guide* (P-H) for more information on communicating with others.

NAME

intro — introduction to commands and application programs

DESCRIPTION

This section describes, in alphabetical order, commands available for the AT&T 3B2 Computer. Certain distinctions of purpose are made in the headings.

The following Utility packages are delivered with the computer:

AT&T Windowing Utilities
Basic Networking Utilities
Cartridge Tape Controller Utilities
Directory and File Management Utilities
Editing Utilities
Essential Utilities
Graphics Utilities
Help Utilities
Inter-process Communications
Line Printer Spooling Utilities
Performance Measurement Utilities
Security Administration Utilities
Spell Utilities
Terminal Filters Utilities
Terminal Information Utilities
User Environment Utilities

The following Utility Packages are available for purchase:

Networking Support Utilities
Remote File Sharing Utilities

Manual Page Command Syntax

Unless otherwise noted, commands described in the **SYNOPSIS** section of a manual page accept options and other arguments according to the following syntax and should be interpreted as explained below.

name [−*option*...] [*cmdarg*...]
where:

[ ] Surround an *option* or *cmdarg* that is not required.

... Indicates multiple occurrences of the *option* or *cmdarg*.

name The name of an executable file.

option (Always preceded by a "−".)
noargletter... or,
argletter optarg[,...]

noargletter A single letter representing an option without an option-argument. Note that more than one *noargletter* option can be grouped after one "−" (Rule 5, below).

argletter A single letter representing an option requiring an option-argument.

optarg An option-argument (character string) satisfying a preceding *argletter*. Note that groups of *optargs* following an *argletter* must be separated by commas, or separated by white space and quoted (Rule 8, below).

cmdarg Path name (or other command argument) *not* beginning with "–", or "–" by itself indicating the standard input.

Command Syntax Standard: Rules

These command syntax rules are not followed by all current commands, but all new commands will obey them. *getopts*(1) should be used by all shell procedures to parse positional parameters and to check for legal options. It supports Rules 3-10 below. The enforcement of the other rules must be done by the command itself.

1. Command names (*name* above) must be between two and nine characters long.
2. Command names must include only lower-case letters and digits.
3. Option names (*option* above) must be one character long.
4. All options must be preceded by "–".
5. Options with no arguments may be grouped after a single "–".
6. The first option-argument (*optarg* above) following an option must be preceded by white space.
7. Option-arguments cannot be optional.
8. Groups of option-arguments following an option must either be separated by commas or separated by white space and quoted (e.g., `-o xxx,z,yy` or `-o "xxx z yy"`).
9. All options must precede operands (*cmdarg* above) on the command line.
10. "––" may be used to indicate the end of the options.
11. The order of the options relative to one another should not matter.
12. The relative order of the operands (*cmdarg* above) may affect their significance in ways determined by the command with which they appear.
13. "–" preceded and followed by white space should only be used to mean standard input.

SEE ALSO

getopts(1).
exit(2), wait(2), getopt(3C) in the *Programmer's Reference Manual.*
How to Get Started, at the front of this document.

DIAGNOSTICS

Upon termination, each command returns two bytes of status, one supplied by the system and giving the cause for termination, and (in the case of "normal" termination) one supplied by the program [see *wait*(2) and *exit*(2)]. The former byte is 0 for normal termination; the latter is customarily 0 for successful execution and non-zero to indicate troubles such as erroneous parameters, or bad or inaccessible data. It is called variously "exit code", "exit status", or "return code", and is described only where special conventions are involved.

WARNINGS

Some commands produce unexpected results when processing files containing null characters. These commands often treat text input lines as strings and therefore become confused upon encountering a null character (the string terminator) within a line.

NAME

300, 300s – handle special functions of DASI 300 and 300s terminals

SYNOPSIS

300 [**+12**] [**−n**] [**−d**t,l,c]

300s [**+12**] [**−n**] [**−d**t,l,c]

DESCRIPTION

The *300* command supports special functions and optimizes the use of the DASI 300 (GSI 300 or DTC 300) terminal; *300s* performs the same functions for the DASI 300s (GSI 300s or DTC 300s) terminal. It converts half-line forward, half-line reverse, and full-line reverse motions to the correct vertical motions. In the following discussion of the *300* command, it should be noted that unless your system contains the DOCUMENTER'S WORKBENCH Software, references to certain commands (e.g., *nroff, neqn, eqn,* etc.) will not work. It also attempts to draw Greek letters and other special symbols. It permits convenient use of 12-pitch text. It also reduces printing time 5 to 70%. The *300* command can be used to print equations neatly, in the sequence:

neqn file ... **|** nroff **|** 300

WARNING: if your terminal has a PLOT switch, make sure it is turned *on* before *300* is used.

The behavior of *300* can be modified by the optional flag arguments to handle 12-pitch text, fractional line spacings, messages, and delays.

+12 permits use of 12-pitch, 6 lines/inch text. DASI 300 terminals normally allow only two combinations: 10-pitch, 6 lines/inch, or 12-pitch, 8 lines/inch. To obtain the 12-pitch, 6 lines per inch combination, the user should turn the PITCH switch to 12, and use the **+12** option.

−n controls the size of half-line spacing. A half-line is, by default, equal to 4 vertical plot increments. Because each increment equals 1/48 of an inch, a 10-pitch line-feed requires 8 increments, while a 12-pitch line-feed needs only 6. The first digit of *n* overrides the default value, thus allowing for individual taste in the appearance of subscripts and superscripts. For example, *nroff* half-lines could be made to act as quarter-lines by using **−2**. The user could also obtain appropriate half-lines for 12-pitch, 8 lines/inch mode by using the option **−3** alone, having set the PITCH switch to 12-pitch.

−d*t,l,c* controls delay factors. The default setting is **−d3,90,30**. DASI 300 terminals sometimes produce peculiar output when faced with very long lines, too many tab characters, or long strings of blankless, non-identical characters. One null (delay) character is inserted in a line for every set of *t* tabs, and for every contiguous string of *c* non-blank, non-tab characters. If a line is longer than *l* bytes, 1+(total length)/20 nulls are inserted at the end of that line. Items can be omitted from the end of the list, implying use of the default values. Also, a value of zero for *t* (*c*) results in two null bytes per tab (character). The former may be needed for C programs, the latter for files like **/etc/passwd**. Because terminal behavior varies according to the specific characters printed and the load on a system, the user may have to experiment with these values to get correct output. The **−d** option exists only as a last resort for those few cases that do not otherwise print properly. For example, the file **/etc/passwd** may be printed using **−d3,30,5**. The value **−d0,1** is a good one to use for C programs that have many levels of indentation.

Note that the delay control interacts heavily with the prevailing carriage return and line-feed delays. The *stty*(1) modes **nl0 cr2** or **nl0 cr3** are recommended for most uses.

The *300* command can be used with the *nroff* **−s** flag or **.rd** requests, when it is necessary to insert paper manually or change fonts in the middle of a document. Instead of hitting the return key in these cases, you must use the line-feed key to get any response.

In many (but not all) cases, the following sequences are equivalent:

```
nroff −T300 files ...    and   nroff files ... | 300
nroff −T300−12 files ...   and   nroff files ... | 300 +12
```

The use of *300* can thus often be avoided unless special delays or options are required; in a few cases, however, the additional movement optimization of *300* may produce better-aligned output.

The *neqn* names of, and resulting output for, the Greek and special characters supported by *300* are shown in *greek*(5).

SEE ALSO

450(1), mesg(1), graph(1G), stty(1), tabs(1), tplot(1G).
eqn(1), nroff(1), tbl(1) in the *DOCUMENTER'S WORKBENCH Software 2.0 Technical Discussion and Reference Manual*
greek(5) in the *Programmer's Reference Manual.*

BUGS

Some special characters cannot be correctly printed in column 1 because the print head cannot be moved to the left from there.
If your output contains Greek and/or reverse line-feeds, use a friction-feed platen instead of a forms tractor; although good enough for drafts, the latter has a tendency to slip when reversing direction, distorting Greek characters and misaligning the first line of text after one or more reverse line-feeds.

NAME

4014 − paginator for the Tektronix 4014 terminal

SYNOPSIS

4014 [**−t**] [**−n**] [**−c**N] [**−p**L] [file]

DESCRIPTION

The output of *4014* is intended for a Tektronix 4014 terminal; *4014* arranges for 66 lines to fit on the screen, divides the screen into *N* columns, and contributes an eight-space page offset in the (default) single-column case. Tabs, spaces, and backspaces are collected and plotted when necessary. Teletype Model 37 half- and reverse-line sequences are interpreted and plotted. At the end of each page, *4014* waits for a new-line (empty line) from the keyboard before continuing on to the next page. In this wait state, the command **!***cmd* will send the *cmd* to the shell.

The command line options are:

−t Do not wait between pages (useful for directing output into a file).

−n Start printing at the current cursor position and never erase the screen.

−c*N* Divide the screen into *N* columns and wait after the last column.

−p*L* Set page length to *L*; *L* accepts the scale factors **i** (inches) and **l** (lines); default is lines.

SEE ALSO

pr(1), tc(1).
troff(1) in the *DOCUMENTER'S WORKBENCH Software Release 2.0 Technical Discussion and Reference Manual.*

NAME

450 − handle special functions of the DASI 450 terminal

SYNOPSIS

450

DESCRIPTION

The *450* command supports special functions of, and optimizes the use of, the DASI 450 terminal, or any terminal that is functionally identical, such as the Diablo 1620 or Xerox 1700. It converts half-line forward, half-line reverse, and full-line reverse motions to the correct vertical motions. It also attempts to draw Greek letters and other special symbols in the same manner as *300*(1). It should be noted that, unless your system contains DOCUMENTER'S WORKBENCH Software, certain commands (e.g., *eqn*, *nroff*, *tbl*, etc.) will not work. Use *450* to print equations neatly, in the sequence:

neqn file ... | nroff | 450

WARNING: make sure that the PLOT switch on your terminal is ON before *450* is used. The SPACING switch should be put in the desired position (either 10- or 12-pitch). In either case, vertical spacing is 6 lines/inch, unless dynamically changed to 8 lines per inch by an appropriate escape sequence.

Use *450* with the *nroff* **−s** flag or **.rd** requests when it is necessary to insert paper manually or change fonts in the middle of a document. Instead of hitting the return key in these cases, you must use the line-feed key to get any response.

In many (but not all) cases, the use of *450* can be eliminated in favor of one of the following:

nroff −T450 files ...

or

nroff −T450−12 files ...

The use of *450* can thus often be avoided unless special delays or options are required; in a few cases, however, the additional movement optimization of *450* may produce better-aligned output.

The *neqn* names of, and resulting output for, the Greek and special characters supported by *450* are shown in *greek*(5).

SEE ALSO

300(1), mesg(1), stty(1), tabs(1), graph(1G), tplot(1G).
eqn(1), nroff(1), tbl(1) in the *DOCUMENTER'S WORKBENCH Software Release 2.0 Technical Discussion and Reference Manual.*
greek(5) in the *Programmer's Reference Manual.*

BUGS

Some special characters cannot be correctly printed in column 1 because the print head cannot be moved to the left from there.
If your output contains Greek and/or reverse line-feeds, use a friction-feed platen instead of a forms tractor; although good enough for drafts, the latter has a tendency to slip when reversing direction, distorting Greek characters and misaligning the first line of text after one or more reverse line-feeds.

NAME

ar − archive and library maintainer for portable archives

SYNOPSIS

ar key [posname] afile [name] ...

DESCRIPTION

The *ar* command maintains groups of files combined into a single archive file. Its main use is to create and update library files as used by the link editor. It can be used, though, for any similar purpose. The magic string and the file headers used by *ar* consist of printable ASCII characters. If an archive is composed of printable files, the entire archive is printable.

When *ar* creates an archive, it creates headers in a format that is portable across all machines. The portable archive format and structure is described in detail in *ar*(4). The archive symbol table [described in *ar*(4)] is used by the link editor [*ld*(1)] to effect multiple passes over libraries of object files in an efficient manner. An archive symbol table is only created and maintained by *ar* when there is at least one object file in the archive. The archive symbol table is in a specially named file which is always the first file in the archive. This file is never mentioned or accessible to the user. Whenever the *ar*(1) command is used to create or update the contents of such an archive, the symbol table is rebuilt. The **s** option described below will force the symbol table to be rebuilt.

Unlike command options, the command key is a required part of *ar*'s command line. The key (which may begin with a −) is formed with one of the following letters: **drqtpmx**. Arguments to the *key*, alternatively, are made with one or more of the following set: **vuaibcls**. *Posname* is an archive member name used as a reference point in positioning other files in the archive. *Afile* is the archive file. The *names* are constituent files in the archive file. The meanings of the *key* characters are as follows:

d Delete the named files from the archive file.

r Replace the named files in the archive file. If the optional character **u** is used with **r**, then only those files with dates of modification later than the archive files are replaced. If an optional positioning character from the set **abi** is used, then the *posname* argument must be present and specifies that new files are to be placed after (**a**) or before (**b** or **i**) *posname*. Otherwise new files are placed at the end.

q Quickly append the named files to the end of the archive file. Optional positioning characters are invalid. The command does not check whether the added members are already in the archive. This option is useful to avoid quadratic behavior when creating a large archive piece-by-piece. Unchecked, the file may grow exponentially up to the second degree.

t Print a table of contents of the archive file. If no names are given, all files in the archive are tabled. If names are given, only those files are tabled.

p Print the named files in the archive.

m Move the named files to the end of the archive. If a positioning character is present, then the *posname* argument must be present and, as in **r**, specifies where the files are to be moved.

x Extract the named files. If no names are given, all files in the archive are extracted. In neither case does **x** alter the archive file.

The meanings of the key arguments are as follows:

v Give a verbose file-by-file description of the making of a new archive file from the old archive and the constituent files. When used with **t**, give a long listing of all information about the files. When used with **x**, precede each file with a name.

c Suppress the message that is produced by default when *afile* is created.

l Place temporary files in the local (current working) directory rather than in the default temporary directory, *TMPDIR*.

s Force the regeneration of the archive symbol table even if *ar*(1) is not invoked with a command which will modify the archive contents. This command is useful to restore the archive symbol table after the *strip*(1) command has been used on the archive.

FILES

*$TMPDIR/** temporary files

$TMPDIR is usually /usr/tmp but can be redefined by setting the environment variable **TMPDIR** [see *tempnam*() in *tmpnam*(3S)].

SEE ALSO

ld(1), lorder(1), strip(1), tmpnam(3S), a.out(4), ar(4)

NOTES

If the same file is mentioned twice in an argument list, it may be put in the archive twice.

NAME

at, batch − execute commands at a later time

SYNOPSIS

at *time* [*date*] [+ *increment*]
at −*r* job...
at -*l* [*job* ...]

batch

DESCRIPTION

at and *batch* read commands from standard input to be executed at a later time. *at* allows you to specify when the commands should be executed, while jobs queued with *batch* will execute when system load level permits. *at* may be used with the following options:

−r Removes jobs previously scheduled with *at*.

−l Reports all jobs scheduled for the invoking user.

Standard output and standard error output are mailed to the user unless they are redirected elsewhere. The shell environment variables, current directory, umask, and ulimit are retained when the commands are executed. Open file descriptors, traps, and priority are lost.

Users are permitted to use *at* if their name appears in the file **/usr/lib/cron/at.allow**. If that file does not exist, the file **/usr/lib/cron/at.deny** is checked to determine if the user should be denied access to *at*. If neither file exists, only root is allowed to submit a job. If **at.deny** is empty, global usage is permitted. The allow/deny files consist of one user name per line. These files can only be modified by the superuser.

The *time* may be specified as 1, 2, or 4 digits. One and two digit numbers are taken to be hours, four digits to be hours and minutes. The time may alternately be specified as two numbers separated by a colon, meaning *hour*:*minute*. A suffix **am** or **pm** may be appended; otherwise a 24-hour clock time is understood. The suffix **zulu** may be used to indicate GMT. The special names **noon**, **midnight**, **now**, and **next** are also recognized.

An optional *date* may be specified as either a month name followed by a day number (and possibly year number preceded by an optional comma) or a day of the week (fully spelled or abbreviated to three characters). Two special "days", **today** and **tomorrow** are recognized. If no *date* is given, **today** is assumed if the given hour is greater than the current hour and **tomorrow** is assumed if it is less. If the given month is less than the current month (and no year is given), next year is assumed.

The optional *increment* is simply a number suffixed by one of the following: **minutes**, **hours**, **days**, **weeks**, **months**, or **years**. (The singular form is also accepted.)

Thus legitimate commands include:

at 0815am Jan 24
at 8:15am Jan 24
at now + 1 day
at 5 pm Friday

at and *batch* write the job number and schedule time to standard error.

batch submits a batch job. It is almost equivalent to "at now", but not quite. For one, it goes into a different queue. For another, "at now" will respond with the error message **too late**.

at **-r** removes jobs previously scheduled by *at* or *batch*. The job number is the number given to you previously by the *at* or *batch* command. You can also get job numbers by typing *at* **-l**. You can only remove your own jobs unless you are the super-user.

EXAMPLES

The *at* and *batch* commands read from standard input the commands to be executed at a later time. *sh*(1) provides different ways of specifying standard input. Within your commands, it may be useful to redirect standard output.

This sequence can be used at a terminal:

batch
sort *filename* >*outfile*
<control-D> (hold down 'control' and depress 'D')

This sequence, which demonstrates redirecting standard error to a pipe, is useful in a shell procedure (the sequence of output redirection specifications is significant):

batch <<!
sort *filename* 2>&1 >*outfile* | mail *loginid*
!

To have a job reschedule itself, invoke *at* from within the shell procedure, by including code similar to the following within the shell file:

echo "sh *shellfile*" | at 1900 thursday next week

FILES

/usr/lib/cron	main cron directory
/usr/lib/cron/at.allow	list of allowed users
/usr/lib/cron/at.deny	list of denied users
/usr/lib/cron/queue	scheduling information
/usr/spool/cron/atjobs	spool area

SEE ALSO

kill(1), mail(1), nice(1), ps(1), sh(1), sort(1).
cron(1M) in the *System Administrator's Reference Manual*.

DIAGNOSTICS

Complains about various syntax errors and times out of range.

NAME

awk – pattern scanning and processing language

SYNOPSIS

awk [**–Fc**] [prog] [parameters] [files]

DESCRIPTION

awk scans each input *file* for lines that match any of a set of patterns specified in *prog*. With each pattern in *prog* there can be an associated action that will be performed when a line of a *file* matches the pattern. The set of patterns may appear literally as *prog*, or in a file specified as **–f** *file*. The *prog* string should be enclosed in single quotes (') to protect it from the shell.

Parameters, in the form x=... y=... etc., may be passed to *awk*.

Files are read in order; if there are no files, the standard input is read. The file name – means the standard input. Each line is matched against the pattern portion of every pattern-action statement; the associated action is performed for each matched pattern.

An input line is made up of fields separated by white space. (This default can be changed by using FS; see below). The fields are denoted **$1**, **$2**, ...; **$0** refers to the entire line.

A pattern-action statement has the form:

```
pattern { action }
```

A missing action means print the line; a missing pattern always matches. An action is a sequence of statements. A statement can be one of the following:

```
if ( conditional ) statement [ else statement ]
while ( conditional ) statement
for ( expression ; conditional ; expression ) statement
break
continue
{ [ statement ] ... }
variable = expression
print [ expression-list ] [ >expression ]
printf format [ , expression-list ] [ >expression ]
next    # skip remaining patterns on this input line
exit    # skip the rest of the input
```

Statements are terminated by semicolons, new-lines, or right braces. An empty expression-list stands for the whole line. Expressions take on string or numeric values as appropriate, and are built using the operators +, –, *, /, %, and concatenation (indicated by a blank). The **C** operators ++, ––, +=, –=, *=, /=, and %= are also available in expressions. Variables may be scalars, array elements (denoted x[i]) or fields. Variables are initialized to the null string. Array subscripts may be any string, not necessarily numeric; this allows for a form of associative memory. String constants are quoted (").

The *print* statement prints its arguments on the standard output (or on a file if >*expr* is present), separated by the current output field separator, and terminated by the output record separator. The *printf* statement formats its expression list according to the format [see *printf*(3S) in the *Programmer's Reference Manual*].

The built-in function *length* returns the length of its argument taken as a string, or of the whole line if no argument. There are also built-in functions *exp, log, sqrt,* and *int*. The last truncates its argument to an integer; *substr(s, m, n)* returns the *n*-character substring of *s* that begins at position *m*. The function *sprintf(fmt, expr, expr, ...)* formats the expressions according to the *printf*(3S) format given by *fmt* and returns the resulting string.

Patterns are arbitrary Boolean combinations (**!**, **||**, **&&**, and parentheses) of regular expressions and relational expressions. Regular expressions must be surrounded by slashes and are as in *egrep* (see *grep*(1)). Isolated regular expressions in a pattern apply to the entire line. Regular expressions may also occur in relational expressions. A pattern may consist of two patterns separated by a comma; in this case, the action is performed for all lines between an occurrence of the first pattern and the next occurrence of the second.

A relational expression is one of the following:

expression matchop regular-expression
expression relop expression

where a relop is any of the six relational operators in C, and a matchop is either (for *contains*) or **!** (for *does not contain*). A conditional is an arithmetic expression, a relational expression, or a Boolean combination of these.

The special patterns BEGIN and END may be used to capture control before the first input line is read and after the last. BEGIN must be the first pattern, END the last.

A single character *c* may be used to separate the fields by starting the program with:

BEGIN { FS = *c* }

or by using the −**F***c* option.

Other variable names with special meanings include NF, the number of fields in the current record; NR, the ordinal number of the current record; FILENAME, the name of the current input file; OFS, the output field separator (default blank); ORS, the output record separator (default new-line); and OFMT, the output format for numbers (default **%.6g**).

EXAMPLES

Print lines longer than 72 characters:

```
length > 72
```

Print first two fields in opposite order:

```
{ print $2, $1 }
```

Add up first column, print sum and average:

```
        { s += $1 }
END     { print "sum is", s, " average is", s/NR }
```

Print fields in reverse order:

```
{ for (i = NF; i > 0; --i) print $i }
```

Print all lines between start/stop pairs:

```
/start/, /stop/
```

Print all lines whose first field is different from previous one:

```
$1 != prev { print; prev = $1 }
```

Print file, filling in page numbers starting at 5:

```
/Page/  { $2 = n++; }
        { print }
```

command line: awk −f program n=5 input

SEE ALSO

grep(1), sed(1).
lex(1), printf(3S) in the *Programmer's Reference Manual.*

BUGS

Input white space is not preserved on output if fields are involved.
There are no explicit conversions between numbers and strings. To force an expression to be treated as a number add 0 to it; to force it to be treated as a string concatenate the null string ("") to it.

NAME

bc − arbitrary-precision arithmetic language

SYNOPSIS

bc [**−c**] [**−l**] [file ...]

DESCRIPTION

bc is an interactive processor for a language that resembles C but provides unlimited precision arithmetic. It takes input from any files given, then reads the standard input. The *bc*(1) utility is actually a preprocessor for *dc*(1), which it invokes automatically unless the **−c** option is present. In this case the *dc* input is sent to the standard output instead. The options are as follows:

−c Compile only. The output is send to the standard output.

−l Argument stands for the name of an arbitrary precision math library.

The syntax for *bc* programs is as follows; L means letter a−z, E means expression, S means statement.

Comments
    are enclosed in /* and */.

Names
    simple variables: L
    array elements: L [E]
    The words "ibase", "obase", and "scale"

Other operands
    arbitrarily long numbers with optional sign and decimal point.
    (E)
    sqrt (E)
    length (E)   number of significant decimal digits
    scale (E)   number of digits right of decimal point
    L (E , ... , E)

Operators
    + − * / % ^ (% is remainder; ^ is power)
    ++ −− (prefix and postfix; apply to names)
    == <= >= != < >
    = =+ =− =* =/ =% =^

Statements
    E
    { S ; ... ; S }
    if (E) S
    while (E) S
    for (E ; E ; E) S
    null statement
    break
    quit

Function definitions
    define L (L ,..., L) {
        auto L, ... , L
        S; ... S

```
                return ( E )
        }
```

Functions in **−l** math library

s(x)	sine
c(x)	cosine
e(x)	exponential
l(x)	log
a(x)	arctangent
j(n,x)	Bessel function

All function arguments are passed by value.

The value of a statement that is an expression is printed unless the main operator is an assignment. Either semicolons or new-lines may separate statements. Assignment to *scale* influences the number of digits to be retained on arithmetic operations in the manner of *dc*(1). Assignments to *ibase* or *obase* set the input and output number radix respectively.

The same letter may be used as an array, a function, and a simple variable simultaneously. All variables are global to the program. "Auto" variables are pushed down during function calls. When using arrays as function arguments or defining them as automatic variables, empty square brackets must follow the array name.

EXAMPLE

```
scale = 20
define e(x){
        auto a, b, c, i, s
        a = 1
        b = 1
        s = 1
        for(i=1; 1==1; i++){
                a = a*x
                b = b*i
                c = a/b
                if(c == 0) return(s)
                s = s+c
        }
}
```

defines a function to compute an approximate value of the exponential function and

```
        for(i=1; i<=10; i++) e(i)
```

prints approximate values of the exponential function of the first ten integers.

FILES

/usr/lib/lib.b	mathematical library
/usr/bin/dc	desk calculator proper

SEE ALSO

dc(1).

BUGS

The *bc* command does not yet recognize the logical operators, **&&** and **||**.
For statement must have all three expressions (E's).
Quit is interpreted when read, not when executed.

NAME

bfs − big file scanner

SYNOPSIS

bfs [−] name

DESCRIPTION

The *bfs* command is (almost) like *ed*(1) except that it is read-only and processes much larger files. Files can be up to 1024K bytes and 32K lines, with up to 512 characters, including new-line, per line (255 for 16-bit machines). *bfs* is usually more efficient than *ed*(1) for scanning a file, since the file is not copied to a buffer. It is most useful for identifying sections of a large file where *csplit*(1) can be used to divide it into more manageable pieces for editing.

Normally, the size of the file being scanned is printed, as is the size of any file written with the **w** command. The optional − suppresses printing of sizes. Input is prompted with * if **P** and a carriage return are typed, as in *ed*(1). Prompting can be turned off again by inputting another **P** and carriage return. Note that messages are given in response to errors if prompting is turned on.

All address expressions described under *ed*(1) are supported. In addition, regular expressions may be surrounded with two symbols besides / and **?**: > indicates downward search without wrap-around, and < indicates upward search without wrap-around. There is a slight difference in mark names: only the letters **a** through **z** may be used, and all 26 marks are remembered.

The **e**, **g**, **v**, **k**, **p**, **q**, **w**, **=**, **!** and null commands operate as described under *ed*(1). Commands such as −−−, +++−, +++=, **−12**, and **+4p** are accepted. Note that **1,10p** and **1,10** will both print the first ten lines. The **f** command only prints the name of the file being scanned; there is no *remembered* file name. The **w** command is independent of output diversion, truncation, or crunching (see the **xo**, **xt** and **xc** commands, below). The following additional commands are available:

xf *file*
: Further commands are taken from the named *file*. When an end-of-file is reached, an interrupt signal is received or an error occurs, reading resumes with the file containing the **xf**. The **xf** commands may be nested to a depth of 10.

xn List the marks currently in use (marks are set by the **k** command).

xo [*file*]
: Further output from the **p** and null commands is diverted to the named *file*, which, if necessary, is created mode 666 (readable and writable by everyone), unless your *umask* setting (see *umask*(1)) dictates otherwise. If *file* is missing, output is diverted to the standard output. Note that each diversion causes truncation or creation of the file.

: *label*
: This positions a *label* in a command file. The *label* is terminated by new-line, and blanks between the : and the start of the *label* are ignored. This command may also be used to insert comments into a command file, since labels need not be referenced.

(. , .)**xb**/*regular expression*/*label*

A jump (either upward or downward) is made to *label* if the command succeeds. It fails under any of the following conditions:

1. Either address is not between **1** and **$**.
2. The second address is less than the first.
3. The regular expression does not match at least one line in the specified range, including the first and last lines.

On success, **.** is set to the line matched and a jump is made to *label*. This command is the only one that does not issue an error message on bad addresses, so it may be used to test whether addresses are bad before other commands are executed. Note that the command

```
xb/^/ label
```

is an unconditional jump.

The **xb** command is allowed only if it is read from someplace other than a terminal. If it is read from a pipe only a downward jump is possible.

xt *number*

Output from the **p** and null commands is truncated to at most *number* characters. The initial number is 255.

xv[*digit*][*spaces*][*value*]

The variable name is the specified *digit* following the **xv**. The commands **xv5100** or **xv5 100** both assign the value **100** to the variable **5**. The command **xv61,100p** assigns the value **1,100p** to the variable **6**. To reference a variable, put a % in front of the variable name. For example, using the above assignments for variables **5** and **6**:

```
1,%5p
1,%5
%6
```

will all print the first 100 lines.

```
g/%5/p
```

would globally search for the characters **100** and print each line containing a match. To escape the special meaning of %, a \ must precede it.

```
g/".*\%[cds]/p
```

could be used to match and list lines containing *printf* of characters, decimal integers, or strings.

Another feature of the **xv** command is that the first line of output from a UNIX system command can be stored into a variable. The only requirement is that the first character of *value* be an **!**. For example:

```
.w junk
xv5!cat junk
!rm junk
!echo "%5"
xv6!expr %6 + 1
```

would put the current line into variable **5**, print it, and increment the variable **6** by one. To escape the special meaning of **!** as the first character of *value*, precede it with a \.

```
xv7\!date
```

stores the value **!date** into variable **7**.

xbz *label*

xbn *label*
These two commands will test the last saved *return code* from the execution of a UNIX system command (**!***command*) or nonzero value, respectively, to the specified label. The two examples below both search for the next five lines containing the string **size**.

```
xv55
: 1
/size/
xv5!expr %5 − 1
!if 0%5 != 0 exit 2
xbn 1
xv45
: 1
/size/
xv4!expr %4 − 1
!if 0%4 = 0 exit 2
xbz 1
```

xc [*switch*]
If *switch* is **1**, output from the **p** and null commands is crunched; if *switch* is **0** it is not. Without an argument, **xc** reverses *switch*. Initially *switch* is set for no crunching. Crunched output has strings of tabs and blanks reduced to one blank and blank lines suppressed.

SEE ALSO
csplit(1), ed(1), umask(1).

DIAGNOSTICS
? for errors in commands, if prompting is turned off. Self-explanatory error messages when prompting is on.

NAME
banner – make posters

SYNOPSIS
banner strings

DESCRIPTION
banner prints its arguments (each up to 10 characters long) in large letters on the standard output.

SEE ALSO
echo(1).

NAME

basename, dirname – deliver portions of path names

SYNOPSIS

basename string [suffix]
dirname string

DESCRIPTION

basename deletes any prefix ending in / and the *suffix* (if present in *string*) from *string*, and prints the result on the standard output. It is normally used inside substitution marks (\` \`) within shell procedures.

Dirname delivers all but the last level of the path name in *string*.

EXAMPLES

The following example, invoked with the argument **/usr/src/cmd/cat.c**, compiles the named file and moves the output to a file named **cat** in the current directory:

```
cc $1
mv a.out `basename $1 '\.c'`
```

The following example will set the shell variable **NAME** to **/usr/src/cmd**:

```
NAME=`dirname /usr/src/cmd/cat.c`
```

SEE ALSO

sh(1).

NAME

bdiff – big diff

SYNOPSIS

bdiff file1 file2 [n] [–**s**]

DESCRIPTION

bdiff is used in a manner analogous to *diff*(1) to find which lines in two files must be changed to bring the files into agreement. Its purpose is to allow processing of files which are too large for *diff*.

The parameters to *bdiff* are:

file1 (file2)
: The name of a file to be used. If *file1 (file2)* is –, the standard input is read.

n
: The number of line segments. The value of *n* is 3500 by default. If the optional third argument is given and it is numeric, it is used as the value for *n*. This is useful in those cases in which 3500-line segments are too large for *diff*, causing it to fail.

–s
: Specifies that no diagnostics are to be printed by *bdiff* (silent option). Note, however, that this does not suppress possible diagnostic messages from *diff*(1), which *bdiff* calls.

bdiff ignores lines common to the beginning of both files, splits the remainder of each file into *n*-line segments, and invokes *diff* upon corresponding segments. If both optional arguments are specified, they must appear in the order indicated above.

The output of *bdiff* is exactly that of *diff*, with line numbers adjusted to account for the segmenting of the files (that is, to make it look as if the files had been processed whole). Note that because of the segmenting of the files, *bdiff* does not necessarily find a smallest sufficient set of file differences.

FILES

/tmp/bd?????

SEE ALSO

diff(1), help(1).

DIAGNOSTICS

Use *help*(1) for explanations.

NAME

cal – print calendar

SYNOPSIS

cal [[month] year]

DESCRIPTION

cal prints a calendar for the specified year. If a month is also specified, a calendar just for that month is printed. If neither is specified, a calendar for the present month is printed. *Year* can be between 1 and 9999. The *month* is a number between 1 and 12. The calendar produced is that for England and the United States.

EXAMPLES

An unusual calendar is printed for September 1752. That is the month 11 days were skipped to make up for lack of leap year adjustments. To see this calendar, type: **cal 9 1752**

BUGS

The year is always considered to start in January even though this is historically naive.

Beware that "cal 83" refers to the early Christian era, not the 20th century.

NAME

calendar – reminder service

SYNOPSIS

calendar [–]

DESCRIPTION

calendar consults the file **calendar** in the current directory and prints out lines that contain today's or tomorrow's date anywhere in the line. Most reasonable month-day dates such as "Aug. 24," "august 24," "8/24," etc., are recognized, but not "24 August" or "24/8". On weekends "tomorrow" extends through Monday.

When an argument is present, *calendar* does its job for every user who has a file **calendar** in his or her login directory and sends them any positive results by *mail*(1). Normally this is done daily by facilities in the UNIX operating system.

FILES

/usr/lib/calprog   to figure out today's and tomorrow's dates

/etc/passwd

/tmp/cal*

SEE ALSO

mail(1).

BUGS

Your calendar must be public information for you to get reminder service.
calendar's extended idea of "tomorrow" does not account for holidays.

NAME

cat – concatenate and print files

SYNOPSIS

cat [**−u**] [**−s**] [**−v** [**−t**] [**−e**]] file ...

DESCRIPTION

cat reads each *file* in sequence and writes it on the standard output. Thus:

cat file

prints the file, and:

cat file1 file2 >file3

concatenates the first two files and places the result on the third.

If no input file is given, or if the argument – is encountered, *cat* reads from the standard input file.

The following options apply to *cat*.

−u The output is not buffered. (The default is buffered output.)

−s *cat* is silent about non-existent files.

−v Causes non-printing characters (with the exception of tabs, new-lines and form-feeds) to be printed visibly. Control characters are printed ^X (control-*x*); the DEL character (octal 0177) is printed ^**?**. Non-ASCII characters (with the high bit set) are printed as **M-***x*, where *x* is the character specified by the seven low order bits.

When used with the **−v** option, the following options may be used.

−t Causes tabs to be printed as ^**I**'s.

−e Causes a **$** character to be printed at the end of each line (prior to the new-line).

The **−t** and **−e** options are ignored if the **−v** option is not specified.

WARNING

Command formats such as

cat file1 file2 >file1

will cause the original data in *file1* to be lost; therefore, take care when using shell special characters.

SEE ALSO

cp(1), pg(1), pr(1).

NAME

cd – change working directory

SYNOPSIS

cd [directory]

DESCRIPTION

If *directory* is not specified, the value of shell parameter **$HOME** is used as the new working directory. If *directory* specifies a complete path starting with /, ., .., *directory* becomes the new working directory. If neither case applies, *cd* tries to find the designated directory relative to one of the paths specified by the **$CDPATH** shell variable. **$CDPATH** has the same syntax as, and similar semantics to, the **$PATH** shell variable. *cd* must have execute (search) permission in *directory*.

Because a new process is created to execute each command, *cd* would be ineffective if it were written as a normal command; therefore, it is recognized and is internal to the shell.

SEE ALSO

pwd(1), sh(1).
chdir(2) in the *Programmer's Reference Manual.*

NAME

chmod – change mode

SYNOPSIS

chmod mode file ...

chmod mode directory ...

DESCRIPTION

The permissions of the named *files* or *directories* are **ch**anged according to **mod**e, which may be symbolic or absolute. Absolute changes to permissions are stated using octal numbers:

chmod *nnn file(s)*

where *n* is a number from 0 to 7. Symbolic changes are stated using mnemonic characters:

chmod *a operator b file(s)*

where *a* is one or more characters corresponding to **user**, **group**, or **other**; where *operator* is +, −, and =, signifying assignment of permissions; and where *b* is one or more characters corresponding to type of permission.

An absolute mode is given as an octal number constructed from the OR of the following modes:

4000	set user ID on execution
20#0	set group ID on execution if # is **7**, **5**, **3**, or **1**
	enable mandatory locking if # is **6**, **4**, **2**, or **0**
1000	sticky bit is turned on ((see *chmod*(2))
0400	read by owner
0200	write by owner
0100	execute (search in directory) by owner
0070	read, write, execute (search) by group
0007	read, write, execute (search) by others

Symbolic changes are stated using letters that correspond both to access classes and to the individual permissions themselves. Permissions to a file may vary depending on your user identification number (UID) or group identification number (GID). Permissions are described in three sequences each having three characters:

User	Group	Other
rwx	rwx	rwx

This example (meaning that **u**ser, **g**roup, and **o**thers all have **r**eading, **w**riting, and e**x**ecution permission to a given file) demonstrates two categories for granting permissions: the access class and the permissions themselves.

Thus, to change the mode of a file's (or directory's) permissions using *chmod*'s symbolic method, use the following syntax for mode:

[*who*] *operator* [*permission(s)*], ...

A command line using the symbolic method would appear as follows:

chmod g+rw *file*

This command would make *file* readable and writable by the group.

The *who* part can be stated as one or more of the following letters:

u	**u**ser's permissions
g	**g**roup's permissions
o	**o**thers permissions

The letter **a** (**a**ll) is equivalent to **ugo** and is the default if *who* is omitted.

Operator can be + to add *permission* to the file's mode, − to take away *permission*, or = to assign *permission* absolutely. (Unlike other symbolic operations, = has an absolute effect in that it resets all other bits.) Omitting *permission* is only useful with = to take away all permissions.

Permission is any compatible combination of the following letters:

r	**r**eading permission
w	**w**riting permission
x	e**x**ecution permission
s	user or group **s**et-ID is turned on
t	sticky bit is turned on
l	mandatory **l**ocking will occur during access

Multiple symbolic modes separated by commas may be given, though no spaces may intervene between these modes. Operations are performed in the order given. Multiple symbolic letters following a single operator cause the corresponding operations to be performed simultaneously. The letter **s** is only meaningful with **u** or **g**, and **t** only works with **u**.

Mandatory file and record locking (**l**) refers to a file's ability to have its reading or writing permissions locked while a program is accessing that file. It is not possible to permit group execution and enable a file to be locked on execution at the same time. In addition, it is not possible to turn on the set-group-ID and enable a file to be locked on execution at the same time. The following examples,

chmod g+x,+l *file*

chmod g+s,+l *file*

are, therefore, illegal usages and will elicit error messages.

Only the owner of a file or directory (or the super-user) may change a file's mode. Only the super-user may set the sticky bit. In order to turn on a file's set-group-ID, your own group ID must correspond to the file's, and group execution must be set.

EXAMPLES

chmod a−x *file*

chmod 444 *file*

The first examples deny execution permission to all. The absolute (octal) example permits only reading permissions.

chmod go+rw *file*

chmod 606 *file*

These examples make a file readable and writable by the group and others.

chmod +l *file*

This causes a file to be locked during access.

chmod =rwx,g+s *file*

chmod 2777 *file*

These last two examples enable all to read, write, and execute the file; and they turn on the set group-ID.

NOTES

In a Remote File Sharing environment, you may not have the permissions that the output of the **ls −l** command leads you to believe. For more information see the "Mapping Remote Users" section of Chapter 10 of the *System Administrator's Guide*.

SEE ALSO

ls(1).
chmod(2) in the *Programmer's Reference Manual*.

NAME

chown, chgrp – change owner or group

SYNOPSIS

chown owner file ...

chown owner directory ...

chgrp group file ...

chgrp group directory ...

DESCRIPTION

chown changes the owner of the *files* or *directories* to *owner*. The owner may be either a decimal user ID or a login name found in the password file.

Chgrp changes the group ID of the *files* or *directories* to *group*. The group may be either a decimal group ID or a group name found in the group file.

If either command is invoked by other than the super-user, the set-user-ID and set-group-ID bits of the file mode, 04000 and 02000 respectively, will be cleared.

Only the owner of a file (or the super-user) may change the owner or group of that file.

FILES

/etc/passwd
/etc/group

NOTES

In a Remote File Sharing environment, you may not have the permissions that the output of the **ls –l** command leads you to believe. For more information see the "Mapping Remote Users" section of Chapter 10 of the *System Administrator's Guide*.

SEE ALSO

chmod(1).
chown(2), group(4), passwd(4) in the *Programmer's Reference Manual*.

NAME

cmp – compare two files

SYNOPSIS

cmp [**–l**] [**–s**] file1 file2

DESCRIPTION

The two files are compared. (If *file1* is –, the standard input is used.) Under default options, *cmp* makes no comment if the files are the same; if they differ, it announces the byte and line number at which the difference occurred. If one file is an initial subsequence of the other, that fact is noted.

Options:

–l Print the byte number (decimal) and the differing bytes (octal) for each difference.

–s Print nothing for differing files; return codes only.

SEE ALSO

comm(1), diff(1).

DIAGNOSTICS

Exit code 0 is returned for identical files, 1 for different files, and 2 for an inaccessible or missing argument.

NAME

col – filter reverse line-feeds

SYNOPSIS

col [–**b**] [–**f**] [–**x**] [–**p**]

DESCRIPTION

col reads from the standard input and writes onto the standard output. It performs the line overlays implied by reverse line feeds (ASCII code **ESC-7**), and by forward and reverse half-line-feeds (**ESC-9** and **ESC-8**). *col* is particularly useful for filtering multicolumn output made with the **.rt** command of *nroff* and output resulting from use of the *tbl*(1) preprocessor.

If the **–b** option is given, *col* assumes that the output device in use is not capable of backspacing. In this case, if two or more characters are to appear in the same place, only the last one read will be output.

Although *col* accepts half-line motions in its input, it normally does not emit them on output. Instead, text that would appear between lines is moved to the next lower full-line boundary. This treatment can be suppressed by the **–f** (fine) option; in this case, the output from *col* may contain forward half-line-feeds (**ESC-9**), but will still never contain either kind of reverse line motion.

Unless the **–x** option is given, *col* will convert white space to tabs on output wherever possible to shorten printing time.

The ASCII control characters **SO** (\017) and **SI** (\016) are assumed by *col* to start and end text in an alternate character set. The character set to which each input character belongs is remembered, and on output **SI** and **SO** characters are generated as appropriate to ensure that each character is printed in the correct character set.

On input, the only control characters accepted are space, backspace, tab, return, new-line, **SI**, **SO**, **VT** (\013), and **ESC** followed by **7**, **8**, or **9**. The **VT** character is an alternate form of full reverse line-feed, included for compatibility with some earlier programs of this type. All other non-printing characters are ignored.

Normally, *col* will ignore any escape sequences unknown to it that are found in its input; the **–p** option may be used to cause *col* to output these sequences as regular characters, subject to overprinting from reverse line motions. The use of this option is highly discouraged unless the user is fully aware of the textual position of the escape sequences.

SEE ALSO

nroff(1), tbl(1) in the *DOCUMENTER's WORKBENCH Software Release 2.0 Technical Discussion and Reference Manual* .

NOTES

The input format accepted by *col* matches the output produced by *nroff* with either the **–T37** or **–Tlp** options. Use **–T37** (and the **–f** option of *col*) if the ultimate disposition of the output of *col* will be a device that can interpret half-line motions, and **–Tlp** otherwise.

BUGS

Cannot back up more than 128 lines.
Allows at most 800 characters, including backspaces, on a line.
Local vertical motions that would result in backing up over the first line of the document are ignored. As a result, the first line must not have any superscripts.

NAME

comm – select or reject lines common to two sorted files

SYNOPSIS

comm [– [**123**]] file1 file2

DESCRIPTION

comm reads *file1* and *file2*, which should be ordered in ASCII collating sequence (see *sort*(1)), and produces a three-column output: lines only in *file1*; lines only in *file2*; and lines in both files. The file name – means the standard input.

Flags 1, 2, or 3 suppress printing of the corresponding column. Thus **comm −12** prints only the lines common to the two files; **comm −23** prints only lines in the first file but not in the second; **comm −123** prints nothing.

SEE ALSO

cmp(1), diff(1), sort(1), uniq(1).

NAME

cp, ln, mv – copy, link or move files

SYNOPSIS

cp file1 [file2 ...] target
ln [**−f**] file1 [file2 ...] target
mv [**−f**] file1 [file2 ...] target

DESCRIPTION

file1 is copied (linked, moved) to *target*. Under no circumstance can *file1* and *target* be the same (take care when using *sh*(1) metacharacters). If *target* is a directory, then one or more files are copied (linked, moved) to that directory. If *target* is a file, its contents are destroyed.

If *mv* or *ln* determines that the mode of *target* forbids writing, it will print the mode (see *chmod*(2)), ask for a response, and read the standard input for one line; if the line begins with **y**, the *mv* or *ln* occurs, if permissable; if not, the command exits. When the **−f** option is used or if the standard input is not a terminal, no questions are asked and the *mv* or *ln* is done.

Only *mv* will allow *file1* to be a directory, in which case the directory rename will occur only if the two directories have the same parent; *file1* is renamed *target*. If *file1* is a file and *target* is a link to another file with links, the other links remain and *target* becomes a new file.

When using *cp*, if *target* is not a file, a new file is created which has the same mode as *file1* except that the sticky bit is not set unless you are super-user; the owner and group of *target* are those of the user. If *target* is a file, copying a file into *target* does not change its mode, owner, nor group. The last modification time of *target* (and last access time, if *target* did not exist) and the last access time of *file1* are set to the time the copy was made. If *target* is a link to a file, all links remain and the file is changed.

SEE ALSO

chmod(1), cpio(1), rm(1).

WARNINGS

ln will not link across file systems. This restriction is necessary because file systems can be added and removed.

BUGS

If *file1* and *target* lie on different file systems, *mv* must copy the file and delete the original. In this case any linking relationship with other files is lost.

NAME

cpio − copy file archives in and out

SYNOPSIS

cpio −o[acBv]

cpio −i[BcdmrtuvfsSb6] [patterns]

cpio −p[adlmuv] directory

DESCRIPTION

cpio −o (copy out) reads the standard input to obtain a list of path names and copies those files onto the standard output together with path name and status information. Output is padded to a 512-byte boundary.

cpio −i (copy in) extracts files from the standard input, which is assumed to be the product of a previous **cpio −o**. Only files with names that match *patterns* are selected. *Patterns* are regular expressions given in the name-generating notation of *sh*(1). In *patterns*, meta-characters **?**, *****, and **[...]** match the slash / character. Multiple *patterns* may be specified and if no *patterns* are specified, the default for *patterns* is * (i.e., select all files). Each *pattern* should be surrounded by double quotes. The extracted files are conditionally created and copied into the current directory tree based upon the options described below. The permissions of the files will be those of the previous **cpio −o**. The owner and group of the files will be that of the current user unless the user is super-user, which causes *cpio* to retain the owner and group of the files of the previous **cpio −o**. NOTE: If **cpio -i** tries to create a file that already exists and the existing file is the same age or newer, **cpio** will output a warning message and not replace the file. (The **-u** option can be used to unconditionally overwrite the existing file.)

cpio −p (pass) reads the standard input to obtain a list of path names of files that are conditionally created and copied into the destination *directory* tree based upon the options described below.

The meanings of the available options are

- **a** Reset *access* times of input files after they have been copied. Access times are not reset for linked files when **cpio -pla** is specified.
- **B** Input/output is to be *blocked* 5,120 bytes to the record (does not apply to the *pass* option; meaningful only with data directed to or from a character special device, e.g. /dev/rmt/0m.
- **d** *Directories* are to be created as needed.
- **c** Write header information in ASCII *character* form for portability. Always use this option when origin and destination machines are different types.
- **r** Interactively *rename* files. If the user types a null line, the file is skipped. (Not available with **cpio -p**.)
- **t** Print a *table of contents* of the input. No files are created.
- **u** Copy *unconditionally* (normally, an older file will not replace a newer file with the same name).
- **v** *Verbose*: causes a list of file names to be printed. When used with the **t** option, the table of contents looks like the output of an **ls −l** command (see *ls*(1)).
- **l** Whenever possible, *link* files rather than copying them. Usable only with the **−p** option.

m Retain previous file *modification* time. This option is ineffective on directories that are being copied.

f Copy in all *files* except those in *patterns*.

s *Swap* bytes within each half word. Use only with the **−i** option.

S *Swap* halfwords within each word. Use only with the **−i** option.

b Reverses the order of the *bytes* within each word. Use only with the **−i** option.

6 Process an old (i.e. UNIX System *Sixth* Edition format) file. Only useful with -i (copy in).

NOTE: **cpio** assumes four-byte words.

If **cpio** reaches end of medium (end of a diskette for example), when writing to (-o) or reading from (-i) a character special device, **cpio** will print the message:

If you want to go on, type device/file name when ready.

To continue, you must replace the medium and type the character special device name (**/dev/rdiskette** for example) and carriage return. You may want to continue by directing **cpio** to use a different device. For example, if you have two floppy drives you may want to switch between them so **cpio** can proceed while you are changing the floppies. (A carriage return alone causes the **cpio** process to exit.)

EXAMPLES

The following examples show three uses of **cpio**.

When standard input is directed through a pipe to **cpio −o,** it groups the files so they can be directed (>) to a single file (../newfile). Instead of "ls," you could use find, echo, cat, etc. to pipe a list of names to cpio. You could direct the output to a device instead of a file.

ls | cpio −o >../*newfile*

cpio −i uses the output file of **cpio −o** (directed through a pipe with cat in the example), takes out those files that match the patterns (memo/a1, memo/b*), creates directories below the current directory as needed (-d option), and places the files in the appropriate directories. If no patterns were given, all files from "newfile" would be placed in the directory.

cat newfile | cpio −id "*memo/a1*" "*memo/b**"

cpio −p takes the file names piped to it and copies or links (-l option) those files to another directory on your machine (*newdir* in the example). The -d options says to create directories as needed. The −m option says retain the modification time. (It is important to use the -depth option of find to generate path names for cpio. This eliminates problems **cpio** could have trying to create files under read-only directories.)

find . −depth −print | cpio −pdlmv *newdir*

SEE ALSO

ar(1), find(1), ls(1), tar(1).
cpio(4) in the *Programmer's Reference Manual.*

NOTES

1) Path names are restricted to 256 characters.
2) Only the super-user can copy special files.
3) Blocks are reported in 512-byte quantities.

NAME

crontab − user crontab file

SYNOPSIS

crontab [file]
crontab −r
crontab −l

DESCRIPTION

crontab copies the specified file, or standard input if no file is specified, into a directory that holds all users' crontabs. The −r option removes a user's crontab from the crontab directory. *crontab* −l will list the crontab file for the invoking user.

Users are permitted to use *crontab* if their names appear in the file **/usr/lib/cron/cron.allow.** If that file does not exist, the file **/usr/lib/cron/cron.deny** is checked to determine if the user should be denied access to *crontab.* If neither file exists, only root is allowed to submit a job. If **cron.allow** does not exist and **cron.deny** exists but is empty, global usage is permitted. The allow/deny files consist of one user name per line.

A crontab file consists of lines of six fields each. The fields are separated by spaces or tabs. The first five are integer patterns that specify the following:

minute (0−59),
hour (0−23),
day of the month (1−31),
month of the year (1−12),
day of the week (0−6 with 0=Sunday).

Each of these patterns may be either an asterisk (meaning all legal values) or a list of elements separated by commas. An element is either a number or two numbers separated by a minus sign (meaning an inclusive range). Note that the specification of days may be made by two fields (day of the month and day of the week). If both are specified as a list of elements, both are adhered to. For example, 0 0 1,15 * 1 would run a command on the first and fifteenth of each month, as well as on every Monday. To specify days by only one field, the other field should be set to * (for example, 0 0 * * 1 would run a command only on Mondays).

The sixth field of a line in a crontab file is a string that is executed by the shell at the specified times. A percent character in this field (unless escaped by \) is translated to a new-line character. Only the first line (up to a % or end of line) of the command field is executed by the shell. The other lines are made available to the command as standard input.

The shell is invoked from your **$HOME** directory with an **arg0** of **sh.** Users who desire to have their *.profile* executed must explicitly do so in the crontab file. *Cron* supplies a default environment for every shell, defining **HOME, LOGNAME, SHELL(=/bin/sh)**, and **PATH(=:/bin:/usr/bin:/usr/lbin)**.

If you do not redirect the standard output and standard error of your commands, any generated output or errors will be mailed to you.

FILES

/usr/lib/cron	main cron directory
/usr/spool/cron/crontabs	spool area
/usr/lib/cron/log	accounting information
/usr/lib/cron/cron.allow	list of allowed users
/usr/lib/cron/cron.deny	list of denied users

SEE ALSO

sh(1).
cron(1M) in the *System Administrator's Reference Manual.*

WARNINGS

If you inadvertently enter the **crontab** command with no argument(s), do not attempt to get out with a CTRL-d. This will cause all entries in your **crontab** file to be removed. Instead, exit with a DEL.

NAME

crypt − encode/decode

SYNOPSIS

crypt [password]
crypt **[−k]**

DESCRIPTION

crypt reads from the standard input and writes on the standard output. The *password* is a key that selects a particular transformation. If no argument is given, *crypt* demands a key from the terminal and turns off printing while the key is being typed in. If the **−k** option is used, *crypt* will use the key assigned to the environment variable CRYPTKEY. *crypt* encrypts and decrypts with the same key:

crypt key <clear >cypher
crypt key <cypher | pr

Files encrypted by *crypt* are compatible with those treated by the editors *ed*(1), *edit*(1), *ex*(1), and *vi*(1) in encryption mode.

The security of encrypted files depends on three factors: the fundamental method must be hard to solve; direct search of the key space must be infeasible; "sneak paths" by which keys or clear text can become visible must be minimized.

crypt implements a one-rotor machine designed along the lines of the German Enigma, but with a 256-element rotor. Methods of attack on such machines are known, but not widely; moreover the amount of work required is likely to be large.

The transformation of a key into the internal settings of the machine is deliberately designed to be expensive, i.e., to take a substantial fraction of a second to compute. However, if keys are restricted to (say) three lower-case letters, then encrypted files can be read by expending only a substantial fraction of five minutes of machine time.

If the key is an argument to the *crypt* command, it is potentially visible to users executing *ps*(1) or a derivative. The choice of keys and key security are the most vulnerable aspect of *crypt*.

FILES

/dev/tty for typed key

SEE ALSO

ed(1), edit(1), ex(1), makekey(1), ps(1), stty(1), vi(1).

WARNING

This command is provided with the Security Administration Utilities, which is only available in the United States. If two or more files encrypted with the same key are concatenated and an attempt is made to decrypt the result, only the contents of the first of the original files will be decrypted correctly.

BUGS

If output is piped to *nroff* and the encryption key is *not* given on the command line, *crypt* can leave terminal modes in a strange state (see *stty*(1)).

NAME

csplit – context split

SYNOPSIS

csplit [**–s**] [**–k**] [**–f** prefix] file arg1 [... argn]

DESCRIPTION

csplit reads *file* and separates it into n+1 sections, defined by the arguments *arg1... argn*. By default the sections are placed in xx00 ... xx*n* (*n* may not be greater than 99). These sections get the following pieces of *file*:

00: From the start of *file* up to (but not including) the line referenced by *arg1*.

01: From the line referenced by *arg1* up to the line referenced by *arg2*.

⋮

n+1: From the line referenced by *argn* to the end of *file*.

If the *file* argument is a – then standard input is used.

The options to *csplit* are:

–s *csplit* normally prints the character counts for each file created. If the **–s** option is present, *csplit* suppresses the printing of all character counts.

–k *csplit* normally removes created files if an error occurs. If the **–k** option is present, *csplit* leaves previously created files intact.

–f *prefix* If the **–f** option is used, the created files are named *prefix***00** ... *prefixn*. The default is **xx00** ... **xx***n*.

The arguments (*arg1* ... *argn*) to *csplit* can be a combination of the following:

/rexp/ A file is to be created for the section from the current line up to (but not including) the line containing the regular expression *rexp*. The current line becomes the line containing *rexp*. This argument may be followed by an optional + or – some number of lines (e.g., **/Page/–5**).

%*rexp*% This argument is the same as */rexp/*, except that no file is created for the section.

lnno A file is to be created from the current line up to (but not including) *lnno*. The current line becomes *lnno*.

{*num*} Repeat argument. This argument may follow any of the above arguments. If it follows a *rexp* type argument, that argument is applied *num* more times. If it follows *lnno*, the file will be split every *lnno* lines (*num* times) from that point.

Enclose all *rexp* type arguments that contain blanks or other characters meaningful to the shell in the appropriate quotes. Regular expressions may not contain embedded new-lines. *csplit* does not affect the original file; it is the users responsibility to remove it.

EXAMPLES

```
csplit −f cobol file '/procedure division/' /par5./ /par16./
```

This example creates four files, **cobol00 ... cobol03**. After editing the "split" files, they can be recombined as follows:

```
cat cobol0[0−3] > file
```

Note that this example overwrites the original file.

```
csplit −k file 100 {99}
```

This example would split the file at every 100 lines, up to 10,000 lines. The **−k** option causes the created files to be retained if there are less than 10,000 lines; however, an error message would still be printed.

```
csplit −k prog.c '%main(%' '/^}/+1' {20}
```

Assuming that **prog.c** follows the normal **C** coding convention of ending routines with a } at the beginning of the line, this example will create a file containing each separate **C** routine (up to 21) in **prog.c**.

SEE ALSO

ed(1), sh(1).
regexp(5) in the *Programmer's Reference Manual*.

DIAGNOSTICS

Self-explanatory except for:

arg − out of range

which means that the given argument did not reference a line between the current position and the end of the file.

NAME

ct − spawn getty to a remote terminal

SYNOPSIS

ct [**−w**n] [**−x**n] [**−h**] [**−v**] [**−s**speed] telno ...

DESCRIPTION

ct dials the telephone number of a modem that is attached to a terminal, and spawns a *getty* process to that terminal. *Telno* is a telephone number, with equal signs for secondary dial tones and minus signs for delays at appropriate places. (The set of legal characters for *telno* is 0 thru 9, -, =, *, and #. The maximum length *telno* is 31 characters). If more than one telephone number is specified, *ct* will try each in succession until one answers; this is useful for specifying alternate dialing paths.

ct will try each line listed in the file **/usr/lib/uucp/Devices** until it finds an available line with appropriate attributes or runs out of entries. If there are no free lines, *ct* will ask if it should wait for one, and if so, for how many minutes it should wait before it gives up. *ct* will continue to try to open the dialers at one-minute intervals until the specified limit is exceeded. The dialogue may be overridden by specifying the **−w***n* option, where *n* is the maximum number of minutes that *ct* is to wait for a line.

The **−x***n* option is used for debugging; it produces a detailed output of the program execution on stderr. The debugging level, *n*, is a single digit; **−x9** is the most useful value.

Normally, *ct* will hang up the current line, so the line can answer the incoming call. The **−h** option will prevent this action. The **−h** option will also wait for the termination of the specified *ct* process before returning control to the user's terminal. If the **−v** option is used, *ct* will send a running narrative to the standard error output stream.

The data rate may be set with the **−s** option, where *speed* is expressed in baud. The default rate is 1200.

After the user on the destination terminal logs out, there are two things that could occur depending on what type of getty is on the line (*getty* or *uugetty*). For the first case, *ct* prompts, **Reconnect?** If the response begins with the letter **n**, the line will be dropped; otherwise, *getty* will be started again and the **login:** prompt will be printed. In the second case, there is already a getty (*uugetty*) on the line, so the **login:** message will appear.

To log out properly, the user must type **control D**.

Of course, the destination terminal must be attached to a modem that can answer the telephone.

FILES

/usr/lib/uucp/Devices
/usr/adm/ctlog

SEE ALSO

cu(1C), login(1), uucp(1C).
getty(1M), uugetty(1M) in the *System Administrator's Reference Manual.*

BUGS

For a shared port, one used for both dial-in and dial-out, the *uugetty* program running on the line must have the **−r** option specified (see *uugetty*(1M)).

NAME

cu − call another UNIX system

SYNOPSIS

cu [−sspeed] [−lline] [**−h**] [**−t**] [**−d**] [**−o** | **−e**] [**−n**] telno
cu [**−s** speed] [**−h**] [**−d**] [**−o** | **−e**] **−l** line
cu [**−h**] [**−d**] [**−o** | **−e**] systemname

DESCRIPTION

cu calls up another UNIX system, a terminal, or possibly a non-UNIX system. It manages an interactive conversation with possible transfers of ASCII files.

cu accepts the following options and arguments:

−s*speed* Specifies the transmission speed (300, 1200, 2400, 4800, 9600); The default value is "Any" speed which will depend on the order of the lines in the **/usr/lib/uucp/Devices** file. Most modems are either 300 or 1200 baud. Directly connected lines may be set to a speed higher than 1200 baud.

−l*line* Specifies a device name to use as the communication line. This can be used to override the search that would otherwise take place for the first available line having the right speed. When the **−l** option is used without the **−s** option, the speed of a line is taken from the Devices file. When the **−l** and **−s** options are both used together, cu will search the Devices file to check if the requested speed for the requested line is available. If so, the connection will be made at the requested speed; otherwise an error message will be printed and the call will not be made. The specified device is generally a directly connected asynchronous line (e.g., **/dev/tty***ab*) in which case a telephone number (*telno*) is not required. The specified device need not be in the **/dev** directory. If the specified device is associated with an auto dialer, a telephone number must be provided. Use of this option with *systemname* rather than *telno* will not give the desired result (see *systemname* below).

−h Emulates local echo, supporting calls to other computer systems which expect terminals to be set to half-duplex mode.

−t Used to dial an ASCII terminal which has been set to auto answer. Appropriate mapping of carriage-return to carriage-return-line-feed pairs is set.

−d Causes diagnostic traces to be printed.

−o Designates that odd parity is to be generated for data sent to the remote system.

−n For added security, will prompt the user to provide the telephone number to be dialed rather than taking it from the command line.

−e Designates that even parity is to be generated for data sent to the remote system.

telno When using an automatic dialer, the argument is the telephone number with equal signs for secondary dial tone or minus signs placed appropriately for delays of 4 seconds.

systemname A uucp system name may be used rather than a telephone number; in this case, *cu* will obtain an appropriate direct line or telephone number from **/usr/lib/uucp/Systems.** Note: the *systemname* option should not be used in conjunction with the **−l** and **−s** options as *cu* will connect to the first available line for the system name specified, ignoring the requested line and speed.

After making the connection, *cu* runs as two processes: the *transmit* process reads data from the standard input and, except for lines beginning with ~, passes it to the remote system; the *receive* process accepts data from the remote system and, except for lines beginning with ~, passes it to the standard output. Normally, an automatic DC3/DC1 protocol is used to control input from the remote so the buffer is not overrun. Lines beginning with ~ have special meanings.

The *transmit* process interprets the following user initiated commands:

~. terminate the conversation.

~! escape to an interactive shell on the local system.

~!*cmd...* run *cmd* on the local system (via **sh −c**).

~$*cmd...* run *cmd* locally and send its output to the remote system.

~%cd change the directory on the local system. Note: **~!cd** will cause the command to be run by a sub-shell, probably not what was intended.

~%take *from* [*to*] copy file *from* (on the remote system) to file *to* on the local system. If *to* is omitted, the *from* argument is used in both places.

~%put *from* [*to*] copy file *from* (on local system) to file *to* on remote system. If *to* is omitted, the *from* argument is used in both places.

For both **~%take** and **put** commands, as each block of the file is transferred, consecutive single digits are printed to the terminal.

~~ *line* send the line ~ *line* to the remote system.

~%break transmit a **BREAK** to the remote system (which can also be specified as **~%b**).

~%debug toggles the **-d** debugging option on or off (which can also be specified as **~%d**).

~t prints the values of the termio structure variables for the user's terminal (useful for debugging).

~l prints the values of the termio structure variables for the remote communication line (useful for debugging).

~%nostop toggles between DC3/DC1 input control protocol and no input control. This is useful in case the remote system is one which does not respond properly to the DC3 and DC1 characters.

The *receive* process normally copies data from the remote system to its standard output. Internally the program accomplishes this by initiating an output diversion to a file when a line from the remote begins with ~.

Data from the remote is diverted (or appended, if >> is used) to *file* on the local system. The trailing ~> marks the end of the diversion.

The use of **~%put** requires *stty*(1) and *cat*(1) on the remote side. It also requires that the current erase and kill characters on the remote system be identical to these current control characters on the local system. Backslashes are inserted at appropriate places.

The use of **~%take** requires the existence of *echo*(1) and *cat*(1) on the remote system. Also, *tabs* mode (See *stty(1))* should be set on the remote system if tabs are to be copied without expansion to spaces.

When *cu* is used on system X to connect to system Y and subsequently used on system Y to connect to system Z, commands on system Y can be executed by using ~~. Executing a tilde command reminds the user of the local system uname. For example, uname can be executed on Z, X, and Y as follows:

```
uname
Z
~[X]!uname
X
~~[Y]!uname
Y
```

In general, ~ causes the command to be executed on the original machine, ~~ causes the command to be executed on the next machine in the chain.

EXAMPLES

To dial a system whose telephone number is 9 201 555 1212 using 1200 baud (where dialtone is expected after the 9):

```
cu −s1200 9=12015551212
```

If the speed is not specified, "Any" is the default value.

To login to a system connected by a direct line:

```
cu −l /dev/ttyXX
```

or

```
cu −l ttyXX
```

To dial a system with the specific line and a specific speed:

```
cu −s1200 −l ttyXX
```

To dial a system using a specific line associated with an auto dialer:

```
cu −l culXX 9=12015551212
```

To use a system name:

cu systemname

FILES

/usr/lib/uucp/Systems
/usr/lib/uucp/Devices
/usr/spool/locks/LCK..(tty-device)

SEE ALSO

cat(1), ct(1C), echo(1), stty(1), uucp(1C), uname(1).

DIAGNOSTICS

Exit code is zero for normal exit, otherwise, one.

WARNINGS

The *cu* command does not do any integrity checking on data it transfers. Data fields with special *cu* characters may not be transmitted properly. Depending on the interconnection hardware, it may be necessary to use a **~.** to terminate the conversion even if **stty 0** has been used. Non-printing characters are not dependably transmitted using either the **~%put** or **~%take** commands. *cu* between an IMBR1 and a penril modem will not return a login prompt immediately upon connection. A carriage return will return the prompt.

BUGS

There is an artificial slowing of transmission by *cu* during the **~%put** operation so that loss of data is unlikely.

NAME

cut – cut out selected fields of each line of a file

SYNOPSIS

cut –**c**list [file ...]
cut –**f**list [–**d**char] [–**s**] [file ...]

DESCRIPTION

Use *cut* to cut out columns from a table or fields from each line of a file; in data base parlance, it implements the projection of a relation. The fields as specified by *list* can be fixed length, i.e., character positions as on a punched card (–**c** option) or the length can vary from line to line and be marked with a field delimiter character like *tab* (–**f** option). *cut* can be used as a filter; if no files are given, the standard input is used. In addition, a file name of "–" explicitly refers to standard input.

The meanings of the options are:

list A comma-separated list of integer field numbers (in increasing order), with optional – to indicate ranges [e.g., **1,4,7**; **1–3,8**; **–5,10** (short for **1–5,10**); or **3–** (short for third through last field)].

–**c***list* The *list* following –**c** (no space) specifies character positions (e.g., **–c1–72** would pass the first 72 characters of each line).

–**f***list* The *list* following –**f** is a list of fields assumed to be separated in the file by a delimiter character (see –**d**); e.g., **–f1,7** copies the first and seventh field only. Lines with no field delimiters will be passed through intact (useful for table subheadings), unless –**s** is specified.

–**d***char* The character following –**d** is the field delimiter (–**f** option only). Default is *tab*. Space or other characters with special meaning to the shell must be quoted.

–**s** Suppresses lines with no delimiter characters in case of –**f** option. Unless specified, lines with no delimiters will be passed through untouched.

Either the –**c** or –**f** option must be specified.

Use *grep*(1) to make horizontal "cuts" (by context) through a file, or *paste*(1) to put files together column-wise (i.e., horizontally). To reorder columns in a table, use *cut* and *paste*.

EXAMPLES

cut –d: –f1,5 /etc/passwd	mapping of user IDs to names
name=\`who am i | cut –f1 –d" "\`	to set **name** to current login name.

DIAGNOSTICS

ERROR: line too long A line can have no more than 1023 characters or fields, or there is no new-line character.

ERROR: bad list for c/f option
Missing –**c** or –**f** option or incorrectly specified *list*. No error occurs if a line has fewer fields than the *list* calls for.

ERROR: no fields The *list* is empty.

ERROR: no delimeter Missing *char* on **−d** option.

ERROR: cannot handle multiple adjacent backspaces
Adjacent backspaces cannot be processed correctly.

WARNING: cannot open <filename>
Either *filename* cannot be read or does not exist. If multiple filenames are present, prcessing continues.

SEE ALSO

grep(1), paste(1).

NAME

date − print and set the date

SYNOPSIS

date [mmddhhmm[yy]] | +format]

DESCRIPTION

If no argument is given, or if the argument begins with +, the current date and time are printed. Otherwise, the current date is set. The first *mm* is the month number; *dd* is the day number in the month; *hh* is the hour number (24 hour system); the second *mm* is the minute number; *yy* is the last 2 digits of the year number and is optional. For example:

date 10080045

sets the date to Oct 8, 12:45 AM. The current year is the default if no year is mentioned. The system operates in GMT. *date* takes care of the conversion to and from local standard and daylight time. Only the superuser may change the date.

If the argument begins with +, the output of *date* is under the control of the user. All output fields are of fixed size (zero padded if necessary). Each field descriptor is preceded by % and will be replaced in the output by its corresponding value. A single % is encoded by %%. All other characters are copied to the output without change. The string is always terminated with a new-line character.

Field Descriptors:

- **n** insert a new-line character
- **t** insert a tab character
- **m** month of year − 01 to 12
- **d** day of month − 01 to 31
- **y** last 2 digits of year − 00 to 99
- **D** date as mm/dd/yy
- **H** hour − 00 to 23
- **M** minute − 00 to 59
- **S** second − 00 to 59
- **T** time as HH:MM:SS
- **j** day of year − 001 to 366
- **w** day of week − Sunday = 0
- **a** abbreviated weekday − Sun to Sat
- **h** abbreviated month − Jan to Dec
- **r** time in AM/PM notation

EXAMPLE

date '+DATE: %m/%d/%y%nTIME: %H:%M:%S'

would have generated as output:

DATE: 08/01/76
TIME: 14:45:05

DIAGNOSTICS

No permission	if you are not the super-user and you try to change the date;
bad conversion	if the date set is syntactically incorrect;
bad format character	if the field descriptor is not recognizable.

FILES

/dev/kmem

WARNING

Should you need to change the date while the system is running multi-user, use *sysadm*(1) *datetime*.

SEE ALSO

sysadm(1).

NAME

dc − desk calculator

SYNOPSIS

dc [file]

DESCRIPTION

dc is an arbitrary precision arithmetic package. Ordinarily it operates on decimal integers, but one may specify an input base, output base, and a number of fractional digits to be maintained. (See *bc*(1), a preprocessor for *dc* that provides infix notation and a C-like syntax that implements functions. *Bc* also provides reasonable control structures for programs.) The overall structure of *dc* is a stacking (reverse Polish) calculator. If an argument is given, input is taken from that file until its end, then from the standard input. The following constructions are recognized:

number
: The value of the number is pushed on the stack. A number is an unbroken string of the digits 0−9. It may be preceded by an underscore (_) to input a negative number. Numbers may contain decimal points.

\+ − / * % ^
: The top two values on the stack are added (+), subtracted (−), multiplied (*), divided (/), remaindered (%), or exponentiated (^). The two entries are popped off the stack; the result is pushed on the stack in their place. Any fractional part of an exponent is ignored.

s*x*
: The top of the stack is popped and stored into a register named *x*, where *x* may be any character. If the **s** is capitalized, *x* is treated as a stack and the value is pushed on it.

l*x*
: The value in register *x* is pushed on the stack. The register *x* is not altered. All registers start with zero value. If the **l** is capitalized, register *x* is treated as a stack and its top value is popped onto the main stack.

d
: The top value on the stack is duplicated.

p
: The top value on the stack is printed. The top value remains unchanged.

P
: Interprets the top of the stack as an ASCII string, removes it, and prints it.

f
: All values on the stack are printed.

q
: Exits the program. If executing a string, the recursion level is popped by two.

Q
: Exits the program. The top value on the stack is popped and the string execution level is popped by that value.

x
: Treats the top element of the stack as a character string and executes it as a string of *dc* commands.

X
: Replaces the number on the top of the stack with its scale factor.

[...] Puts the bracketed ASCII string onto the top of the stack.

<*x* >*x* =*x*
The top two elements of the stack are popped and compared. Register *x* is evaluated if they obey the stated relation.

v Replaces the top element on the stack by its square root. Any existing fractional part of the argument is taken into account, but otherwise the scale factor is ignored.

! Interprets the rest of the line as a UNIX system command.

c All values on the stack are popped.

i The top value on the stack is popped and used as the number radix for further input. **I** Pushes the input base on the top of the stack.

o The top value on the stack is popped and used as the number radix for further output.

O Pushes the output base on the top of the stack.

k The top of the stack is popped, and that value is used as a non-negative scale factor: the appropriate number of places are printed on output, and maintained during multiplication, division, and exponentiation. The interaction of scale factor, input base, and output base will be reasonable if all are changed together.

z The stack level is pushed onto the stack.

Z Replaces the number on the top of the stack with its length.

? A line of input is taken from the input source (usually the terminal) and executed.

; : are used by *bc*(1) for array operations.

EXAMPLE

This example prints the first ten values of n!:

```
[la1+dsa*pla10>y]sy
0sa1
lyx
```

SEE ALSO

bc(1).

DIAGNOSTICS

x is unimplemented
where *x* is an octal number.

stack empty
for not enough elements on the stack to do what was asked.

Out of space
when the free list is exhausted (too many digits).

Out of headers
for too many numbers being kept around.

Out of pushdown
for too many items on the stack.

Nesting Depth
for too many levels of nested execution.

NAME

dd – convert and copy a file

SYNOPSIS

dd [option=value] ...

DESCRIPTION

dd copies the specified input file to the specified output with possible conversions. The standard input and output are used by default. The input and output block size may be specified to take advantage of raw physical I/O.

option	*values*
if=*file*	input file name; standard input is default
of=*file*	output file name; standard output is default
ibs=*n*	input block size *n* bytes (default 512)
obs=*n*	output block size (default 512)
bs=*n*	set both input and output block size, superseding *ibs* and *obs*; also, if no conversion is specified, it is particularly efficient since no in-core copy need be done
cbs=*n*	conversion buffer size
skip=*n*	skip *n* input blocks before starting copy
seek=*n*	seek *n* blocks from beginning of output file before copying
count=*n*	copy only *n* input blocks
conv=ascii	convert EBCDIC to ASCII
ebcdic	convert ASCII to EBCDIC
ibm	slightly different map of ASCII to EBCDIC
lcase	map alphabetics to lower case
ucase	map alphabetics to upper case
swab	swap every pair of bytes
noerror	do not stop processing on an error
sync	pad every input block to *ibs*
... , ...	several comma-separated conversions

Where sizes are specified, a number of bytes is expected. A number may end with **k**, **b**, or **w** to specify multiplication by 1024, 512, or 2, respectively; a pair of numbers may be separated by **x** to indicate multiplication.

cbs is used only if *conv=ascii* or *conv=ebcdic* is specified. In the former case, *cbs* characters are placed into the conversion buffer (converted to ASCII). Trailing blanks are trimmed and a new-line added before sending the line to the output. In the latter case, ASCII characters are read into the conversion buffer (converted to EBCDIC). Blanks are added to make up an output block of size *cbs*.

After completion, *dd* reports the number of whole and partial input and output blocks.

DIAGNOSTICS

f+p blocks in(out) numbers of full and partial blocks read(written)

NAME

deroff – remove nroff/troff, tbl, and eqn constructs

SYNOPSIS

deroff [−**m**x] [−**w**] [files]

DESCRIPTION

deroff reads each of the *files* in sequence and removes all *troff*(1) requests, macro calls, backslash constructs, *eqn*(1) constructs (between **.EQ** and **.EN** lines, and between delimiters), and *tbl*(1) descriptions, perhaps replacing them with white space (blanks and blank lines), and writes the remainder of the file on the standard output. *deroff* follows chains of included files (**.so** and **.nx** *troff* commands); if a file has already been included, a **.so** naming that file is ignored and a **.nx** naming that file terminates execution. If no input file is given, *deroff* reads the standard input.

The −**m** option may be followed by an **m**, **s**, or **l**. The −**mm** option causes the macros to be interpreted so that only running text is output (i.e., no text from macro lines.) The −**ml** option forces the −**mm** option and also causes deletion of lists associated with the **mm** macros.

If the −**w** option is given, the output is a word list, one "word" per line, with all other characters deleted. Otherwise, the output follows the original, with the deletions mentioned above. In text, a "word" is any string that *contains* at least two letters and is composed of letters, digits, ampersands (**&**), and apostrophes ('); in a macro call, however, a "word" is a string that *begins* with at least two letters and contains a total of at least three letters. Delimiters are any characters other than letters, digits, apostrophes, and ampersands. Trailing apostrophes and ampersands are removed from "words."

SEE ALSO

eqn(1), nroff(1), tbl(1), troff(1) in the *DOCUMENTER'S WORKBENCH Software Release 2.0 Technical Discussion and Reference Manual.*

BUGS

deroff is not a complete *troff* interpreter, so it can be confused by subtle constructs. Most such errors result in too much rather than too little output.
The −**ml** option does not handle nested lists correctly.

NAME

df – report number of free disk blocks and i-nodes

SYNOPSIS

df [**-lt**] [**-f**] [*file-system* | *directory* | *mounted-resource*]

DESCRIPTION

The **df** command prints out the number of free blocks and free i-nodes in mounted file systems, directories, or mounted resources by examining the counts kept in the super-blocks.

file-system may be specified either by device name (e.g., **/dev/dsk/c1d0s2**) or by mount point directory name (e.g., **/usr**).

directory can be a directory name. The report presents information for the device that contains the directory.

mounted-resource can be a remote resource name. The report presents information for the remote device that contains the resource.

If no arguments are used, the free space on all locally and remotely mounted file systems is printed.

The **df** command uses the following options:

–l only reports on local file systems.

–t causes the figures for total allocated blocks and i-nodes to be reported as well as the free blocks and i-nodes.

–f an actual count of the blocks in the free list is made, rather than taking the figure from the super-block (free i-nodes are not reported). This option will not print any information about mounted remote resources.

NOTE

If multiple remote resources are listed that reside on the same file system on a remote machine, each listing after the first one will be marked with an asterisk.

FILES

/dev/dsk/*
/etc/mnttab

SEE ALSO

mount(1M).
fs(4), mnttab(4) in the *Programmer's Reference Manual*.

NAME

diff − differential file comparator

SYNOPSIS

diff [**−efbh**] file1 file2

DESCRIPTION

diff tells what lines must be changed in two files to bring them into agreement. If *file1* (*file2*) is −, the standard input is used. If *file1* (*file2*) is a directory, then a file in that directory with the name *file2* (*file1*) is used. The normal output contains lines of these forms:

n1 **a** *n3,n4*
n1,n2 **d** *n3*
n1,n2 **c** *n3,n4*

These lines resemble *ed* commands to convert *file1* into *file2*. The numbers after the letters pertain to *file2*. In fact, by exchanging **a** for **d** and reading backward one may ascertain equally how to convert *file2* into *file1*. As in *ed*, identical pairs, where *n1* = *n2* or *n3* = *n4*, are abbreviated as a single number.

Following each of these lines come all the lines that are affected in the first file flagged by <, then all the lines that are affected in the second file flagged by >.

The **−b** option causes trailing blanks (spaces and tabs) to be ignored and other strings of blanks to compare equal.

The **−e** option produces a script of *a, c,* and *d* commands for the editor *ed*, which will recreate *file2* from *file1*. The **−f** option produces a similar script, not useful with *ed*, in the opposite order. In connection with **−e**, the following shell program may help maintain multiple versions of a file. Only an ancestral file ($1) and a chain of version-to-version *ed* scripts ($2,$3,...) made by *diff* need be on hand. A "latest version" appears on the standard output.

```
(shift; cat $*; echo '1,$p') | ed − $1
```

Except in rare circumstances, *diff* finds a smallest sufficient set of file differences.

Option **−h** does a fast, half-hearted job. It works only when changed stretches are short and well separated, but does work on files of unlimited length. Options **−e** and **−f** are unavailable with **−h**.

FILES

/tmp/d?????
/usr/lib/diffh for **−h**

SEE ALSO

bdiff(1), cmp(1), comm(1), ed(1).

DIAGNOSTICS

Exit status is 0 for no differences, 1 for some differences, 2 for trouble.

BUGS

Editing scripts produced under the **−e** or **−f** option are naive about creating lines consisting of a single period (.).

WARNINGS

Missing newline at end of file X

indicates that the last line of file X did not have a new-line. If the lines are different, they will be flagged and output; although the output will seem to indicate they are the same.

NAME

diff3 − 3-way differential file comparison

SYNOPSIS

diff3 [**−ex3**] file1 file2 file3

DESCRIPTION

diff3 compares three versions of a file, and publishes disagreeing ranges of text flagged with these codes:

====	all three files differ
====1	*file1* is different
====2	*file2* is different
====3	*file3* is different

The type of change suffered in converting a given range of a given file to some other is indicated in one of these ways:

f : *n1* **a**	Text is to be appended after line number *n1* in file *f*, where *f* = 1, 2, or 3.
f : *n1* , *n2* **c**	Text is to be changed in the range line *n1* to line *n2*. If *n1* = *n2*, the range may be abbreviated to *n1*.

The original contents of the range follows immediately after a **c** indication. When the contents of two files are identical, the contents of the lower-numbered file is suppressed.

Under the **−e** option, *diff3* publishes a script for the editor *ed* that will incorporate into *file1* all changes between *file2* and *file3*, i.e., the changes that normally would be flagged ==== and ====3. Option **−x** (**−3**) produces a script to incorporate only changes flagged ==== (====3). The following command will apply the resulting script to *file1*.

```
(cat script; echo '1,$p') | ed − file1
```

FILES

/tmp/d3∗
/usr/lib/diff3prog

SEE ALSO

diff(1).

BUGS

Text lines that consist of a single **.** will defeat **−e**.
Files longer than 64K bytes will not work.

NAME

dircmp − directory comparison

SYNOPSIS

dircmp [**−d**] [**−s**] [**−w***n*] dir1 dir2

DESCRIPTION

dircmp examines *dir1* and *dir2* and generates various tabulated information about the contents of the directories. Listings of files that are unique to each directory are generated for all the options. If no option is entered, a list is output indicating whether the file names common to both directories have the same contents.

−d Compare the contents of files with the same name in both directories and output a list telling what must be changed in the two files to bring them into agreement. The list format is described in *diff*(1).

−s Suppress messages about identical files.

−w*n* Change the width of the output line to *n* characters. The default width is 72.

SEE ALSO

cmp(1), diff(1).

NAME

du − summarize disk usage

SYNOPSIS

du [**−sar**] [names]

DESCRIPTION

du reports the number of blocks contained in all files and (recursively) directories within each directory and file specified by the *names* argument. The block count includes the indirect blocks of the file. If *names* is missing, the current directory is used.

The optional arguments are as follows:

−s causes only the grand total (for each of the specified *names*) to be given.

−a causes an output line to be generated for each file.

If neither **−s** or **−a** is specified, an output line is generated for each directory only.

−r will cause *du* to generate messages about directories that cannot be read, files that cannot be opened, etc., rather than being silent (the default).

A file with two or more links is only counted once.

BUGS

If the **−a** option is not used, non-directories given as arguments are not listed.
If there are links between files in different directories where the directories are on separate branches of the file system hierarchy, *du* will count the excess files more than once.
Files with holes in them will get an incorrect block count. (See Chapter 5, File System Administration, in the *System Administrator's Guide*)

NAME

echo – echo arguments

SYNOPSIS

echo [arg] ...

DESCRIPTION

echo writes its arguments separated by blanks and terminated by a new-line on the standard output. It also understands C-like escape conventions; beware of conflicts with the shell's use of \:

\b	backspace
\c	print line without new-line
\f	form-feed
\n	new-line
\r	carriage return
\t	tab
\v	vertical tab
\\	backslash
\0*n*	where *n* is the 8-bit character whose ASCII code is the 1-, 2- or 3-digit octal number representing that character.

echo is useful for producing diagnostics in command files and for sending known data into a pipe.

SEE ALSO

sh(1).

CAVEATS

When representing an 8-bit character by using the escape convention **\0***n*, the *n* must **always** be preceded by the digit zero (0).

For example, typing: **echo 'WARNING:\07'** will print the phrase **WARNING:** and sound the "bell" on your terminal. The use of single (or double) quotes (or two backslashes) is required to protect the "\" that precedes the "07".

For the octal equivalents of each character, see ascii(5), in the *Programmer's Reference Manual.*

NAME

ed, red – text editor

SYNOPSIS

ed [**–s**] [**–p** string] [**–x**] [file]

red [**–s**] [**–p** string] [**–x**] [file]

DESCRIPTION

ed is the standard text editor. If the *file* argument is given, *ed* simulates an *e* command (see below) on the named file; that is to say, the file is read into *ed*'s buffer so that it can be edited.

–s Suppresses the printing of character counts by *e*, *r*, and *w* commands, of diagnostics from *e* and *q* commands, and of the **!** prompt after a **!***shell command*. Also, see the **WARNING** section at the end of this manual page.

–p Allows the user to specify a prompt string.

–x Encryption option; when this option is used, the file will be encrypted as it is being written and will require an encryption key to be read (see *crypt*(1)). Also, see the **WARNING** section at the end of this manual page.

ed operates on a copy of the file it is editing; changes made to the copy have no effect on the file until a *w* (write) command is given. The copy of the text being edited resides in a temporary file called the *buffer*. There is only one buffer.

red is a restricted version of *ed*. It will only allow editing of files in the current directory. It prohibits executing shell commands via **!***shell command*. Attempts to bypass these restrictions result in an error message (*restricted shell*).

Both *ed* and *red* support the *fspec*(4) formatting capability. After including a format specification as the first line of *file* and invoking *ed* with your terminal in **stty –tabs** or **stty tab3** mode (see *stty*(1)), the specified tab stops will automatically be used when scanning *file*. For example, if the first line of a file contained:

<:t5,10,15 s72:>

tab stops would be set at columns 5, 10, and 15, and a maximum line length of 72 would be imposed. NOTE: while inputing text, tab characters when typed are expanded to every eighth column as is the default.

Commands to *ed* have a simple and regular structure: zero, one, or two *addresses* followed by a single-character *command*, possibly followed by parameters to that command. These addresses specify one or more lines in the buffer. Every command that requires addresses has default addresses, so that the addresses can very often be omitted.

In general, only one command may appear on a line. Certain commands allow the input of text. This text is placed in the appropriate place in the buffer. While *ed* is accepting text, it is said to be in *input mode*. In this mode, *no* commands are recognized; all input is merely collected. Input mode is left by typing a period (.) alone at the beginning of a line, followed immediately by a carriage return.

ed supports a limited form of *regular expression* notation; regular expressions are used in addresses to specify lines and in some commands (e.g., *s*) to specify portions of a line that are to be substituted. A regular expression (RE) specifies a set of character strings. A member of this set of strings is said to be *matched* by the RE. The REs allowed by *ed* are constructed as follows:

The following *one-character RE*s match a *single* character:

1.1 An ordinary character (*not* one of those discussed in 1.2 below) is a one-character RE that matches itself.

1.2 A backslash (\) followed by any special character is a one-character RE that matches the special character itself. The special characters are:

   a. ., *, **[**, and \ (period, asterisk, left square bracket, and backslash, respectively), which are always special, *except* when they appear within square brackets (**[]**; see 1.4 below).

   b. ^ (caret or circumflex), which is special at the *beginning* of an *entire* RE (see 3.1 and 3.2 below), or when it immediately follows the left of a pair of square brackets (**[]**) (see 1.4 below).

   c. **$** (dollar sign), which is special at the *end* of an entire RE (see 3.2 below).

   d. The character used to bound (i.e., delimit) an entire RE, which is special for that RE (for example, see how slash (/) is used in the *g* command, below.)

1.3 A period (.) is a one-character RE that matches any character except new-line.

1.4 A non-empty string of characters enclosed in square brackets (**[]**) is a one-character RE that matches *any one* character in that string. If, however, the first character of the string is a circumflex (^), the one-character RE matches any character *except* new-line and the remaining characters in the string. The ^ has this special meaning *only* if it occurs first in the string. The minus (−) may be used to indicate a range of consecutive ASCII characters; for example, **[0−9]** is equivalent to **[0123456789]**. The − loses this special meaning if it occurs first (after an initial ^, if any) or last in the string. The right square bracket (**]**) does not terminate such a string when it is the first character within it (after an initial ^, if any); e.g., **[]a−f]** matches either a right square bracket (**]**) or one of the letters **a** through **f** inclusive. The four characters listed in 1.2.a above stand for themselves within such a string of characters.

The following rules may be used to construct *RE*s from one-character REs:

2.1 A one-character RE is a RE that matches whatever the one-character RE matches.

2.2 A one-character RE followed by an asterisk (*) is a RE that matches *zero* or more occurrences of the one-character RE. If there is any choice, the longest leftmost string that permits a match is chosen.

2.3 A one-character RE followed by \{*m*\}, \{*m*,\}, or \{*m*,*n*\} is a RE that matches a *range* of occurrences of the one-character RE. The values of *m* and *n* must be non-negative integers less than 256; \{*m*\} matches *exactly* *m* occurrences; \{*m*,\} matches *at least m* occurrences; \{*m*,*n*\} matches *any number* of occurrences *between m* and *n* inclusive. Whenever a choice exists, the RE matches as many occurrences as possible.

2.4 The concatenation of REs is a RE that matches the concatenation of the strings matched by each component of the RE.

2.5 A RE enclosed between the character sequences **\(** and **\)** is a RE that matches whatever the unadorned RE matches.

2.6 The expression *n* matches the same string of characters as was matched by an expression enclosed between **\(** and **\)** *earlier* in the same RE. Here *n* is a digit; the sub-expression specified is that beginning with the *n*-th occurrence of **\(** counting from the left. For example, the expression **^\(.*\)\1$** matches a line consisting of two repeated appearances of the same string.

Finally, an *entire RE* may be constrained to match only an initial segment or final segment of a line (or both).

3.1 A circumflex (**^**) at the beginning of an entire RE constrains that RE to match an *initial* segment of a line.

3.2 A dollar sign (**$**) at the end of an entire RE constrains that RE to match a *final* segment of a line.

The construction **^***entire RE***$** constrains the entire RE to match the entire line.

The null RE (e.g., **//**) is equivalent to the last RE encountered. See also the last paragraph before *FILES* below.

To understand addressing in *ed* it is necessary to know that at any time there is a *current line*. Generally speaking, the current line is the last line affected by a command; the exact effect on the current line is discussed under the description of each command. *Addresses* are constructed as follows:

1. The character **.** addresses the current line.
2. The character **$** addresses the last line of the buffer.
3. A decimal number *n* addresses the *n*-th line of the buffer.
4. '*x* addresses the line marked with the mark name character *x*, which must be a lower-case letter. Lines are marked with the *k* command described below.
5. A RE enclosed by slashes (**/**) addresses the first line found by searching *forward* from the line *following* the current line toward the end of the buffer and stopping at the first line containing a string matching the RE. If necessary, the search wraps around to the beginning of the buffer and

continues up to and including the current line, so that the entire buffer is searched. See also the last paragraph before *FILES* below.

6. A RE enclosed in question marks (**?**) addresses the first line found by searching *backward* from the line *preceding* the current line toward the beginning of the buffer and stopping at the first line containing a string matching the RE. If necessary, the search wraps around to the end of the buffer and continues up to and including the current line. See also the last paragraph before *FILES* below.

7. An address followed by a plus sign (+) or a minus sign (−) followed by a decimal number specifies that address plus (respectively minus) the indicated number of lines. The plus sign may be omitted.

8. If an address begins with + or −, the addition or subtraction is taken with respect to the current line; e.g, **−5** is understood to mean **.−5**.

9. If an address ends with + or −, then 1 is added to or subtracted from the address, respectively. As a consequence of this rule and of Rule 8, immediately above, the address − refers to the line preceding the current line. (To maintain compatibility with earlier versions of the editor, the character ^ in addresses is entirely equivalent to −.) Moreover, trailing + and − characters have a cumulative effect, so −− refers to the current line less 2.

10. For convenience, a comma (**,**) stands for the address pair **1,$**, while a semicolon (**;**) stands for the pair **.,$**.

Commands may require zero, one, or two addresses. Commands that require no addresses regard the presence of an address as an error. Commands that accept one or two addresses assume default addresses when an insufficient number of addresses is given; if more addresses are given than such a command requires, the last one(s) are used.

Typically, addresses are separated from each other by a comma (**,**). They may also be separated by a semicolon (**;**). In the latter case, the current line (**.**) is set to the first address, and only then is the second address calculated. This feature can be used to determine the starting line for forward and backward searches (see Rules 5 and 6, above). The second address of any two-address sequence must correspond to a line that follows, in the buffer, the line corresponding to the first address.

In the following list of *ed* commands, the default addresses are shown in parentheses. The parentheses are *not* part of the address; they show that the given addresses are the default.

It is generally illegal for more than one command to appear on a line. However, any command (except *e*, *f*, *r*, or *w*) may be suffixed by **l**, **n**, or **p** in which case the current line is either listed, numbered or printed, respectively, as discussed below under the *l*, *n*, and *p* commands.

(.)a
<text>
.

The *a*ppend command reads the given text and appends it after the addressed line; **.** is left at the last inserted line, or, if there were none, at the addressed line. Address 0 is legal for this command: it causes the "appended" text to be placed at the beginning of the buffer. The maximum number of characters that may be entered from a terminal is 256 per line (including the new-line character).

(.)c
<text>
.

The *c*hange command deletes the addressed lines, then accepts input text that replaces these lines; **.** is left at the last line input, or, if there were none, at the first line that was not deleted.

(.,.)d

The *d*elete command deletes the addressed lines from the buffer. The line after the last line deleted becomes the current line; if the lines deleted were originally at the end of the buffer, the new last line becomes the current line.

e *file*

The *e*dit command causes the entire contents of the buffer to be deleted, and then the named file to be read in; **.** is set to the last line of the buffer. If no file name is given, the currently-remembered file name, if any, is used (see the *f* command). The number of characters read is typed; *file* is remembered for possible use as a default file name in subsequent *e*, *r*, and *w* commands. If *file* is replaced by **!**, the rest of the line is taken to be a shell (*sh*(1)) command whose output is to be read. Such a shell command is *not* remembered as the current file name. See also *DIAGNOSTICS* below.

E *file*

The *E*dit command is like *e*, except that the editor does not check to see if any changes have been made to the buffer since the last *w* command.

f *file*

If *file* is given, the *f*ile-name command changes the currently-remembered file name to *file*; otherwise, it prints the currently-remembered file name.

(1,$)g/*RE*/*command list*

In the *g*lobal command, the first step is to mark every line that matches the given RE. Then, for every such line, the given *command list* is executed with **.** initially set to that line. A single command or the first of a list of commands appears on the same line as the global command. All lines of a multi-line list except the last line must be ended with a \; *a*, *i*, and *c* commands and associated input are permitted. The **.** terminating input mode may be omitted if it would be the last line of the *command list*. An empty *command list* is equivalent to the *p* command. The *g*, *G*, *v*, and *V* commands are *not* permitted in the *command list*. See also *BUGS* and the last paragraph before *FILES* below.

(1,$)G/*RE*/

In the interactive *G*lobal command, the first step is to mark every line that matches the given RE. Then, for every such line, that line is printed, **.** is changed to that line, and any *one* command (other than one of the *a*, *c*, *i*, *g*, *G*, *v*, and *V* commands) may be input and is executed. After the execution of that command, the next marked line is printed, and so on; a new-line acts as a null command; an **&** causes the re-execution of the most recent command executed within the current invocation of *G*. Note that the commands input as part of the execution of the *G* command may address and affect *any* lines in the buffer. The *G* command can be terminated by an interrupt signal (ASCII DEL or BREAK).

h

The *h*elp command gives a short error message that explains the reason for the most recent **?** diagnostic.

H

The *H*elp command causes *ed* to enter a mode in which error messages are printed for all subsequent **?** diagnostics. It will also explain the previous **?** if there was one. The *H* command alternately turns this mode on and off; it is initially off.

(.)i
<text>
.

The *i*nsert command inserts the given text before the addressed line; **.** is left at the last inserted line, or, if there were none, at the addressed line. This command differs from the *a* command only in the placement of the input text. Address 0 is not legal for this command. The maximum number of characters that may be entered from a terminal is 256 per line (including the new-line character).

(.,.+1)j

The *j*oin command joins contiguous lines by removing the appropriate new-line characters. If exactly one address is given, this command does nothing.

(.)k*x*

The mar*k* command marks the addressed line with name *x*, which must be a lower-case letter. The address '*x* then addresses this line; **.** is unchanged.

(.,.)l

The *l*ist command prints the addressed lines in an unambiguous way: a few non-printing characters (e.g., *tab*, *backspace*) are represented by visually mnemonic overstrikes. All other non-printing characters are printed in octal, and long lines are folded. An *l* command may be appended to any other command other than *e*, *f*, *r*, or *w*.

(.,.)m*a*

The *m*ove command repositions the addressed line(s) after the line addressed by *a*. Address 0 is legal for *a* and causes the addressed line(s) to be moved to the beginning of the file. It is an error if address *a* falls within the range of moved lines; **.** is left at the last line moved.

(.,.)n

The *n*umber command prints the addressed lines, preceding each line by its line number and a tab character; **.** is left at the last line printed. The *n* command may be appended to any other command other than *e*, *f*, *r*, or *w*.

(.,.)p

The *p*rint command prints the addressed lines; **.** is left at the last line printed. The *p* command may be appended to any other command other than *e*, *f*, *r*, or *w*. For example, *dp* deletes the current line and prints the new current line.

P

The editor will prompt with a * for all subsequent commands. The *P* command alternately turns this mode on and off; it is initially off.

q

The *q*uit command causes *ed* to exit. No automatic write of a file is done; however, see *DIAGNOSTICS*, below.

Q

The editor exits without checking if changes have been made in the buffer since the last *w* command.

($)r *file*

The *r*ead command reads in the given file after the addressed line. If no file name is given, the currently-remembered file name, if any, is used (see *e* and *f* commands). The currently-remembered file name is *not* changed unless *file* is the very first file name mentioned since *ed* was invoked. Address 0 is legal for *r* and causes the file to be read at the beginning of the buffer. If the read is successful, the number of characters read is typed; **.** is set to the last line read in. If *file* is replaced by **!**, the rest of the line is taken to be a shell (*sh*(1)) command whose output is to be read. For example, "$r !ls" appends current directory to the end of the file being edited. Such a shell command is *not* remembered as the current file name.

(.,.)s/*RE***/***replacement***/** or
(.,.)s/*RE***/***replacement***/g** or
(.,.)s/*RE***/***replacement***/n** n = 1-512

The *s*ubstitute command searches each addressed line for an occurrence of the specified RE. In each line in which a match is found, all (non-overlapped) matched strings are replaced by the *replacement* if the global replacement indicator **g** appears after the command. If the global indicator does not appear, only the first occurrence of the matched string is replaced. If a number n appears after the command, only the n th occurrence of the matched string on each addressed line is replaced. It is an error for the substitution to fail on *all* addressed lines. Any character other than space or new-line may be used instead of / to delimit the RE and the *replacement*; **.** is left at the last line on which a substitution occurred. See also the last paragraph before *FILES* below.

An ampersand (**&**) appearing in the *replacement* is replaced by the string matching the RE on the current line. The special meaning of **&** in this context may be suppressed by preceding it by \. As a more general feature, the characters *n*, where *n* is a digit, are replaced by the text matched by the *n*-th regular subexpression of the specified RE enclosed between \(and \). When nested parenthesized subexpressions are present, *n* is determined by counting occurrences of \(starting from the left. When the character % is the only character in the *replacement*, the *replacement* used in the most recent substitute command is used as the *replacement* in the current substitute command. The % loses its special meaning when it is in a replacement string of more than one character or is preceded by a \.

A line may be split by substituting a new-line character into it. The new-line in the *replacement* must be escaped by preceding it by \. Such substitution cannot be done as part of a *g* or *v* command list.

(.,.)t*a*

This command acts just like the *m* command, except that a *copy* of the addressed lines is placed after address *a* (which may be 0); **.** is left at the last line of the copy.

u

The *u*ndo command nullifies the effect of the most recent command that modified anything in the buffer, namely the most recent *a*, *c*, *d*, *g*, *i*, *j*, *m*, *r*, *s*, *t*, *v*, *G*, or *V* command.

(1,$)v/*RE***/***command list*

This command is the same as the global command *g* except that the *command list* is executed with **.** initially set to every line that does *not* match the RE.

(1,$)V/*RE***/**

This command is the same as the interactive global command *G* except that the lines that are marked during the first step are those that do *not* match the RE.

(1,$)w *file*

The *w*rite command writes the addressed lines into the named file. If the file does not exist, it is created with mode 666 (readable and writable by everyone), unless your *umask* setting (see *umask*(1)) dictates otherwise. The currently-remembered file name is *not* changed unless *file* is the very first file name mentioned since *ed* was invoked. If no file name is given, the currently-remembered file name, if any, is used (see *e* and *f* commands); **.** is unchanged. If the command is successful, the number of characters written is typed. If *file* is replaced by **!**, the rest of the line is taken to be a shell (*sh*(1)) command whose standard input is the addressed lines. Such a shell command is *not* remembered as the current file name.

X

An encryption key is requested from the standard input. Subsequent *e*, *r*, and *w* commands will use this key to encrypt or decrypt the text (see *crypt*(1)). An explicitly empty key turns off encryption. Also, see the **−x** option of *ed*.

($)=

The line number of the addressed line is typed; **.** is unchanged by this command.

!*shell command*

The remainder of the line after the **!** is sent to the UNIX system shell (*sh*(1)) to be interpreted as a command. Within the text of that command, the unescaped character % is replaced with the remembered file name; if a **!** appears as the first character of the shell command, it is replaced with the text of the previous shell command. Thus, **!!** will repeat the last shell command. If any expansion is performed, the expanded line is echoed; **.** is unchanged.

(.+1)<new-line>

An address alone on a line causes the addressed line to be printed. A new-line alone is equivalent to **.+1p**; it is useful for stepping forward through the buffer.

If an interrupt signal (ASCII DEL or BREAK) is sent, *ed* prints a **?** and returns to *its* command level.

Some size limitations: 512 characters per line, 256 characters per global command list, and 64 characters per file name. The limit on the number of lines depends on the amount of user memory: each line takes 1 word.

When reading a file, *ed* discards ASCII NUL characters. Files (e.g., **a.out**) that contain characters not in the ASCII set (bit 8 on) cannot be edited by *ed*.

If a file is not terminated by a new-line character, **ed** adds one and outputs a message explaining what it did.

If the closing delimiter of a RE or of a replacement string (e.g., /) would be the last character before a new-line, that delimiter may be omitted, in which case the addressed line is printed. The following pairs of commands are equivalent:

```
s/s1/s2   s/s1/s2/p
g/s1      g/s1/p
?s1       ?s1?
```

FILES

/usr/tmp	default directory for temporary work file.
$TMPDIR	if this environmental variable is not null, its value is used in place of /usr/tmp as the directory name for the temporary work file.
ed.hup	work is saved here if the terminal is hung up.

DIAGNOSTICS

?	for command errors.
?*file*	for an inaccessible file.
	(use the *h*elp and *H*elp commands for detailed explanations).

If changes have been made in the buffer since the last *w* command that wrote the entire buffer, *ed* warns the user if an attempt is made to destroy *ed*'s buffer via the *e* or *q* commands. It prints **?** and allows one to continue editing. A second *e* or *q* command at this point will take effect. The **−s** command-line option inhibits this feature.

SEE ALSO

edit(1), ex(1), grep(1), sed(1), sh(1), stty(1), umask(1), vi(1).
fspec(4), regexp(5) in the *Programmer's Reference Manual*.

BUGS

A *!* command cannot be subject to a *g* or a *v* command.

The *!* command and the **!** escape from the *e*, *r*, and *w* commands cannot be used if the editor is invoked from a restricted shell (see *sh*(1)).

The sequence **\n** in a RE does not match a new-line character.

Characters are masked to 7 bits on input.

If the editor input is coming from a command file (e.g., ed file < ed-cmd-file), the editor will exit at the first failure.

WARNINGS

The **−x** option is provided with the Security Administration Utilities, which is available only in the United States.

The − option, although supported in this release for upward compatibility, will no longer be supported in the next major release of the system. Convert shell scripts that use the − option to use the **−s** option, instead.

NAME

edit – text editor (variant of ex for casual users)

SYNOPSIS

edit [**−r**] [**−x**] *name* ...

DESCRIPTION

edit is a variant of the text editor *ex* recommended for new or casual users who wish to use a command-oriented editor.

−r Recover file after an editor or system crash.

−x Encryption option; when this option is used, the file will be encrypted as it is being written and will require an encryption key to be read (see *crypt*(1)). Also, see the **WARNING** section at the end of this manual page.

The following brief introduction should help you get started with *edit.* If you are using a CRT terminal you may want to learn about the display editor *vi.*

To edit the contents of an existing file you begin with the command "edit name" to the shell. *edit* makes a copy of the file which you can then edit, and tells you how many lines and characters are in the file. To create a new file, just make up a name for the file and try to run *edit* on it; you will cause an error diagnostic, but do not worry.

edit prompts for commands with the character ':', which you should see after starting the editor. If you are editing an existing file, then you will have some lines in *edit's* buffer (its name for the copy of the file you are editing). Most commands to *edit* use its "current line" if you do not tell them which line to use. Thus if you say **print** (which can be abbreviated **p**) and hit carriage return (as you should after all *edit* commands) this current line will be printed. If you **delete** (**d**) the current line, *edit* will print the new current line. When you start editing, *edit* makes the last line of the file the current line. If you **delete** this last line, then the new last line becomes the current one. In general, after a **delete,** the next line in the file becomes the current line. (Deleting the last line is a special case.)

If you start with an empty file or wish to add some new lines, then the **append** (**a**) command can be used. After you give this command (typing a carriage return after the word **append**) *edit* will read lines from your terminal until you give a line consisting of just a "**.**", placing these lines after the current line. The last line you type then becomes the current line. The command **insert** (**i**) is like **append** but places the lines you give before, rather than after, the current line.

edit numbers the lines in the buffer, with the first line having number 1. If you give the command "1" then *edit* will type this first line. If you then give the command **delete** *edit* will delete the first line, line 2 will become line 1, and *edit* will print the current line (the new line 1) so you can see where you are. In general, the current line will always be the last line affected by a command.

You can make a change to some text within the current line by using the **substitute** (**s**) command. You say "s/*old*/*new*/" where *old* is replaced by the old characters you want to get rid of and *new* is the new characters you want to replace it with.

The command **file** (**f**) will tell you how many lines there are in the buffer you are editing and will say "[Modified]" if you have changed it. After modifying a file you can put the buffer text back to replace the file by giving a **write** (**w**) command. You can then leave the editor by issuing a **quit** (**q**) command. If you run *edit* on a file, but do not change it, it is not necessary (but does no harm) to **write** the file back. If you try to **quit** from *edit* after modifying the buffer without writing it out, you will be warned that there has been "No **write** since last change" and *edit* will await another command. If you wish not to **write** the buffer out then you can issue another **quit** command. The buffer is then irretrievably discarded, and you return to the shell.

By using the **delete** and **append** commands, and giving line numbers to see lines in the file you can make any changes you desire. You should learn at least a few more things, however, if you are to use *edit* more than a few times.

The **change** (**c**) command will change the current line to a sequence of lines you supply (as in **append** you give lines up to a line consisting of only a "."). You can tell **change** to change more than one line by giving the line numbers of the lines you want to change, i.e., "3,5change". You can print lines this way too. Thus "1,23p" prints the first 23 lines of the file.

The **undo** (**u**) command will reverse the effect of the last command you gave which changed the buffer. Thus if you give a **substitute** command which does not do what you want, you can say **undo** and the old contents of the line will be restored. You can also **undo** an **undo** command so that you can continue to change your mind. *edit* will give you a warning message when commands you do affect more than one line of the buffer. If the amount of change seems unreasonable, you should consider doing an *undo* and looking to see what happened. If you decide that the change is ok, then you can *undo* again to get it back. Note that commands such as *write* and *quit* cannot be undone.

To look at the next line in the buffer you can just hit carriage return. To look at a number of lines hit ^D (control key and, while it is held down D key, then let up both) rather than carriage return. This will show you a half screen of lines on a CRT or 12 lines on a hardcopy terminal. You can look at the text around where you are by giving the command "z.". The current line will then be the last line printed; you can get back to the line where you were before the "z." command by saying "''". The **z** command can also be given other following characters "z−" prints a screen of text (or 24 lines) ending where you are; "z+" prints the next screenful. If you want less than a screenful of lines, type in "z.12" to get 12 lines total. This method of giving counts works in general; thus you can delete 5 lines starting with the current line with the command "delete 5".

To find things in the file, you can use line numbers if you happen to know them; since the line numbers change when you insert and delete lines this is somewhat unreliable. You can search backwards and forwards in the file for strings by giving commands of the form **/text/** to search forward for *text* or **?text?** to search backward for *text.* If a search reaches the end of the file without finding the text it wraps, end around, and continues to search back to the line where you are. A useful feature here is a search of the form **/^text/** which searches for *text* at the beginning of a line. Similarly **/text$/** searches for *text* at the end of a line. You can leave off the trailing / or ? in these commands.

The current line has a symbolic name "**.**"; this is most useful in a range of lines as in ".,$print" which prints the rest of the lines in the file. To get to the last line in the file you can refer to it by its symbolic name "$". Thus the command "$ delete" or "$d" deletes the last line in the file, no matter which line was the current line before. Arithmetic with line references is also possible. Thus the line "$−5" is the fifth before the last, and ".+20" is 20 lines after the present.

You can find out which line you are at by doing ".=". This is useful if you wish to move or copy a section of text within a file or between files. Find out the first and last line numbers you wish to copy or move (say 10 to 20). For a move you can then say "10,20delete a" which deletes these lines from the file and places them in a buffer named *a*. *edit* has 26 such buffers named *a* through *z*. You can later get these lines back by doing "put a" to put the contents of buffer *a* after the current line. If you want to move or copy these lines between files you can give an **edit** (**e**) command after copying the lines, following it with the name of the other file you wish to edit, i.e., "edit chapter2". By changing *delete* to *yank* above you can get a pattern for copying lines. If the text you wish to move or copy is all within one file then you can just say "10,20move $" for example. It is not necessary to use named buffers in this case (but you can if you wish).

SEE ALSO

ed(1), ex(1), vi(1).

WARNING

The **−x** option is provided with the Security Administration Utilities, which is available only in the United States.

NAME

egrep − search a file for a pattern using full regular expressions

SYNOPSIS

egrep [options] full regular expression [file ...]

DESCRIPTION

egrep (*expression grep*) searches files for a pattern of characters and prints all lines that contain that pattern. *egrep* uses full regular expressions (expressions that have string values that use the full set of alphanumeric and special characters) to match the patterns. It uses a fast deterministic algorithm that sometimes needs exponential space.

egrep accepts full regular expressions as in *ed*(1), except for \(and \), with the addition of:

1. A full regular expression followed by + that matches one or more occurrences of the full regular expression.
2. A full regular expression followed by **?** that matches 0 or 1 occurrences of the full regular expression.
3. Full regular expressions separated by **|** or by a new-line that match strings that are matched by any of the expressions.
4. A full regular expression that may be enclosed in parentheses **()** for grouping.

Be careful using the characters **$**, *****, **[**, **^**, **|**, **(**, **)**, and \ in *full regular expression*, because they are also meaningful to the shell. It is safest to enclose the entire *full regular expression* in single quotes '...'.

The order of precedence of operators is **[]**, then ***?+**, then concatenation, then **|** and new-line.

If no files are specified, *egrep* assumes standard input. Normally, each line found is copied to the standard output. The file name is printed before each line found if there is more than one input file.

Command line options are:

−b Precede each line by the block number on which it was found. This can be useful in locating block numbers by context (first block is 0).

−c Print only a count of the lines that contain the pattern.

−i Ignore upper/lower case distinction during comparisons.

−l Print the names of files with matching lines once, separated by newlines. Does not repeat the names of files when the pattern is found more than once.

−n Precede each line by its line number in the file (first line is 1).

−v Print all lines except those that contain the pattern.

−e *special_expression*
Search for a *special expression* (*full regular expression* that begins with a −).

−f *file*
Take the list of *full regular expressions* from *file*.

SEE ALSO

ed(1), fgrep(1), grep(1), sed(1), sh(1).

DIAGNOSTICS

Exit status is 0 if any matches are found, 1 if none, 2 for syntax errors or inaccessible files (even if matches were found).

BUGS

Ideally there should be only one *grep* command, but there is not a single algorithm that spans a wide enough range of space-time tradeoffs. Lines are limited to BUFSIZ characters; longer lines are truncated. BUFSIZ is defined in **/usr/include/stdio.h.**

NAME

enable, disable – enable/disable LP printers

SYNOPSIS

enable printers
disable [−**c**] [−**r**[reason]] printers

DESCRIPTION

enable activates the named *printers*, enabling them to print requests taken by *lp*(1). Use *lpstat*(1) to find the status of printers.

Disable deactivates the named *printers*, disabling them from printing requests taken by *lp*(1). By default, any requests that are currently printing on the designated printers will be reprinted in their entirety either on the same printer or on another member of the same class. Use *lpstat*(1) to find the status of printers. Options useful with *disable* are:

−**c** Cancel any requests that are currently printing on any of the designated printers.

−**r**[*reason*] Associates a *reason* with the deactivation of the printers. This reason applies to all printers mentioned up to the next −**r** option. If the −**r** option is not present or the −**r** option is given without a reason, then a default reason will be used. *Reason* is reported by *lpstat*(1).

FILES

/usr/spool/lp/*

SEE ALSO

lp(1), lpstat(1).

NAME

env – set environment for command execution

SYNOPSIS

env [–] [name=value] ... [command args]

DESCRIPTION

env obtains the current *environment*, modifies it according to its arguments, then executes the command with the modified environment. Arguments of the form *name=value* are merged into the inherited environment before the command is executed. The – flag causes the inherited environment to be ignored completely, so that the command is executed with exactly the environment specified by the arguments.

If no command is specified, the resulting environment is printed, one name-value pair per line.

SEE ALSO

sh(1).
exec(2), profile(4), environ(5) in the *Programmer's Reference Manual*.

NAME

ex – text editor

SYNOPSIS

ex [–] [**–v**] [**–t** *tag*] [**–r**] [**–R**] [**–x**] [+*command*] *name* ...

DESCRIPTION

ex is the root of a family of editors: *ex* and *vi*. *ex* is a superset of *ed*, with the most notable extension being a display editing facility. Display based editing is the focus of *vi*.

If you have a CRT terminal, you may wish to use a display based editor; in this case see *vi*(1), which is a command which focuses on the display editing portion of *ex*.

For ed Users

If you have used *ed* you will find that *ex* has a number of new features useful on CRT terminals. Intelligent terminals and high speed terminals are very pleasant to use with *vi*. Generally, the editor uses far more of the capabilities of terminals than *ed* does, and uses the terminal capability data base (see *Terminal Information Utilities Guide*) and the type of the terminal you are using from the variable TERM in the environment to determine how to drive your terminal efficiently. The editor makes use of features such as insert and delete character and line in its **visual** command (which can be abbreviated **vi**) and which is the central mode of editing when using *vi*(1).

ex contains a number of new features for easily viewing the text of the file. The **z** command gives easy access to windows of text. Hitting ^D causes the editor to scroll a half-window of text and is more useful for quickly stepping through a file than just hitting return. Of course, the screen-oriented **visual** mode gives constant access to editing context.

ex gives you more help when you make mistakes. The **undo** (**u**) command allows you to reverse any single change which goes astray. *ex* gives you a lot of feedback, normally printing changed lines, and indicates when more than a few lines are affected by a command so that it is easy to detect when a command has affected more lines than it should have.

The editor also normally prevents overwriting existing files unless you edited them so that you do not accidentally clobber with a *write* a file other than the one you are editing. If the system (or editor) crashes, or you accidentally hang up the telephone, you can use the editor **recover** command to retrieve your work. This will get you back to within a few lines of where you left off.

ex has several features for dealing with more than one file at a time. You can give it a list of files on the command line and use the **next** (**n**) command to deal with each in turn. The **next** command can also be given a list of file names, or a pattern as used by the shell to specify a new set of files to be dealt with. In general, file names in the editor may be formed with full shell metasyntax. The metacharacter '%' is also available in forming file names and is replaced by the name of the current file.

For moving text between files and within a file the editor has a group of buffers, named *a* through *z*. You can place text in these named buffers and carry it over when you edit another file.

There is a command **&** in *ex* which repeats the last **substitute** command. In addition there is a confirmed substitute command. You give a range of substitutions to be done and the editor interactively asks whether each substitution is desired.

It is possible to ignore case of letters in searches and substitutions. *ex* also allows regular expressions which match words to be constructed. This is convenient, for example, in searching for the word "edit" if your document also contains the word "editor."

ex has a set of *options* which you can set to tailor it to your liking. One option which is very useful is the *autoindent* option which allows the editor to automatically supply leading white space to align text. You can then use the ^D key as a backtab and space and tab forward to align new code easily.

Miscellaneous new useful features include an intelligent **join** (**j**) command which supplies white space between joined lines automatically, commands < and > which shift groups of lines, and the ability to filter portions of the buffer through commands such as *sort*.

INVOCATION OPTIONS

The following invocation options are interpreted by *ex*:

–	Suppress all interactive-user feedback. This is useful in processing editor scripts.
–v	Invokes *vi*
–t *tagfR*	Edit the file containing the *tag* and position the editor at its definition.
–r *file*	Recover *file* after an editor or system crash. If *file* is not specified a list of all saved files will be printed.
–R	*Readonly* mode set, prevents accidentally overwriting the file.
–x	Encryption option; when this option is used, the file will be encrypted as it is being written and will require an encryption key to be read (see *crypt*(1)). Also, see the **WARNING** section at the end of this manual page.
+*command*	Begin editing by executing the specified editor search or positioning *command*.

The *name* argument indicates files to be edited.

ex States

Command	Normal and initial state. Input prompted for by **:**. Your kill character cancels partial command.
Insert	Entered by **a**, **i**, or **c**. Arbitrary text may be entered. Insert is normally terminated by a line having only **.** on it, or abnormally with an interrupt.
Visual	Entered by **vi**, terminates with **Q** or ^\\.

ex command names and abbreviations

abbrev	**ab**	next	**n**	undo	**u**
append	**a**	number	**nu**	unmap	**unm**
args	**ar**	preserve	**pre**	version	**ve**
change	**c**	print	**p**	visual	**vi**
copy	**co**	put	**pu**	write	**w**
delete	**d**	quit	**q**	xit	**x**
edit	**e**	read	**re**	yank	**ya**
file	**f**	recover	**rec**	window	**z**
global	**g**	rewind	**rew**	escape	**!**
insert	**i**	set	**se**	lshift	<
join	**j**	shell	**sh**	print next	CR
list	**l**	source	**so**	resubst	**&**
map		stop	**st**	rshift	>
mark	**ma**	substitute	**s**	scroll	^D
move	**m**	unabbrev	**una**		

ex Command Addresses

n	line *n*	*/pat*	next with *pat*
.	current	*?pat*	previous with *pat*
$	last	*x-n*	*n* before *x*
+	next	*x,y*	*x* through *y*
−	previous	*'x*	marked with *x*
+*n*	*n* forward	''	previous context
%	1,$		

Initializing options

EXINIT	place **set**'s here in environment var.
$HOME/.exrc	editor initialization file
./.exrc	editor initialization file
set *x*	enable option
set no*x*	disable option
set *x=val*	give value *val*
set	show changed options
set all	show all options
set *x*?	show value of option *x*

Most useful options

autoindent	ai	supply indent
autowrite	aw	write before changing files
ignorecase	ic	in scanning
list		print ^I for tab, $ at end
magic		**. [*** special in patterns
number	nu	number lines
paragraphs	para	macro names which start ...
redraw		simulate smart terminal
scroll		command mode lines
sections	sect	macro names ...
shiftwidth	sw	for < >, and input ^D
showmatch	sm	to **)** and } as typed
showmode	smd	show insert mode in *vi*

slowopen	slow	stop updates during insert
window		visual mode lines
wrapscan	ws	around end of buffer?
wrapmargin	wm	automatic line splitting

Scanning pattern formation

^	beginning of line
$	end of line
.	any character
\<	beginning of word
\>	end of word
[*str*]	any char in *str*
[↑*str*]	... not in *str*
[*x*−*y*]	... between *x* and *y*
*	any number of preceding

AUTHOR

Vi and *ex* are based on software developed by The University of California, Berkeley California, Computer Science Division, Department of Electrical Engineering and Computer Science.

FILES

/usr/lib/ex?.?strings	error messages
/usr/lib/ex?.?recover	recover command
/usr/lib/ex?.?preserve	preserve command
/usr/lib/*/*	describes capabilities of terminals
$HOME/.exrc	editor startup file
./.exrc	editor startup file
/tmp/Ex*nnnnn*	editor temporary
/tmp/Rx*nnnnn*	named buffer temporary
/usr/preserve/*login*	preservation directory (where *login* is the user's login)

SEE ALSO

awk(1), ed(1), edit(1), grep(1), sed(1), vi(1).
curses(3X), term(4), terminfo(4) in the *Programmer's Reference Manual.*
The *Terminal Information Utilities Guide.*

WARNING

The **−x** option is provided with the Security Administration Utilities, which is available only in the United States.

BUGS

The *undo* command causes all marks to be lost on lines changed and then restored if the marked lines were changed.

Undo never clears the buffer modified condition.

The *z* command prints a number of logical rather than physical lines. More than a screen full of output may result if long lines are present.

File input/output errors do not print a name if the command line '−' option is used.

There is no easy way to do a single scan ignoring case.

The editor does not warn if text is placed in named buffers and not used before exiting the editor.

Null characters are discarded in input files and cannot appear in resultant files.

NAME

expr − evaluate arguments as an expression

SYNOPSIS

expr arguments

DESCRIPTION

The arguments are taken as an expression. After evaluation, the result is written on the standard output. Terms of the expression must be separated by blanks. Characters special to the shell must be escaped. Note that **0** is returned to indicate a zero value, rather than the null string. Strings containing blanks or other special characters should be quoted. Integer-valued arguments may be preceded by a unary minus sign. Internally, integers are treated as 32-bit, 2s complement numbers.

The operators and keywords are listed below. Characters that need to be escaped are preceded by \. The list is in order of increasing precedence, with equal precedence operators grouped within {} symbols.

expr \| *expr*
: returns the first *expr* if it is neither null nor **0**, otherwise returns the second *expr*.

expr \& *expr*
: returns the first *expr* if neither *expr* is null or **0**, otherwise returns **0**.

expr { =, \>, \>=, \<, \<=, != } *expr*
: returns the result of an integer comparison if both arguments are integers, otherwise returns the result of a lexical comparison.

expr { +, − } *expr*
: addition or subtraction of integer-valued arguments.

expr { *, /, % } *expr*
: multiplication, division, or remainder of the integer-valued arguments.

expr : *expr*
: The matching operator **:** compares the first argument with the second argument which must be a regular expression. Regular expression syntax is the same as that of *ed*(1), except that all patterns are "anchored" (i.e., begin with ^) and, therefore, ^ is not a special character, in that context. Normally, the matching operator returns the number of characters matched (**0** on failure). Alternatively, the **\(...\)** pattern symbols can be used to return a portion of the first argument.

EXAMPLES

1. a=\`expr $a + 1\`

   adds 1 to the shell variable **a**.

2. # 'For $a equal to either "/usr/abc/file" or just "file"'
   expr $a : '.*/\(.*\)' \| $a

   returns the last segment of a path name (i.e., file). Watch out for / alone as an argument: *expr* will take it as the division operator (see BUGS below).

3. # A better representation of example 2.
```
expr //$a : '.*/\(.*\)'
```

The addition of the // characters eliminates any ambiguity about the division operator and simplifies the whole expression.

4.
```
expr $VAR : '.*'
```

returns the number of characters in **$VAR**.

SEE ALSO

ed(1), sh(1).

DIAGNOSTICS

As a side effect of expression evaluation, *expr* returns the following exit values:

0	if the expression is neither null nor **0**
1	if the expression *is* null or **0**
2	for invalid expressions.

syntax error	for operator/operand errors
non-numeric argument	if arithmetic is attempted on such a string

BUGS

After argument processing by the shell, *expr* cannot tell the difference between an operator and an operand except by the value. If **$a** is an =, the command:

```
expr $a = '='
```

looks like:

```
expr = = =
```

as the arguments are passed to *expr* (and they will all be taken as the = operator). The following works:

```
expr X$a = X=
```

NAME

factor – obtain the prime factors of a number

SYNOPSIS

factor [integer]

DESCRIPTION

When you use *factor* without an argument, it waits for you to give it an integer. After you give it a positive integer less than or equal to 10^{14}, it factors the integer, prints its prime factors the proper number of times, and then waits for another integer. *factor* exits if it encounters a zero or any non-numeric character.

If you invoke *factor* with an argument, it factors the integer as described above, and then it exits.

The maximum time to factor an integer is proportional to $\cdot\ \bar{n}$. *factor* will take this time when n is prime or the square of a prime.

DIAGNOSTICS

factor prints the error message, "Ouch," for input out of range or for garbage input.

NAME

fgrep − search a file for a character string

SYNOPSIS

fgrep [options] string [file ...]

DESCRIPTION

fgrep (fast *grep*) seaches files for a character string and prints all lines that contain that string. *fgrep* is different from *grep(1)* and *egrep(1)* because it searches for a string, instead of searching for a pattern that matches an expression. It uses a fast and compact algorithm.

The characters **$**, *****, **[**, **^**, **|**, **(**, **)**, and \ are interpreted literally by *fgrep*, that is, *fgrep* does not recognize full regular expressions as does *egrep*. Since these characters have special meaning to the shell, it is safest to enclose the entire *string* in single quotes '...'.

If no files are specified, *fgrep* assumes standard input. Normally, each line found is copied to the standard output. The file name is printed before each line found if there is more than one input file.

Command line options are:

−b Precede each line by the block number on which it was found. This can be useful in locating block numbers by context (first block is 0).

−c Print only a count of the lines that contain the pattern.

−i Ignore upper/lower case distinction during comparisons.

−l Print the names of files with matching lines once, separated by new-lines. Does not repeat the names of files when the pattern is found more than once.

−n Precede each line by its line number in the file (first line is 1).

−v Print all lines except those that contain the pattern.

−x Print only lines matched entirely.

−e *special_string*
Search for a *special string* (*string* begins with a −).

−f *file*
Take the list of *strings* from *file*.

SEE ALSO

ed(1), egrep(1), grep(1), sed(1), sh(1).

DIAGNOSTICS

Exit status is 0 if any matches are found, 1 if none, 2 for syntax errors or inaccessible files (even if matches were found).

BUGS

Ideally there should be only one *grep* command, but there is not a single algorithm that spans a wide enough range of space-time tradeoffs. Lines are limited to BUFSIZ characters; longer lines are truncated. BUFSIZ is defined in **/usr/include/stdio.h**.

NAME

file − determine file type

SYNOPSIS

file [**−c**] [**−f** ffile] [**−m** mfile] arg ...

DESCRIPTION

file performs a series of tests on each argument in an attempt to classify it. If an argument appears to be ASCII, *file* examines the first 512 bytes and tries to guess its language. If an argument is an executable **a.out**, *file* will print the version stamp, provided it is greater than 0.

−c The −c option causes *file* to check the magic file for format errors. This validation is not normally carried out for reasons of efficiency. No file typing is done under **−c**.

−f If the **−f** option is given, the next argument is taken to be a file containing the names of the files to be examined.

−m The **−m** option instructs *file* to use an alternate magic file.

file uses the file **/etc/magic** to identify files that have some sort of *magic number*, that is, any file containing a numeric or string constant that indicates its type. Commentary at the beginning of **/etc/magic** explains its format.

FILES

/etc/magic

SEE ALSO

filehdr(4) in the *Programmer's Reference Manual.*

NAME

find − find files

SYNOPSIS

find path-name-list expression

DESCRIPTION

find recursively descends the directory hierarchy for each path name in the *path-name-list* (that is, one or more path names) seeking files that match a boolean *expression* written in the primaries given below. In the descriptions, the argument *n* is used as a decimal integer where +*n* means more than *n*, −*n* means less than *n* and *n* means exactly *n*. Valid expressions are:

−name *file* — True if *file* matches the current file name. Normal shell argument syntax may be used if escaped (watch out for **[**, **?** and *****).

[−perm] −*onum* — True if the file permission flags exactly match the octal number *onum* (see *chmod*(1)). If *onum* is prefixed by a minus sign, only the bits that are set in *onum* are compared with the file permission flags, and the expression evaluates true if they match.

−type *c* — True if the type of the file is *c*, where *c* is **b**, **c**, **d**, **p**, or **f** for block special file, character special file, directory, fifo (a.k.a named pipe), or plain file respectively.

−links *n* — True if the file has *n* links.

−user *uname* — True if the file belongs to the user *uname*. If *uname* is numeric and does not appear as a login name in the **/etc/passwd** file, it is taken as a user ID.

−group *gname* — True if the file belongs to the group *gname*. If *gname* is numeric and does not appear in the **/etc/group** file, it is taken as a group ID.

−size *n*[**c**] — True if the file is *n* blocks long (512 bytes per block). If *n* is followed by a **c**, the size is in characters.

−atime *n* — True if the file has been accessed in *n* days. The access time of directories in *path-name-list* is changed by *find* itself.

−mtime *n* — True if the file has been modified in *n* days.

−ctime *n* — True if the file has been changed in *n* days.

−exec *cmd* — True if the executed *cmd* returns a zero value as exit status. The end of *cmd* must be punctuated by an escaped semicolon. A command argument {} is replaced by the current path name.

−ok *cmd* — Like **−exec** except that the generated command line is printed with a question mark first, and is executed only if the user responds by typing **y**.

−print — Always true; causes the current path name to be printed.

−cpio *device* — Always true; write the current file on *device* in *cpio*(1) format (5120-byte records).

−newer *file* True if the current file has been modified more recently than the argument *file*.

−depth Always true; causes descent of the directory hierarchy to be done so that all entries in a directory are acted on before the directory itself. This can be useful when *find* is used with *cpio*(1) to transfer files that are contained in directories without write permission.

−mount Always true; restricts the search to the file system containing the directory specified, or if no directory was specified, the current directory.

−local True if the file physically resides on the local system.

(*expression* **)** True if the parenthesized expression is true (parentheses are special to the shell and must be escaped).

The primaries may be combined using the following operators (in order of decreasing precedence):

1) The negation of a primary (**!** is the unary *not* operator).
2) Concatenation of primaries (the *and* operation is implied by the juxtaposition of two primaries).
3) Alternation of primaries (**−o** is the *or* operator).

EXAMPLE

To remove all files named **a.out** or ***.o** that have not been accessed for a week:

find / \(−name a.out −o −name '*.o' \) −atime +7 −exec rm {} \;

FILES

/etc/passwd, /etc/group

SEE ALSO

chmod(1), cpio(1), sh(1), test(1).
stat(2), umask(2), fs(4) in the *Programmer's Reference Manual.*

BUGS

find / −depth always fails with the message: "find: stat failed: : No such file or directory".

NAME

gdev: hpd, erase, hardcopy, tekset, td − graphical device routines and filters

SYNOPSIS

hpd [−options] [GPS file ...]
erase
hardcopy
tekset
td [−**ern***n*] [GPS file ...]

DESCRIPTION

All of the commands described below reside in **/usr/bin/graf** (see *graphics*(1G)).

hpd *hpd* translates a GPS (graphical primitive string; see *gps*(4)) to instructions for the Hewlett-Packard 7221A Graphics Plotter. A viewing window is computed from the maximum and minimum points in *file* unless the −**u** or −**r** *option* is provided. If no *file* is given, the standard input is assumed. *options* are:

- **c***n* Select character set *n*, *n* between 0 and 5 (see the *HP7221A Plotter Operating and Programming Manual, Appendix A*).
- **p***n* Select pen numbered *n*, *n* between 1 and 4 inclusive.
- **r***n* Window on GPS region *n*, *n* between 1 and 25 inclusive.
- **s***n* Slant characters *n* degrees clockwise from the vertical.
- **u** Window on the entire GPS universe.
- **xd***n* Set x displacement of the viewport's lower left corner to *n* inches.
- **xv***n* Set width of viewport to *n* inches.
- **yd***n* Set y displacement of the viewport's lower left corner to *n* inches.
- **yv***n* Set height of viewport to *n* inches.

erase *Erase* sends characters to a Tektronix 4010 series storage terminal to erase the screen.

hardcopy When issued at a Tektronix display terminal with a hard copy unit, *hardcopy* generates a screen copy on the unit.

tekset *tekset* sends characters to a Tektronix terminal to clear the display screen, set the display mode to alpha, and set characters to the smallest font.

td *td* translates a GPS to scope code for a Tektronix 4010 series storage terminal. A viewing window is computed from the maximum and minimum points in *file* unless the −**u** or −**r** *option* is provided. If no *file* is given, the standard input is assumed. Options are:

e Do not erase screen before initiating display.

r*n* Display GPS region *n*, *n* between 1 and 25 inclusive.

u Display the entire GPS universe.

SEE ALSO

ged(1G), graphics(1G).
gps(4) in the *Programmer's Reference Manual*.

NAME

ged − graphical editor

SYNOPSIS

ged [**−eruR**]*n*] [GPS file ...]

DESCRIPTION

ged is an interactive graphical editor used to display, construct, and edit GPS files on Tektronix 4010 series display terminals. If GPS *file*(s) are given, *ged* reads them into an internal display buffer and displays the buffer. The GPS in the buffer can then be edited. If − is given as a file name, *ged* reads a GPS from the standard input.

ged accepts the following command line options:

e Do not erase the screen before the initial display.

r*n* Display region number *n*.

u Display the entire GPS *universe*.

R Restricted shell invoked on use of **!**.

A GPS file is composed of instances of three graphical objects: *lines, arc,* and *text. Arc* and *lines* objects have a start point, or *object-handle,* followed by zero or more points, or *point-handles. Text* has only an object-handle. The objects are positioned within a Cartesian plane, or *universe,* having 64K (−32K to +32K) points, or *universe-units,* on each axis. The universe is divided into 25 equal sized areas called *regions.* Regions are arranged in five rows of five squares each, numbered 1 to 25 from the lower left of the universe to the upper right.

ged maps rectangular areas, called *windows,* from the universe onto the display screen. Windows allow the user to view pictures from different locations and at different magnifications. The *universe-window* is the window with minimum magnification, i.e., the window that views the entire universe. The *home-window* is the window that completely displays the contents of the display buffer.

COMMANDS

ged commands are entered in *stages*. Typically each stage ends with a <**cr**> (return). Prior to the final <**cr**> the command may be aborted by typing **rubout**. The input of a stage may be edited during the stage using the erase and kill characters of the calling shell. The prompt * indicates that *ged* is waiting at stage 1.

Each command consists of a subset of the following stages:

1. *Command line*

   A *command line* consists of a command *name* followed by *argument*(s) followed by a <**cr**>. A command *name* is a single character. Command *arguments* are either *option*(s) or a *file-name. Options* are indicated by a leading −.

2. *Text* *Text* is a sequence of characters terminated by an unescaped <**cr**> (120 lines of text maximum).

3. *Points* *Points* is a sequence of one or more screen locations (maximum of 30) indicated either by the terminal crosshairs or by name. The

prompt for entering *points* is the appearance of the crosshairs. When the crosshairs are visible, typing:

sp (space) enters the current location as a *point*. The *point* is identified with a number.

$*n* enters the previous *point* numbered *n*.

>*x* labels the last *point* entered with the upper case letter *x*.

$*x* enters the *point* labeled *x*.

. establishes the previous *points* as the current *points*. At the start of a command the previous *points* are those locations given with the previous command.

= echoes the current *points*.

$.*n* enters the *point* numbered *n* from the previous *points*.

erases the last *point* entered.

@ erases all of the *points* entered.

4. *Pivot* The *pivot* is a single location, entered by typing **<cr>** or by using the **$** operator, and indicated with a *.

5. *Destination*
The *destination* is a single location entered by typing **<cr>** or by using **$**.

COMMAND SUMMARY

In the summary, characters typed by the user are printed in **bold**. Command stages are printed in *italics*. Arguments surrounded by brackets "**[]**" are optional. Parentheses "**()**" surrounding arguments separated by "or" means that exactly one of the arguments must be given.

Construct commands:

Arc	[−**e**cho,**s**tyle,**w**eight] *points*
Box	[−**e**cho,**s**tyle,**w**eight] *points*
Circle	[−**e**cho,**s**tyle,**w**eight] *points*
Hardware	[−**e**cho] *text points*
Lines	[−**e**cho,**s**tyle,**w**eight] *points*
Text	[−**a**ngle,**e**cho,**h**eight,**m**id-point,**r**ight-point,**t**ext,**w**eight] *text points*

Edit commands:

Delete	(− (**u**niverse or **v**iew) or *points*)
Edit	[−**a**ngle,**e**cho,**h**eight,**s**tyle,**w**eight] (− (**u**niverse or **v**iew) or *points*)
Kopy	[−**e**cho,**p**oints,**x**] *points pivot destination*

Move	[−**echo**,**points**,**x**] *points pivot destination*
Rotate	[−**a**ngle,**echo**,**kopy**,**x**] *points pivot destination*
Scale	[−**echo**,**factor**,**kopy**,**x**] *points pivot destination*

View commands:

coordinates	*points*
erase	
new-display	
object-handles	(− (**u**niverse or **v**iew) or *points*)
point-handles	(− (**l**abelled-points or **u**niverse or **v**iew) or *points*)
view	(− (**h**ome or **u**niverse or **r**egion) or [−**x**] *pivot destination*)
x	[−**v**iew] *points*
zoom	[−**o**ut] *points*

Other commands:

quit or **Q**uit	
read	[−**a**ngle,**e**cho,**h**eight,**m**id-point,**r**ight-point,**t**ext,**w**eight *file-name* [*destination*]
set	[−**a**ngle,**e**cho,**f**actor,**h**eight,**k**opy,**m**id-point,**p**oints, **r**ight-point,**s**tyle,**t**ext,**w**eight,**x**]
write	*file-name*
!*command*	
?	

Options:

Options specify parameters used to construct, edit, and view graphical objects. If a parameter used by a command is not specifed as an *option*, the default value for the parameter will be used (see **s**et below). The format of command *options* is:

−*option*[,*option*]

where *option* is *keyletter*[*value*]. Flags take on the *values* of true or false indicated by + and − respectively. If no *value* is given with a flag, true is assumed.

Object options:

angle*n*	Angle of *n* degrees.
echo	When true, echo additions to the display buffer.
factor*n*	**S**cale factor is *n* percent.
height*n*	Height of *text* is *n* universe-units ($0 \leqslant n < 1280$).

kopy	When true, copy rather than move.
mid-point	When true, mid-point is used to locate text string.
points	When true, operate on points; otherwise operate on objects.
right-point	When true, right-point is used to locate *text* string.
style*type*	Line style set to one of following *types*: **so** solid **da** dashed **dd** dot-dashed **do** dotted **ld** long-dashed
text	When false, *text* strings are outlined rather than drawn.
weight*type*	Sets line weight to one of following *types*: **n** narrow **m** medium **b** bold

Area options:

home	Reference the home-window.
out	Reduce magnification.
region*n*	Reference region *n*.
universe	Reference the universe-window.
view	Reference those objects currently in view.
x	Indicate the center of the referenced area.

COMMAND DESCRIPTIONS

Construct commands:

Arc and **L**ines

behave similarly. Each consists of a *command line* followed by *points*. The first *point* entered is the object-handle. Successive *points* are point-handles. **L**ines connect the handles in numerical order. **A**rc fits a curve to the handles (currently a maximum of 3 points will be fit with a circular arc; splines will be added in a later version).

Box and **C**ircle

are special cases of **L**ines and **A**rc, respectively. **B**ox generates a rectangle with sides parallel to the universe axes. A diagonal of the rectangle would connect the first *point* entered with the last *point*. The first *point* is the object-handle. Point-handles are created at each of the vertices. **C**ircle generates a circular arc centered about the *point* numbered zero and passing through the last *point*. The circle's object-handle coincides with the last *point*. A point-handle is generated 180 degrees around the circle from the object-handle.

Text and **H**ardware

generate *text* objects. Each consists of a *command line, text* and *points*. *Text* is a sequence of characters delimited by <**cr**>. Multiple lines of text may be entered by preceding a **cr** with a backslash (i.e., **cr**). The **T**ext command creates software-generated characters. Each line of software text is treated as a separate *text* object. The first *point* entered is the object-handle for the first line of text. The **H**ardware command sends the characters in *text* uninterpreted to the terminal.

Edit commands:

Edit commands operate on portions of the display buffer called *defined areas*. A defined area is referenced either with an area *option* or interactively. If an area *option* is not given, the perimeter of the defined area is indicated by *points*. If no *point* is entered, a small defined area is built around the location of the <**cr**>. This is useful to reference a single *point*. If only one *point* is entered, the location of the <**cr**> is taken in conjunction with the *point* to indicate a diagonal of a rectangle. A defined area referenced by *points* will be outlined with dotted lines.

Delete

removes all objects whose object-handle lies within a defined area. The **u**niverse option removes all objects and erases the screen.

Edit modifies the parameters of the objects within a defined area. Parameters that can be edited are:

angle	angle of *text*
height	height of *text*
style	style of *lines* and *arc*
weight	weight of *lines, arc,* and *text*.

Kopy (or **M**ove)

copies (or moves) object- and/or point-handles within a defined area by the displacement from the *pivot* to the *destination*.

Rotate

rotates objects within a defined area around the *pivot*. If the **k**opy flag is true then the objects are copied rather than moved.

Scale

For objects whose object handles are within a defined area, point displacements from the *pivot* are scaled by **f**actor percent. If the **k**opy flag is true then the objects are copied rather than moved.

View commands:

coordinates

prints the location of *point*(s) in universe- and screen-units.

erase

clears the screen (but not the display buffer).

new-display

erases the screen then displays the display buffer.

object-handles (or **p**oint-handles)
labels object-handles (and/or point-handles) that lie within the defined area with **O** (or **P**). **P**oint-handles identifies labeled points when the **l**abelled-points flag is true.

view
moves the window so that the universe point corresponding to the *pivot* coincides with the screen point corresponding to the *destination*. Options for **h**ome, **u**niverse, and **r**egion display particular windows in the universe.

x indicates the center of a defined area. Option **v**iew indicates the center of the screen.

zoom
decreases (**z**oom **o**ut) or increases the magnification of the viewing window based on the defined area. For increased magnification, the window is set to circumscribe the defined area. For a decrease in magnification the current window is inscribed within the defined area.

Other commands:

quit or **Q**uit
exit from *ged*. **Q**uit responds with **?** if the display buffer has not been written since the last modification.

read inputs the contents of a file. If the file contains a GPS it is read directly. If the file contains text it is converted into *text* object(s). The first line of a text file begins at *destination*.

set when given *option*(s) resets default parameters, otherwise it prints current default values.

write
outputs the contents of the display buffer to a file.

! escapes *ged* to execute a UNIX system command.

? lists *ged* commands.

SEE ALSO
gdev(1G), graphics(1G), sh(1).
gps(4) in the *Programmer's Reference Manual*.
"Graphics Editor" chapter in the *Graphics Utilities Guide*.

WARNING
See Appendix A of the *Tektronix 4014 Computer Display Terminal User's Manual* for a discussion of the appropriate terminal strap options.

NAME

getopt – parse command options

SYNOPSIS

set -- `getopt** optstring **$*`

DESCRIPTION

WARNING: Start using the new command *getopts*(1) in place of *getopt*(1). *getopt*(1) will not be supported in the next major release. For more information, see the **WARNINGS** section, below.

getopt is used to break up options in command lines for easy parsing by shell procedures and to check for legal options. *optstring* is a string of recognized option letters (see *getopt*(3C)); if a letter is followed by a colon, the option is expected to have an argument which may or may not be separated from it by white space. The special option -- is used to delimit the end of the options. If it is used explicitly, *getopt* will recognize it; otherwise, *getopt* will generate it; in either case, *getopt* will place it at the end of the options. The positional parameters ($1 $2 ...) of the shell are reset so that each option is preceded by a – and is in its own positional parameter; each option argument is also parsed into its own positional parameter.

EXAMPLE

The following code fragment shows how one might process the arguments for a command that can take the options **a** or **b**, as well as the option **o**, which requires an argument:

```
set -- `getopt abo: $*`
if [ $? != 0 ]
then
        echo $USAGE
        exit 2
fi
for i in $*
do
        case $i in
        -a | -b)    FLAG=$i; shift;;
        -o)         OARG=$2; shift 2;;
        --)         shift; break;;
        esac
done
```

This code will accept any of the following as equivalent:

```
cmd -aoarg file file
cmd -a -o arg file file
cmd -oarg -a file file
cmd -a -oarg -- file file
```

SEE ALSO

getopts(1), sh(1).
getopt(3C) in the *Programmer's Reference Manual.*

DIAGNOSTICS

getopt prints an error message on the standard error when it encounters an option letter not included in *optstring*.

WARNINGS

getopt(1) does not support the part of Rule 8 of the command syntax standard (see *intro*(1)) that permits groups of option-arguments following an option to be separated by white space and quoted. For example,

```
cmd -a -b -o "xxx z yy" file
```

is not handled correctly). To correct this deficiency, use the new command *getopts*(1) in place of *getopt*(1).

getopt(1) will not be supported in the next major release. For this release a conversion tool has been provided, *getoptcvt*. For more information about *getopts* and *getoptcvt*, see the *getopts*(1) manual page.

If an option that takes an option-argument is followed by a value that is the same as one of the options listed in *optstring* (referring to the earlier EXAMPLE section, but using the following command line: `cmd -o -a file`), *getopt* will always treat **−a** as an option-argument to **−o**; it will never recognize **−a** as an option. For this case, the **for** loop in the example will shift past the *file* argument.

NAME

getopts, getoptcvt – parse command options

SYNOPSIS

getopts optstring name [arg ...]

/usr/lib/getoptcvt [–**b**] file

DESCRIPTION

getopts is used by shell procedures to parse positional parameters and to check for legal options. It supports all applicable rules of the command syntax standard (see Rules 3-10, *intro*(1)). It should be used in place of the *getopt*(1) command. (See the **WARNING**, below.)

optstring must contain the option letters the command using *getopts* will recognize; if a letter is followed by a colon, the option is expected to have an argument, or group of arguments, which must be separated from it by white space.

Each time it is invoked, *getopts* will place the next option in the shell variable *name* and the index of the next argument to be processed in the shell variable **OPTIND**. Whenever the shell or a shell procedure is invoked, **OPTIND** is initialized to **1**.

When an option requires an option-argument, *getopts* places it in the shell variable **OPTARG**.

If an illegal option is encountered, **?** will be placed in *name*.

When the end of options is encountered, *getopts* exits with a non-zero exit status. The special option "––" may be used to delimit the end of the options.

By default, *getopts* parses the positional parameters. If extra arguments (*arg* ...) are given on the *getopts* command line, *getopts* will parse them instead.

/usr/lib/getoptcvt reads the shell script in *file*, converts it to use *getopts*(1) instead of *getopt*(1), and writes the results on the standard output.

–**b** the results of running */usr/lib/getoptcvt* will be portable to earlier releases of the UNIX system. */usr/lib/getoptcvt* modifies the shell script in *file* so that when the resulting shell script is executed, it determines at run time whether to invoke *getopts*(1) or *getopt*(1).

So all new commands will adhere to the command syntax standard described in *intro*(1), they should use *getopts*(1) or *getopt*(3C) to parse positional parameters and check for options that are legal for that command (see **WARNINGS**, below).

EXAMPLE

The following fragment of a shell program shows how one might process the arguments for a command that can take the options **a** or **b**, as well as the option **o**, which requires an option-argument:

```
while getopts abo: c
do
        case $c in
        a | b)      FLAG=$c;;
        o)          OARG=$OPTARG;;
        \?)         echo $USAGE
                    exit 2;;
        esac
done
shift `expr $OPTIND - 1`
```

This code will accept any of the following as equivalent:

```
cmd -a -b -o "xxx z yy" file
cmd -a -b -o "xxx z yy" -- file
cmd -ab -o xxx,z,yy file
cmd -ab -o "xxx z yy" file
cmd -o xxx,z,yy -b -a file
```

SEE ALSO

intro(1), sh(1).
getopts(3C) in the *Programmer's Reference Manual*.
UNIX System V Release 3.0 Release Notes.

WARNING

Although the following command syntax rule (see *intro*(1)) relaxations are permitted under the current implementation, they should not be used because they may not be supported in future releases of the system. As in the **EXAMPLE** section above, **a** and **b** are options, and the option **o** requires an option-argument:

`cmd -aboxxx file` (Rule 5 violation: options with option-arguments must not be grouped with other options)
`cmd -ab -oxxx file` (Rule 6 violation: there must be white space after an option that takes an option-argument)

Changing the value of the shell variable **OPTIND** or parsing different sets of arguments may lead to unexpected results.

DIAGNOSTICS

getopts prints an error message on the standard error when it encounters an option letter not included in *optstring*.

NAME

glossary – definitions of common UNIX system terms and symbols

SYNOPSIS

[**help**] **glossary** [term]

DESCRIPTION

The UNIX system Help Facility command *glossary* provides definitions of common technical terms and symbols.

Without an argument, *glossary* displays a menu screen listing the terms and symbols that are currently included in *glossary*. A user may choose one of the terms or may exit to the shell by typing q (for "quit"). When a term is selected, its definition is retrieved and displayed. By selecting the appropriate menu choice, the list of terms and symbols can be redisplayed.

A term's definition may also be requested directly from shell level (as shown above), causing a definition to be retrieved and the list of terms and symbols not to be displayed. Some of the symbols must be escaped if requested at shell level in order for the facility to understand the symbol. The following is a table which list the symbols and their escape sequence.

<table>
<tr><th>SYMBOL</th><th>ESCAPE SEQUENCE</th></tr>
<tr><td>""</td><td>\"\"</td></tr>
<tr><td>''</td><td>\'\'</td></tr>
<tr><td>[]</td><td>\\[\\]</td></tr>
<tr><td>``</td><td>\`\`</td></tr>
<tr><td>#</td><td>\#</td></tr>
<tr><td>&</td><td>\&</td></tr>
<tr><td>*</td><td>*</td></tr>
<tr><td>\</td><td>\\\\</td></tr>
<tr><td>|</td><td>\|</td></tr>
</table>

From any screen in the Help Facility, a user may execute a command via the shell (*sh*(1)) by typing a ! and the command to be executed. The screen will be redrawn if the command that was executed was entered at a first level prompt. If entered at any other prompt level, only the prompt will be redrawn.

By default, the Help Facility scrolls the data that is presented to the user. If you prefer to have the screen clear before printing the data (non-scrolling), the shell variable **SCROLL** must be set to **no** and exported so it will become part of your environment. This is done by adding the following line to your *.profile* file (see *profile*(4)): "`export SCROLL ; SCROLL=no`". If you later decide that scrolling is desired, **SCROLL** must be set to **yes**.

Information on each of the Help Facility commands (*starter, locate, usage, glossary*, and *help*) is located on their respective manual pages.

SEE ALSO

help(1), helpadm(1M), locate(1), sh(1), starter(1), usage(1).
term(5) in the *Programmer's Reference Manual*.

WARNINGS

If the shell variable **TERM** (see *sh*(1)) is not set in the user's *.profile* file, then **TERM** will default to the terminal value type 450 (a hard-copy terminal). For a list of valid terminal types, refer to *term*(5).

NAME

graph − draw a graph

SYNOPSIS

graph [options]

DESCRIPTION

graph with no options takes pairs of numbers from the standard input as abscissas and ordinates of a graph. Successive points are connected by straight lines. The graph is encoded on the standard output for display by the *tplot*(1G) filters.

If the coordinates of a point are followed by a non-numeric string, that string is printed as a label beginning on the point. Labels may be surrounded with quotes ", in which case they may be empty or contain blanks and numbers; labels never contain new-lines.

The following options are recognized, each as a separate argument:

−a	Supply abscissas automatically (they are missing from the input); spacing is given by the next argument (default 1). A second optional argument is the starting point for automatic abscissas (default 0 or lower limit given by **−x**).
−b	Break (disconnect) the graph after each label in the input.
−c	Character string given by next argument is default label for each point.
−g	Next argument is grid style, 0 no grid, 1 frame with ticks, 2 full grid (default).
−l	Next argument is label for graph.
−m	Next argument is mode (style) of connecting lines: 0 disconnected, 1 connected (default). Some devices give distinguishable line styles for other small integers (e.g., the Tektronix 4014: 2=dotted, 3=dash-dot, 4=short-dash, 5=long-dash).
−s	Save screen, do not erase before plotting.
−x [**l**]	If **l** is present, x axis is logarithmic. Next 1 (or 2) arguments are lower (and upper) *x* limits. Third argument, if present, is grid spacing on *x* axis. Normally these quantities are determined automatically.
−y [**l**]	Similarly for *y*.
−h	Next argument is fraction of space for height.
−w	Similarly for width.
−r	Next argument is fraction of space to move right before plotting.
−u	Similarly to move up before plotting.
−t	Transpose horizontal and vertical axes. (Option **−x** now applies to the vertical axis.)

A legend indicating grid range is produced with a grid unless the **−s** option is present. If a specified lower limit exceeds the upper limit, the axis is reversed.

SEE ALSO

graphics(1G), spline(1G), tplot(1G).

BUGS

graph stores all points internally and drops those for which there is no room.
Segments that run out of bounds are dropped, not windowed.
Logarithmic axes may not be reversed.

NAME

graphics – access graphical and numerical commands

SYNOPSIS

graphics [**–r**]

DESCRIPTION

graphics prefixes the path name **/usr/bin/graf** to the current **$PATH** value, changes the primary shell prompt to ^, and executes a new shell. The directory **/usr/bin/graf** contains all of the Graphics subsystem commands. If the **–r** option is given, access to the graphical commands is created in a restricted environment; that is, **$PATH** is set to

:/usr/bin/graf:/rbin:/usr/rbin

and the restricted shell, *rsh*, is invoked. To restore the environment that existed prior to issuing the *graphics* command, type **EOT** (control-d on most terminals). To logoff from the graphics environment, type **quit**.

The command line format for a command in *graphics* is *command name* followed by *argument*(s). An *argument* may be a *file name* or an *option string*. A *file name* is the name of any UNIX system file except those beginning with –. The *file name* – is the name for the standard input. An *option string* consists of – followed by one or more *option*(s). An *option* consists of a keyletter possibly followed by a value. *Options* may be separated by commas.

The graphical commands have been partitioned into four groups.

Commands that manipulate and plot numerical data; see *stat*(1G).

Commands that generate tables of contents; see *toc*(1G).

Commands that interact with graphical devices; see *gdev*(1G) and *ged*(1G).

A collection of graphical utility commands; see *gutil*(1G).

A list of the *graphics* commands can be generated by typing **whatis** in the *graphics* environment.

SEE ALSO

gdev(1G), ged(1G), gutil(1G), stat(1G), toc(1G).
gps(4) in the *Programmer's Reference Manual*.

NAME

greek – select terminal filter

SYNOPSIS

greek [**–T**terminal]

DESCRIPTION

greek is a filter that reinterprets the extended character set, as well as the reverse and half-line motions, of a 128-character Teletype Model 37 terminal for certain other terminals. Special characters are simulated by overstriking, if necessary and possible. If the argument is omitted, *greek* attempts to use the environment variable **$TERM** (see *environ*(5)). Currently, the following *terminal*s are recognized:

300	DASI 300.
300-12	DASI 300 in 12-pitch.
300s	DASI 300s.
300s-12	DASI 300s in 12-pitch.
450	DASI 450.
450-12	DASI 450 in 12-pitch.
1620	Diablo 1620 (alias DASI 450).
1620-12	Diablo 1620 (alias DASI 450) in 12-pitch.
2621	Hewlett-Packard 2621, 2640, and 2645.
2640	Hewlett-Packard 2621, 2640, and 2645.
2645	Hewlett-Packard 2621, 2640, and 2645.
4014	Tektronix 4014.
hp	Hewlett-Packard 2621, 2640, and 2645.
tek	Tektronix 4014.

FILES

/usr/bin/300
/usr/bin/300s
/usr/bin/4014
/usr/bin/450
/usr/bin/hp

SEE ALSO

300(1), 4014(1), 450(1), hp(1), tplot(1G).
eqn(1), mm(1), nroff(1) in the *DOCUMENTER'S WORKBENCH Software Release 2.0 Technical Discussion and Reference Manual.*
environ(5), greek(5), term(5) in the *Programmer's Reference Manual.*

NAME

grep − search a file for a pattern

SYNOPSIS

grep [options] limited regular expression [file ...]

DESCRIPTION

grep searches files for a pattern and prints all lines that contain that pattern. *grep* uses limited regular expressions (expressions that have string values that use a subset of the possible alphanumeric and special characters) like those used with *ed (1)* to match the patterns. It uses a compact non-deterministic algorithm.

Be careful using the characters **$**, *****, **[**, **^**, **|**, **(**, **)**, and \ in the *limited regular expression* because they are also meaningful to the shell. It is safest to enclose the entire *limited regular expression* in single quotes '...'.

If no files are specified, *grep* assumes standard input. Normally, each line found is copied to standard output. The file name is printed before each line found if there is more than one input file.

Command line options are:

−b Precede each line by the block number on which it was found. This can be useful in locating block numbers by context (first block is 0).

−c Print only a count of the lines that contain the pattern.

−i Ignore upper/lower case distinction during comparisons.

−l Print the names of files with matching lines once, separated by new-lines. Does not repeat the names of files when the pattern is found more than once.

−n Precede each line by its line number in the file (first line is 1).

−s Suppress error messages about nonexistent or unreadable files

−v Print all lines except those that contain the pattern.

SEE ALSO

ed(1), egrep(1), fgrep(1), sed(1), sh(1).

DIAGNOSTICS

Exit status is 0 if any matches are found, 1 if none, 2 for syntax errors or inaccessible files (even if matches were found).

BUGS

Lines are limited to BUFSIZ characters; longer lines are truncated. BUFSIZ is defined in **/usr/include/stdio.h**.
If there is a line with embedded nulls, *grep* will only match up to the first null; if it matches, it will print the entire line.

NAME

gutil – graphical utilities
gutil: utilities – bel; cvrtopt; gd; gtop; pd; ptog; quit; remcom; whatis; yoo

SYNOPSIS

command-name [options] [files]

DESCRIPTION

Below is a list of miscellaneous device independent utility commands found in **/usr/bin/graf**. If no *files* are given, input is from the standard input. All output is to the standard output. Graphical data is stored in GPS format; see *gps*(4).

bel – send bel character to terminal

cvrtopt [=**s***string* **f***string* **i***string* **t***string*] [*args*] – options converter
Cvrtopt reformats *args* (usually the command line arguments of a calling shell procedure) to facilitate processing by shell procedures. An *arg* is either a file name (a string not beginning with a –, or a – by itself) or an option string (a string of options beginning with a –). Output is of the form:

–option –option . . . file name(s)

All options appear singularly and preceding any file names. Options that take values (e.g., –r1.1) or are two letters long must be described through options to *cvrtopt*.

Cvrtopt is usually used with *set* in the following manner as the first line of a shell procedure:

set – cvrtopt =[*options***] $@**

Options to *cvrtopt* are:

s*string* *String* accepts string values.

f*string* *String* accepts floating point numbers as values.

i*string* *String* accepts integers as values.

t*string* *String* is a two-letter option name that takes no value.

String is a one- or two-letter option name.

gd [GPS *files*] – GPS dump
Gd prints a human readable listing of GPS.

gtop [–**r***n* **u**] [GPS *files*] – GPS to *plot*(4) filter
Gtop transforms a GPS into *plot*(4) commands displayable by *plot* filters. GPS objects are translated if they fall within the window that circumscribes the first *file* unless an *option* is given.
Options:

r*n* translate objects in GPS **r**egion *n*.

u translate all objects in the GPS **u**niverse.

pd [*plot*(5) *files*] – *plot*(4) dump
Pd prints a human readable listing of *plot*(4) format graphical commands.

ptog [*plot*(5) *files*] – *plot*(4) to GPS filter
Ptog transforms *plot*(4) commands into a GPS.

quit – terminate session

remcom [*files*] – remove comments
Remcom copies its input to its output with comments removed. Comments are as defined in C (i.e., /* comment */).

whatis [–**o**] [*names*] – brief on-line documentation
Whatis prints a brief description of each *name* given. If no *name* is given, then the current list of description *names* is printed. The command **whatis** * prints out every description.
Option:

o just print command **o**ptions

yoo *file* – pipe fitting
Yoo is a piping primitive that deposits the output of a pipeline into a *file* used in the pipeline. Note that, without *yoo*, this is not usually successful as it causes a read and write on the same file simultaneously.

SEE ALSO

graphics(1G).
gps(4), plot(4) in the *Programmer's Reference Manual*.

NAME

help – UNIX system Help Facility

SYNOPSIS

help
[**help**] **starter**
[**help**] **usage** [**–d**] [**–e**] [**–o**] [command_name]
[**help**] **locate** [keyword1 [keyword2] ...]
[**help**] **glossary** [term]
help arg ...

DESCRIPTION

The UNIX system Help Facility provides on-line assistance for UNIX system users, whether they desire general information or specific assistance for use of the Source Code Control System (SCCS) commands.

Without arguments, *help* prints a menu of available on-line assistance commands with a short description of their functions. The commands and their descriptions are:

COMMAND	DESCRIPTION
starter	information about the UNIX system for the beginning user
locate	locate UNIX system commands using function-related keywords
usage	UNIX system command usage information
glossary	definitions of UNIX system technical terms

The user may choose one of the above commands by entering its corresponding letter (given in the menu), or may exit to the shell by typing q (for "quit").

With arguments, *help* directly invokes the named on-line assistance command, bypassing the initial *help* menu. The commands *starter*, *locate*, *usage*, and *glossary*, optionally preceded by the word *help*, may also be specified at shell level. When executing *glossary* from shell level some of the symbols listed in the glossary must be escaped (preceded by one or more backslashes, "\") to be understood by the Help Facility. For a list of symbols and how many backslashes to use for each, refer to the *glossary*(1) manual page.

From any screen in the Help Facility, a user may execute a command via the shell (*sh*(1)) by typing a ! and the command to be executed. The screen will be redrawn if the command that was executed was entered at a first level prompt. If entered at any other prompt level, only the prompt will be redrawn.

By default, the Help Facility scrolls the data that is presented to the user. If you prefer to have the screen clear before printing the data (non-scrolling), the shell variable **SCROLL** must be set to **no** and exported so it will become part of your environment. This is done by adding the following line to your *.profile* file (see *profile*(4)): "`export SCROLL ; SCROLL=no`". If you later decide that scrolling is desired, **SCROLL** must be set to **yes**.

Information on each of the Help Facility commands (*starter*, *locate*, *usage*, *glossary*, and *help*) is located on their respective manual pages.

The Help Facility can be tailored to a customer's needs by use of the *helpadm*(1M) command.

If the first argument to *help* is different from *starter, usage, locate,* or *glossary, help* assumes information is being requested about the SCCS Facility. The arguments may be either message numbers (which normally appear in parentheses following messages) or command names, of one of the following types:

type1 Begins with non-numerics, ends in numerics. The non-numeric prefix is usually an abbreviation for the program or set of routines which produced the message (e.g., ge3 for message 3 from the *get* command).

type2 Does not contain numerics (as a command, such as get).

type3 Is all numeric (e.g., 212).

SEE ALSO

glossary(1), helpadm(1M), locate(1), sh(1), starter(1), usage(1).
admin(1), cdc(1), comb(1), delta(1), get(1), prs(1), rmdel(1), sact(1), sccsdiff(1), unget(1), val(1), vc(1), what(1), profile(4), sccsfile(4), term(5) in the *Programmer's Reference Manual.*

WARNINGS

If the shell variable **TERM** (see *sh*(1)) is not set in the user's *.profile* file, then **TERM** will default to the terminal value type 450 (a hard-copy terminal). For a list of valid terminal types, refer to *term*(5).

NAME

helpadm – make changes to the Help Facility database

SYNOPSIS

/etc/helpadm

DESCRIPTION

The UNIX system Help Facility Administration command, *helpadm* , allows UNIX system administrators and command developers to define the content of the Help Facility database for specific commands and to monitor use of the Help Facility. The *helpadm* command can only be executed by login root, login bin, or a login that is a member of group bin.

The *helpadm* command prints a menu of 3 types of Help Facility data which can be modified, and 2 choices relating to monitoring use of the Help Facility. The five choices are:

- modify *startup* data
- add, modify, or delete a *glossary* term
- add, modify, or delete command data (description, options, examples, and keywords)
- prevent monitoring use of the Help Facility (login root and login bin only)
- permit monitoring use of the Help Facility (login root and login bin only)

The user may make one of the above choices by entering its corresponding letter (given in the menu), or may exit to the shell by typing q (for "quit").

If one of the first three choices is chosen, then the user is prompted for additional information; specifically, which *startup* screen, *glossary* term definition, or command description is to be modified. The user may also be prompted for information to identify whether the changes to the database are additions, modifications, or deletions. If the user is modifying existing data or adding new data, then they are prompted to make the appropriate modifications/additions. If the user is deleting a *glossary* term or a command from the database, then they must respond affirmatively to the next query in order for the deletion to be done. In any case, before the user's changes are final, they must respond affirmatively when asked whether they are sure they want their requested database changes to be done.

By default, *helpadm* will put the user into *ed*(1) to make additions/modifications to database information. If the user wishes to be put into a different editor, then they should set the environment variable **EDITOR** in their environment to the desired editor, and then export **EDITOR .**

If the user chooses to monitor/prevent monitoring use of the Help Facility, the choice made is acted on with no further interaction by the user.

SEE ALSO

ed(1), glossary(1), help(1), locate(1), starter(1), usage(1).

WARNINGS

When the UNIX system is delivered to a customer, **/etc/profile** exports the environment variable **LOGNAME .** If **/etc/profile** has been changed so that **LOGNAME** is not exported, then the options to monitor/prevent monitoring use of the Help Facility may not work properly.

FILES

HELPLOG	/usr/lib/help/HELPLOG
helpclean	/usr/lib/help/helpclean

NAME

hp − handle special functions of Hewlett-Packard terminals

SYNOPSIS

hp [**−e**] [**−m**]

DESCRIPTION

hp supports special functions of the Hewlett-Packard 2640 series of terminals, with the primary purpose of producing accurate representations of most *nroff* output. A typical usage is in conjunction with DOCUMENTER'S WORKBENCH Software:

nroff −h files ... | hp

Regardless of the hardware options on your terminal, *hp* tries to do sensible things with underlining and reverse line-feeds. If the terminal has the "display enhancements" feature, subscripts and superscripts can be indicated in distinct ways. If it has the "mathematical-symbol" feature, Greek and other special characters can be displayed.

The flags are as follows:

−e It is assumed that your terminal has the "display enhancements" feature, and so maximal use is made of the added display modes. Overstruck characters are presented in the Underline mode. Superscripts are shown in Half-bright mode, and subscripts in Half-bright, Underlined mode. If this flag is omitted, *hp* assumes that your terminal lacks the "display enhancements" feature. In this case, all overstruck characters, subscripts, and superscripts are displayed in Inverse Video mode, i.e., dark-on-light, rather than the usual light-on-dark.

−m Requests minimization of output by removal of new-lines. Any contiguous sequence of 3 or more new-lines is converted into a sequence of only 2 new-lines; i.e., any number of successive blank lines produces only a single blank output line. This allows you to retain more actual text on the screen.

With regard to Greek and other special characters, *hp* provides the same set as does *300*(1), except that "not" is approximated by a right arrow, and only the top half of the integral sign is shown.

DIAGNOSTICS

"line too long" if the representation of a line exceeds 1,024 characters.
The exit codes are **0** for normal termination, **2** for all errors.

SEE ALSO

300(1), greek(1).
col(1), eqn(1), nroff(1), tbl(1) in the *DOCUMENTER'S WORKBENCH Software Release 2.0 Technical Discussion and Reference Manual.*

BUGS

An "overstriking sequence" is defined as a printing character followed by a backspace followed by another printing character. In such sequences, if either printing character is an underscore, the other printing character is shown underlined or in Inverse Video; otherwise, only the first printing character is shown (again, underlined or in Inverse Video). Nothing special is done if a backspace is adjacent to an ASCII control character. Sequences of control characters (e.g.,

reverse line-feeds, backspaces) can make text "disappear"; in particular, tables generated by *tbl*(1) that contain vertical lines will often be missing the lines of text that contain the "foot" of a vertical line, unless the input to *hp* is piped through *col*(1).
Although some terminals do provide numerical superscript characters, no attempt is made to display them.

NAME

hpio – Hewlett-Packard 2645A terminal tape file archiver

SYNOPSIS

hpio –o[**rc**] file ...

hpio –i[**rta**] [**–n** count]

DESCRIPTION

hpio is designed to take advantage of the tape drives on Hewlett-Packard 2645A terminals. Up to 255 UNIX system files can be archived onto a tape cartridge for off-line storage or for transfer to another UNIX system. The actual number of files depends on the sizes of the files. One file of about 115,000 bytes will almost fill a tape cartridge. Almost 300 1-byte files will fit on a tape, but the terminal will not be able to retrieve files after the first 255. This manual page is not intended to be a guide for using tapes on Hewlett-Packard 2645A terminals, but tries to give enough information to be able to create and read tape archives and to position a tape for access to a desired file in an archive.

hpio –o (copy out) copies the specified *file*(s), together with path name and status information to a tape drive on your terminal (which is assumed to be positioned at the beginning of a tape or immediately after a tape mark). The left tape drive is used by default. Each *file* is written to a separate tape file and terminated with a tape mark. When *hpio* finishes, the tape is positioned following the last tape mark written.

hpio –i (copy in) extracts a file(s) from a tape drive (which is assumed to be positioned at the beginning of a file that was previously written by a **hpio –o**). The default action extracts the next file from the left tape drive.

hpio always leaves the tape positioned after the last file read from or written to the tape. Tapes should always be rewound before the terminal is turned off. To rewind a tape depress the green function button, then function key 5, and then select the appropriate tape drive by depressing either function key 5 for the left tape drive or function key 6 for the right. If several files have been archived onto a tape, the tape may be positioned at the beginning of a specific file by depressing the green function button, then function key 8, followed by typing the desired file number (1–255) with no RETURN, and finally function key 5 for the left tape or function key 6 for the right. The desired file number may also be specified by a signed number relative to the current file number.

The meanings of the available options are:

r Use the right tape drive.

c Include a checksum at the end of each *file*. The checksum is always checked by **hpio –i** for each file written with this option by **hpio –o**.

n *count* The number of input files to be extracted is set to *count*. If this option is not given, *count* defaults to 1. An arbitrarily large *count* may be specified to extract all files from the tape. *hpio* will stop at the end of data mark on the tape.

t Print a table of contents only. No files are created. Printed information gives the file size in bytes, the file name, the file access modes, and whether or not a checksum is included for the file.

a Ask before creating a file. **hpio −i** normally prints the file size and name, creates and reads in the file, and prints a status message when the file has been read in. If a checksum is included with the file, it reports whether the checksum matched its computed value. With this option, the file size and name are printed followed by a **?**. Any response beginning with **y** or **Y** will cause the file to be copied in as above. Any other response will cause the file to be skipped.

FILES

/dev/tty?? to block messages while accessing a tape

SEE ALSO

cu(1C).

DIAGNOSTICS

BREAK

An interrupt signal terminated processing.

Can't create '*file*'.

File system access permissions did not allow *file* to be created.

Can't get tty options on stdout.

hpio was unable to get the input-output control settings associated with the terminal.

Can't open '*file*'.

File could not be accessed to copy it to tape.

End of Tape.

No tape record was available when a read from a tape was requested. An end of data mark is the usual reason for this, but it may also occur if the wrong tape drive is being accessed and no tape is present.

'*file*' not a regular file.

File is a directory or other special file. Only regular files will be copied to tape.

Readcnt = *rc*, termcnt = *tc*.

hpio expected to read *rc* bytes from the next block on the tape, but the block contained *tc* bytes. This is caused by having the tape improperly positioned or by a tape block being mangled by interference from other terminal I/O.

Skip to next file failed.

An attempt to skip over a tape mark failed.

Tape mark write failed.

An attempt to write a tape mark at the end of a file failed.

Write failed.

A tape write failed. This is most frequently caused by specifying the wrong tape drive, running off the end of the tape, or trying to write on a tape that is write protected.

WARNINGS

Tape I/O operations may copy bad data if any other I/O involving the terminal occurs. Do not attempt any type ahead while *hpio* is running. *hpio* turns off write permissions for other users while it is running, but processes started asynchronously from your terminal can still interfere. The most common indication of this problem, while a tape is being written, is the appearance of characters on the display screen that should have been copied to tape.

The keyboard, including the terminal BREAK key, is locked during tape write operations; the BREAK key is only functional between writes.

hpio must have complete control of the attributes of the terminal to communicate with the tape drives. Interaction with commands such as *cu*(1C) may interfere and prevent successful operation.

BUGS

Some binary files contain sequences that will confuse the terminal.

An **hpio −i** that encounters the end of data mark on the tape (e.g., scanning the entire tape with **hpio −itn 300**), leaves the tape positioned *after* the end of data mark. If a subsequent **hpio −o** is done at this point, the data will not be retrievable. The tape must be repositioned manually using the terminal FIND FILE −1 operation (depress the green function button, function key 8, and then function key 5 for the left tape or function key 6 for the right tape) before the **hpio −o** is started.

If an interrupt is received by *hpio* while a tape is being written, the terminal may be left with the keyboard locked. If this happens, the terminal's RESET TERMINAL key will unlock the keyboard.

NAME

id – print user and group IDs and names

SYNOPSIS

id

DESCRIPTION

id outputs the user and group IDs and the corresponding names of the invoking process. If the effective and real IDs are different, both are printed.

SEE ALSO

logname(1) in the *User's Reference Manual*.
getuid(2) in the *Programmer's Reference Manual*.

NAME

ipcrm – remove a message queue, semaphore set or shared memory id

SYNOPSIS

ipcrm [*options*]

DESCRIPTION

ipcrm will remove one or more specified messages, semaphore or shared memory identifiers. The identifiers are specified by the following *options*:

–q *msqid* removes the message queue identifier *msqid* from the system and destroys the message queue and data structure associated with it.

–m *shmid* removes the shared memory identifier *shmid* from the system. The shared memory segment and data structure associated with it are destroyed after the last detach.

–s *semid* removes the semaphore identifier *semid* from the system and destroys the set of semaphores and data structure associated with it.

–Q *msgkey* removes the message queue identifier, created with key *msgkey*, from the system and destroys the message queue and data structure associated with it.

–M *shmkey* removes the shared memory identifier, created with key *shmkey*, from the system. The shared memory segment and data structure associated with it are destroyed after the last detach.

–S *semkey* removes the semaphore identifier, created with key *semkey*, from the system and destroys the set of semaphores and data structure associated with it.

The details of the removes are described in *msgctl*(2), *shmctl*(2), and *semctl*(2). The identifiers and keys may be found by using *ipcs*(1).

SEE ALSO

ipcs(1).
msgctl(2), msgget(2), msgop(2), semctl(2), semget(2), semop(2), shmctl(2), shmget(2), shmop(2) in the *Programmer's Reference Manual*.

NAME

ipcs − report inter-process communication facilities status

SYNOPSIS

ipcs [options]

DESCRIPTION

ipcs prints certain information about active inter-process communication facilities. Without *options*, information is printed in short format for message queues, shared memory, and semaphores that are currently active in the system. Otherwise, the information that is displayed is controlled by the following *options*:

−q Print information about active message queues.

−m Print information about active shared memory segments.

−s Print information about active semaphores.

If any of the options **−q**, **−m**, or **−s** are specified, information about only those indicated will be printed. If none of these three are specified, information about all three will be printed subject to these options:

−b Print biggest allowable size information. (Maximum number of bytes in messages on queue for message queues, size of segments for shared memory, and number of semaphores in each set for semaphores.) See below for meaning of columns in a listing.

−c Print creator's login name and group name. See below.

−o Print information on outstanding usage. (Number of messages on queue and total number of bytes in messages on queue for message queues and number of processes attached to shared memory segments.)

−p Print process number information. (Process ID of last process to send a message and process ID of last process to receive a message on message queues and process ID of creating process and process ID of last process to attach or detach on shared memory segments) See below.

−t Print time information. (Time of the last control operation that changed the access permissions for all facilities. Time of last *msgsnd* and last *msgrcv* on message queues, last *shmat* and last *shmdt* on shared memory, last *semop*(2) on semaphores.) See below.

−a Use all print *options*. (This is a shorthand notation for **−b**, **−c**, **−o**, **−p**, and **−t**.)

−C *corefile*
Use the file *corefile* in place of **/dev/kmem**.

−N *namelist*
The argument will be taken as the name of an alternate *namelist* (**/unix** is the default).

The column headings and the meaning of the columns in an *ipcs* listing are given below; the letters in parentheses indicate the *options* that cause the corresponding heading to appear; **all** means that the heading always appears.

Note that these *options* only determine what information is provided for each facility; they do *not* determine which facilities will be listed.

T (all)
Type of the facility:
- **q** message queue;
- **m** shared memory segment;
- **s** semaphore.

ID (all)
The identifier for the facility entry.

KEY (all)
The key used as an argument to *msgget*, *semget*, or *shmget* to create the facility entry. (Note: The key of a shared memory segment is changed to **IPC_PRIVATE** when the segment has been removed until all processes attached to the segment detach it.)

MODE (all)
The facility access modes and flags: The mode consists of 11 characters that are interpreted as follows:
The first two characters are:
- **R** if a process is waiting on a *msgrcv;*
- **S** if a process is waiting on a *msgsnd;*
- **D** if the associated shared memory segment has been removed. It will disappear when the last process attached to the segment detaches it;
- **C** if the associated shared memory segment is to be cleared when the first attach is executed;
- – if the corresponding special flag is not set.

The next 9 characters are interpreted as three sets of three bits each. The first set refers to the owner's permissions; the next to permissions of others in the user-group of the facility entry; and the last to all others. Within each set, the first character indicates permission to read, the second character indicates permission to write or alter the facility entry, and the last character is currently unused.

The permissions are indicated as follows:
- **r** if read permission is granted;
- **w** if write permission is granted;
- **a** if alter permission is granted;
- – if the indicated permission is *not* granted.

OWNER (all)
The login name of the owner of the facility entry.

GROUP (all)
The group name of the group of the owner of the facility entry.

CREATOR (a,c)
The login name of the creator of the facility entry.

CGROUP (a,c)
The group name of the group of the creator of the facility entry.

CBYTES (a,o)
The number of bytes in messages currently outstanding on the associated message queue.

QNUM (a,o)
The number of messages currently outstanding on the associated message queue.

QBYTES (a,b)
The maximum number of bytes allowed in messages outstanding on the associated message queue.

LSPID (a,p)
The process ID of the last process to send a message to the associated queue.

LRPID (a,p)
The process ID of the last process to receive a message from the associated queue.

STIME (a,t)
The time the last message was sent to the associated queue.

RTIME (a,t)
The time the last message was received from the associated queue.

CTIME (a,t)
The time when the associated entry was created or changed.

NATTCH (a,o)
The number of processes attached to the associated shared memory segment.

SEGSZ (a,b)
The size of the associated shared memory segment.

CPID (a,p)
The process ID of the creator of the shared memory entry.

LPID (a,p)
The process ID of the last process to attach or detach the shared memory segment.

ATIME (a,t)
The time the last attach was completed to the associated shared memory segment.

DTIME (a,t)
The time the last detach was completed on the associated shared memory segment.

NSEMS (a,b)
The number of semaphores in the set associated with the semaphore entry.

OTIME (a,t)
The time the last semaphore operation was completed on the set associated with the semaphore entry.

FILES

/unix	system namelist
/dev/kmem	memory
/etc/passwd	user names
/etc/group	group names

SEE ALSO

msgop(2), semop(2), shmop(2) in the *Programmer's Reference Manual.*

BUGS

Things can change while *ipcs* is running; the picture it gives is only a close approximation to reality.

NAME

ismpx – return windowing terminal state

SYNOPSIS

ismpx [**–s**]

DESCRIPTION

The *ismpx* command reports whether its standard input is connected to a multiplexed *xt*(7) channel; i.e., whether it's running under *layers*(1) or not. It is useful for shell scripts that download programs to a windowing terminal or depend on screen size.

ismpx prints **yes** and returns **0** if invoked under *layers*(1), and prints **no** and returns **1** otherwise.

–s Do not print anything; just return the proper exit status.

EXIT STATUS

Returns **0** if invoked under *layers*(1), **1** if not.

SEE ALSO

layers(1), jwin(1).
xt(7) in the *System Administrator's Reference Manual.*

EXAMPLE

```
if ismpx -s
then
        jwin
fi
```

NAME

join − relational database operator

SYNOPSIS

join [options] file1 file2

DESCRIPTION

join forms, on the standard output, a join of the two relations specified by the lines of *file1* and *file2*. If *file1* is −, the standard input is used.

File1 and *file2* must be sorted in increasing ASCII collating sequence on the fields on which they are to be joined, normally the first in each line [see *sort*(1)].

There is one line in the output for each pair of lines in *file1* and *file2* that have identical join fields. The output line normally consists of the common field, then the rest of the line from *file1*, then the rest of the line from *file2*.

The default input field separators are blank, tab, or new-line. In this case, multiple separators count as one field separator, and leading separators are ignored. The default output field separator is a blank.

Some of the below options use the argument *n*. This argument should be a **1** or a **2** referring to either *file1* or *file2*, respectively. The following options are recognized:

−a*n* In addition to the normal output, produce a line for each unpairable line in file *n*, where *n* is 1 or 2.

−e *s* Replace empty output fields by string *s*.

−j*n m* Join on the *m*th field of file *n*. If *n* is missing, use the *m*th field in each file. Fields are numbered starting with **1**.

−o *list* Each output line comprises the fields specified in *list*, each element of which has the form *n.m*, where *n* is a file number and *m* is a field number. The common field is not printed unless specifically requested.

−t*c* Use character *c* as a separator (tab character). Every appearance of *c* in a line is significant. The character *c* is used as the field separator for both input and output.

EXAMPLE

The following command line will join the password file and the group file, matching on the numeric group ID, and outputting the login name, the group name and the login directory. It is assumed that the files have been sorted in ASCII collating sequence on the group ID fields.

```
join −j1 4 −j2 3 −o 1.1 2.1 1.6 −t: /etc/passwd /etc/group
```

SEE ALSO

awk(1), comm(1), sort(1), uniq(1).

BUGS

With default field separation, the collating sequence is that of **sort −b**; with **−t**, the sequence is that of a plain sort.

The conventions of *join, sort, comm, uniq* and *awk*(1) are wildly incongruous.

Filenames that are numeric may cause conflict when the **-o** option is used right before listing filenames.

NAME

jterm – reset layer of windowing terminal

SYNOPSIS

jterm

DESCRIPTION

The *jterm* command is used to reset a layer of a windowing terminal after downloading a terminal program that changes the terminal attributes of the layer. It is useful only under *layers*(1). In practice, it is most commonly used to restart the default terminal emulator after using an alternate one provided with a terminal-specific application package. For example, on the AT&T Teletype 5620 DMD terminal, after executing the *hp2621*(1) command in a layer, issuing the *jterm* command will restart the default terminal emulator in that layer.

EXIT STATUS

Returns **0** upon successful completion, **1** otherwise.

NOTE

The layer that is reset is the one attached to standard error; that is, the window you are in when you type the *jterm* command.

SEE ALSO

layers(1).

NAME

jwin – print size of layer

SYNOPSIS

jwin

DESCRIPTION

jwin runs only under *layers*(1) and is used to determine the size of the layer associated with the current process. It prints the width and the height of the layer in bytes (number of characters across and number of lines, respectively). For bit-mapped terminals only, it also prints the width and height of the layer in bits.

EXIT STATUS

Returns **0** on successful completion, **1** otherwise.

DIAGNOSTICS

If *layers*(1) has not been invoked, an error message is printed:

```
jwin: not mpx
```

NOTE

The layer whose size is printed is the one attached to standard input; that is, the window you are in when you type the *jwin* command.

SEE ALSO

layers(1).

EXAMPLE

```
jwin
bytes:   86 25
bits:    780 406
```

NAME

kill – terminate a process

SYNOPSIS

kill [−signo] PID ...

DESCRIPTION

kill sends signal 15 (terminate) to the specified processes. This will normally kill processes that do not catch or ignore the signal. The process number of each asynchronous process started with **&** is reported by the shell (unless more than one process is started in a pipeline, in which case the number of the last process in the pipeline is reported). Process numbers can also be found by using *ps*(1).

The details of the kill are described in *kill*(2). For example, if process number 0 is specified, all processes in the process group are signaled.

The killed process must belong to the current user unless he is the super-user.

If a signal number preceded by – is given as first argument, that signal is sent instead of terminate (see *signal*(2)). In particular "kill −9 ..." is a sure kill.

SEE ALSO

ps(1), sh(1).
kill(2), signal(2) in the *Programmer's Reference Manual.*

NAME

layers – layer multiplexor for windowing terminals

SYNOPSIS

layers [**–s**] [**–t**] [**–d**] [**–p**] [**–f** file] [layersys-prgm]

DESCRIPTION

layers manages asynchronous windows (see *layers*(5)) on a windowing terminal. Upon invocation, *layers* finds an unused *xt*(7) channel group and associates it with the terminal line on its standard output. It then waits for commands from the terminal.

Command-line options:

–s Reports protocol statistics on standard error at the end of the session after you exit from *layers*. The statistics may be printed during a session by invoking the program *xts*(1M).

–t Turns on *xt*(7) driver packet tracing, and produces a trace dump on standard error at the end of the session after you exit from *layers*. The trace dump may be printed during a session by invoking the program *xtt*(1M).

–d If a firmware patch has been downloaded, prints out the sizes of the text, data, and bss portions of the firmware patch on standard error.

–p If a firmware patch has been downloaded, prints the down-loading protocol statistics and a trace on standard error.

–f *file* Starts *layers* with an initial configuration specified by *file*. Each line of the file represents a layer to be created, and has the following format:

```
origin_x origin_y corner_x corner_y command_list
```

The coordinates specify the size and position of the layer on the screen in the terminal's coordinate system. If all four are *0*, the user must define the layer interactively. *command_list*, a list of one or more commands, must be provided. It is executed in the newlayer using the user's shell (by executing: **$SHELL -i -c** "*command_list*"). This means that the last command should invoke a shell, such as */bin/sh*. (If the last command is not a shell, then, when the last command has completed, the layer will not be functional.)

layersys-prgm
A file containing a firmware patch that the *layers* command downloads to the terminal before layers are created and *command_list* is executed.

Each layer is in most ways functionally identical to a separate terminal. Characters typed on the keyboard are sent to the standard input of the UNIX system process attached to the current layer (called the host process), and characters written on the standard output by the host process appear in that layer. When a layer is created, a separate shell is established and bound to the layer. If the environment variable **SHELL** is set, the user will get that shell: otherwise, */bin/sh* will be used. In order to enable communications with other users via *write*(1), *layers* invokes the command *relogin*(1M) when the first layer is created.

relogin(1M) will reassign that layer as the user's logged-in terminal. An alternative layer can be designated by using *relogin*(1M) directly. *layers* will restore the original assignment on termination.

Layers are created, deleted, reshaped, and otherwise manipulated in a terminal-dependent manner. For instance, the AT&T Teletype 5620 DMD terminal provides a mouse-activated pop-up menu of layer operations. The method of ending a *layers* session is also defined by the terminal.

If a user wishes to take advantage of a terminal-specific application software package, the environment variable **DMD** should be set to the pathname of the directory where the package was installed. Otherwise **DMD** should not be set.

EXAMPLE

```
layers -f startup
```

where **startup** contains

```
8 8 700 200 date ; pwd ; exec $SHELL
8 300 780 850 exec $SHELL
```

NOTES

The *xt*(7) driver supports an alternate data transmission scheme known as ENCODING MODE. This mode makes *layers* operation possible even over data links which intercept control characters or do not transmit 8-bit characters. ENCODING MODE is selected either by setting a configuration option on your windowing terminal or by setting the environment variable **DMDLOAD** to the value *hex* before running *layers*:

```
export DMDLOAD; DMDLOAD=hex
```

If, after executing **layers -f** *file*, the terminal does not respond in one or more of the layers, often the last command in the *command-list* for that layer did not invoke a shell.

WARNING

To access this version of *layers*, make sure */usr/bin* appears before any other directory, such as *$DMD/bin*, you have in your path that contains a layers program. (For information about defining the shell environmental variable **PATH** in your *.profile*, see *profile*(4)) Otherwise, if there is a terminal-dependent version of *layers*, you may get it instead of the correct one.

When invoking *layers* with the **−s**, **−t**, **−d**, or **−p** options, it is best to redirect standard error to another file to save the statistics and tracing output (e.g., **layers −s 2>stats**); otherwise all or some of the output may be lost.

FILES

/dev/xt??[0-7]
/usr/lib/layersys/lsys.8;7;3
$DMD/lib/layersys/lsys.8;?;?

SEE ALSO

sh(1), write(1).
layers(5), libwindows(3X) in the *Programmer's Reference Manual*.
relogin(1M), xt(7), xts(1M), xtt(1M), wtinit(1M) in the *System Administrator's Reference Manual*.

NAME

line – read one line

SYNOPSIS

line

DESCRIPTION

line copies one line (up to a new-line) from the standard input and writes it on the standard output. It returns an exit code of 1 on **EOF** and always prints at least a new-line. It is often used within shell files to read from the user's terminal.

SEE ALSO

sh(1).
read(2) in the *Programmer's Reference Manual.*

NAME

locate – identify a UNIX system command using keywords

SYNOPSIS

[**help**] **locate**
[**help**] **locate** [keyword1 [keyword2] ...]

DESCRIPTION

The *locate* command is part of the UNIX system Help Facility, and provides on-line assistance with identifying UNIX system commands.

Without arguments, the initial *locate* screen is displayed from which the user may enter keywords functionally related to the action of the desired UNIX system commands they wish to have identified. A user may enter keywords and receive a list of UNIX system commands whose functional attributes match those in the keyword list, or may exit to the shell by typing q (for "quit"). For example, if you wish to print the contents of a file, enter the keywords "print" and "file". The *locate* command would then print the names of all commands related to these keywords.

Keywords may also be entered directly from the shell, as shown above. In this case, the initial screen is not displayed, and the resulting command list is printed.

More detailed information on a command in the list produced by *locate* can be obtained by accessing the *usage* module of the UNIX system Help Facility. Access is made by entering the appropriate menu choice after the command list is displayed.

From any screen in the Help Facility, a user may execute a command via the shell (*sh*(1)) by typing a ! and the command to be executed. The screen will be redrawn if the command that was executed was entered at a first level prompt. If entered at any other prompt level, only the prompt will be redrawn.

By default, the Help Facility scrolls the data that is presented to the user. If you prefer to have the screen clear before printing the data (non-scrolling), the shell variable **SCROLL** must be set to **no** and exported so it will become part of your environment. This is done by adding the following line to your *.profile* file (see *profile*(4)): "`export SCROLL ; SCROLL=no`". If you later decide that scrolling is desired, **SCROLL** must be set to **yes**.

Information on each of the Help Facility commands (*starter, locate, usage, glossary,* and *help*) is located on their respective manual pages.

SEE ALSO

glossary(1), help(1), sh(1), starter(1), usage(1).
term(5) in the *Programmer's Reference Manual.*

WARNINGS

If the shell variable **TERM** (see *sh*(1)) is not set in the user's *.profile* file, then **TERM** will default to the terminal value type 450 (a hard-copy terminal). For a list of valid terminal types, refer to *term*(5).

NAME

login − sign on

SYNOPSIS

login [name [env-var ...]]

DESCRIPTION

The *login* command is used at the beginning of each terminal session and allows you to identify yourself to the system. It may be invoked as a command or by the system when a connection is first established. Also, it is invoked by the system when a previous user has terminated the initial shell by typing a *cntrl-d* to indicate an "end-of-file." (See *How to Get Started* at the beginning of this volume for instructions on how to dial up initially.)

If *login* is invoked as a command it must replace the initial command interpreter. This is accomplished by typing:

exec login

from the initial shell.

login asks for your user name (if not supplied as an argument), and, if appropriate, your password. Echoing is turned off (where possible) during the typing of your password, so it will not appear on the written record of the session.

At some installations, an option may be invoked that will require you to enter a second "dialup" password. This will occur only for dial-up connections, and will be prompted by the message "dialup password:". Both passwords are required for a successful login.

If you do not complete the login successfully within a certain period of time (e.g., one minute), you are likely to be silently disconnected.

After a successful login, accounting files are updated, the procedure **/etc/profile** is performed, the message-of-the-day, if any, is printed, the user-ID, the group-ID, the working directory, and the command interpreter (usually *sh*(1)) is initialized, and the file **.profile** in the working directory is executed, if it exists. These specifications are found in the **/etc/passwd** file entry for the user. The name of the command interpreter is − followed by the last component of the interpreter's path name (i.e., **−sh**). If this field in the password file is empty, then the default command interpreter, **/bin/sh** is used. If this field is "*", then the named directory becomes the root directory, the starting point for path searches for path names beginning with a **/**. At that point *login* is re-executed at the new level which must have its own root structure, including **/etc/login** and **/etc/passwd**.

The basic *environment* is initialized to:

HOME=*your-login-directory*
PATH=:/bin:/usr/bin
SHELL=*last-field-of-passwd-entry*
MAIL=/usr/mail/*your-login-name*
TZ=*timezone-specification*

The environment may be expanded or modified by supplying additional arguments to *login*, either at execution time or when *login* requests your login name.

The arguments may take either the form *xxx* or *xxx=yyy*. Arguments without an equal sign are placed in the environment as

L*n*=xxx

where *n* is a number starting at 0 and is incremented each time a new variable name is required. Variables containing an = are placed into the environment without modification. If they already appear in the environment, then they replace the older value. There are two exceptions. The variables **PATH** and **SHELL** cannot be changed. This prevents people, logging into restricted shell environments, from spawning secondary shells which are not restricted. Both *login* and *getty* understand simple single-character quoting conventions. Typing a backslash in front of a character quotes it and allows the inclusion of such things as spaces and tabs.

FILES

/etc/utmp	accounting
/etc/wtmp	accounting
/usr/mail/*your-name*	mailbox for user *your-name*
/etc/motd	message-of-the-day
/etc/passwd	password file
/etc/profile	system profile
.profile	user's login profile

SEE ALSO

mail(1), newgrp(1), sh(1), su(1M).
passwd(4), profile(4), environ(5) in the *Programmer's Reference Manual.*

DIAGNOSTICS

login incorrect if the user name or the password cannot be matched.

No shell, cannot open password file, or *no directory*: consult a UNIX system programming counselor.

No utmp entry. You must exec "login" from the lowest level "sh" if you attempted to execute *login* as a command without using the shell's *exec* internal command or from other than the initial shell.

NAME

logname – get login name

SYNOPSIS

logname

DESCRIPTION

logname returns the contents of the environment variable **$LOGNAME**, which is set when a user logs into the system.

FILES

/etc/profile

SEE ALSO

env(1), login(1).
logname(3X), environ(5) in the *Programmer's Reference Manual*.

NAME

lp, cancel – send/cancel requests to an LP line printer

SYNOPSIS

lp [**–c**] [**–d**dest] [**–m**] [**–n**number] [**–o**option] [**–s**] [**–t**title] [**–w**] files
cancel [ids] [printers]

DESCRIPTION

lp arranges for the named files and associated information (collectively called a *request*) to be printed by a line printer. If no file names are mentioned, the standard input is assumed. The file name – stands for the standard input and may be supplied on the command line in conjunction with named *files*. The order in which *files* appear is the same order in which they will be printed.

lp associates a unique *id* with each request and prints it on the standard output. This *id* can be used later to cancel (see *cancel*) or find the status (see *lpstat*(1)) of the request.

The following options to *lp* may appear in any order and may be intermixed with file names:

–c Make copies of the *files* to be printed immediately when *lp* is invoked. Normally, *files* will not be copied, but will be linked whenever possible. If the **–c** option is not given, then the user should be careful not to remove any of the *files* before the request has been printed in its entirety. It should also be noted that in the absence of the **–c** option, any changes made to the named *files* after the request is made but before it is printed will be reflected in the printed output.

–d*dest* Choose *dest* as the printer or class of printers that is to do the printing. If *dest* is a printer, then the request will be printed only on that specific printer. If *dest* is a class of printers, then the request will be printed on the first available printer that is a member of the class. Under certain conditions (printer unavailability, file space limitation, etc.), requests for specific destinations may not be accepted (see *accept*(1M) and *lpstat*(1)). By default, *dest* is taken from the environment variable **LPDEST** (if it is set). Otherwise, a default destination (if one exists) for the computer system is used. Destination names vary between systems (see *lpstat*(1)).

–m Send mail (see *mail(1))* after the files have been printed. By default, no mail is sent upon normal completion of the print request.

–n*number* Print *number* copies (default of 1) of the output.

–o*option* Specify printer-dependent or class-dependent *options*. Several such *options* may be collected by specifying the **–o** keyletter more than once. For more information about what is valid for *options*, see **Models** in *lpadmin*(1M).

–s Suppress messages from *lp*(1) such as "request id is ...".

–t*title* Print *title* on the banner page of the output.

−w Write a message on the user's terminal after the *files* have been printed. If the user is not logged in, then mail will be sent instead.

Cancel cancels line printer requests that were made by the *lp*(1) command. The command line arguments may be either request *ids* (as returned by *lp*(1)) or *printer* names (for a complete list, use *lpstat*(1)). Specifying a request *id* cancels the associated request even if it is currently printing. Specifying a *printer* cancels the request which is currently printing on that printer. In either case, the cancellation of a request that is currently printing frees the printer to print its next available request.

FILES

/usr/spool/lp/*

SEE ALSO

enable(1), lpstat(1), mail(1).
accept(1M), lpadmin(1M), lpsched(1M) in the *System Administrator's Reference Manual.*

NAME

lpstat — print LP status information

SYNOPSIS

lpstat [options]

DESCRIPTION

lpstat prints information about the current status of the LP spooling system.

If no *options* are given, then *lpstat* prints the status of all requests made to *lp*(1) by the user. Any arguments that are not *options* are assumed to be request *ids* (as returned by *lp*). *lpstat* prints the status of such requests. *Options* may appear in any order and may be repeated and intermixed with other arguments. Some of the keyletters below may be followed by an optional *list* that can be in one of two forms: a list of items separated from one another by a comma, or a list of items enclosed in double quotes and separated from one another by a comma and/or one or more spaces. For example:

−u"user1, user2, user3"

The omission of a *list* following such keyletters causes all information relevant to the keyletter to be printed, for example:

lpstat −o

prints the status of all output requests.

−a[*list*] Print acceptance status (with respect to *lp*) of destinations for requests. *List* is a list of intermixed printer names and class names.

−c[*list*] Print class names and their members. *List* is a list of class names.

−d Print the system default destination for *lp*.

−o[*list*] Print the status of output requests. *List* is a list of intermixed printer names, class names, and request *ids*.

−p[*list*] Print the status of printers. *List* is a list of printer names.

−r Print the status of the LP request scheduler

−s Print a status summary, including the system default destination, a list of class names and their members, and a list of printers and their associated devices.

−t Print all status information.

−u[*list*] Print status of output requests for users. *List* is a list of login names.

−v[*list*] Print the names of printers and the path names of the devices associated with them. *List* is a list of printer names.

FILES

/usr/spool/lp/*

SEE ALSO

enable(1), lp(1).

NAME

ls − list contents of directory

SYNOPSIS

ls [**−RadCxmlnogrtucpFbqisf**] [names]

DESCRIPTION

For each directory argument, *ls* lists the contents of the directory; for each file argument, *ls* repeats its name and any other information requested. The output is sorted alphabetically by default. When no argument is given, the current directory is listed. When several arguments are given, the arguments are first sorted appropriately, but file arguments appear before directories and their contents.

There are three major listing formats. The default format is to list one entry per line, the **−C** and **−x** options enable multi-column formats, and the **−m** option enables stream output format. In order to determine output formats for the **−C**, **−x**, and **−m** options, *ls* uses an environment variable, **COLUMNS**, to determine the number of character positions available on one output line. If this variable is not set, the *terminfo*(4) database is used to determine the number of columns, based on the environment variable **TERM**. If this information cannot be obtained, 80 columns are assumed.

The *ls* command has the following options:

−R Recursively list subdirectories encountered.

−a List all entries, including those that begin with a dot (.), which are normally not listed.

−d If an argument is a directory, list only its name (not its contents); often used with **−l** to get the status of a directory.

−C Multi-column output with entries sorted down the columns.

−x Multi-column output with entries sorted across rather than down the page.

−m Stream output format; files are listed across the page, separated by commas.

−l List in long format, giving mode, number of links, owner, group, size in bytes, and time of last modification for each file (see below). If the file is a special file, the size field will instead contain the major and minor device numbers rather than a size.

−n The same as **−l**, except that the owner's **UID** and group's **GID** numbers are printed, rather than the associated character strings.

−o The same as **−l**, except that the group is not printed.

−g The same as **−l**, except that the owner is not printed.

−r Reverse the order of sort to get reverse alphabetic or oldest first as appropriate.

−t Sort by time stamp (latest first) instead of by name. The default is the last modification time. (See **−n** and **−c**.)

−u Use time of last access instead of last modification for sorting (with the **−t** option) or printing (with the **−l** option).

−c Use time of last modification of the i-node (file created, mode changed, etc.) for sorting (**−t**) or printing (**−l**).

−p Put a slash (/) after each filename if that file is a directory.

−F Put a slash (/) after each filename if that file is a directory and put an asterisk (*) after each filename if that file is executable.

−b Force printing of non-graphic characters to be in the octal **ddd** notation.

−q Force printing of non-graphic characters in file names as the character (**?**).

−i For each file, print the i-number in the first column of the report.

−s Give size in blocks, including indirect blocks, for each entry.

−f Force each argument to be interpreted as a directory and list the name found in each slot. This option turns off **−l, −t, −s,** and **−r,** and turns on **−a;** the order is the order in which entries appear in the directory.

The mode printed under the **−l** option consists of ten characters. The first character may be one of the following:

d the entry is a directory;
b the entry is a block special file;
c the entry is a character special file;
p the entry is a fifo (a.k.a. "named pipe") special file;
− the entry is an ordinary file.

The next 9 characters are interpreted as three sets of three bits each. The first set refers to the owner's permissions; the next to permissions of others in the user-group of the file; and the last to all others. Within each set, the three characters indicate permission to read, to write, and to execute the file as a program, respectively. For a directory, "execute" permission is interpreted to mean permission to search the directory for a specified file.

ls −l (the **l**ong list) prints its output as follows:

```
−rwxrwxrwx  1 smith  dev    10876  May 16 9:42 part2
```

This horizontal configuration provides a good deal of information. Reading from right to left, you see that the current directory holds one file, named "part2." Next, the last time that file's contents were modified was 9:42 A.M. on May 16. The file is moderately sized, containing 10,876 characters, or bytes. The owner of the file, or the user, belongs to the group "dev" (perhaps indicating "development"), and his or her login name is "smith." The number, in this case "1," indicates the number of links to file "part2." Finally, the row of dash and letters tell you that user, group, and others have permissions to read, write, execute "part2."

The execute (**x**) symbol here occupies the third position of the three-character sequence. A – in the third position would have indicated a denial of execution permissions.

The permissions are indicated as follows:

- **r** the file is readable
- **w** the file is writable
- **x** the file is executable
- **–** the indicated permission is *not* granted
- **l** mandatory locking will occur during access (the set-group-ID bit is on and the group execution bit is off)
- **s** the **s**et-user-ID or **s**et-group-ID bit is on, and the corresponding user or group execution bit is also on
- **S** undefined bit-state (the set-user-ID bit is on and the user execution bit if off)
- **t** the 1000 (octal) bit, or sticky bit, is on (see **chmod(1)**), and execution is on
- **T** the 1000 bit is turned on, and execution is off (undefined bit-state)

For user and group permissions, the third position is sometimes occupied by a character other than **x** or **–**. **s** also may occupy this position, referring to the state of the **s**et-ID bit, whether it be the user's or the group's. The ability to assume the same ID as the user during execution is, for example, used during login when you begin as root but need to assume the identity of the user stated at "login."

In the case of the sequence of group permissions, **l** may occupy the third position. **l** refers to mandatory file and record **l**ocking. This permission describes a file's ability to allow other files to lock its reading or writing permissions during access.

For others permissions, the third position may be occupied by **t** or **T**. These refer to the state of the sticky bit and execution permissions.

EXAMPLES

The first set of examples refers to permissions:

–rwxr––r––

This describes a file that is readable, writable, and executable by the user and readable by the group and others.

–rwsr–xr–x

The second example describes a file that is readable, writable, and executable by the user, readable and executable by the group and others, and allows its user-ID to be assumed, during execution, by the user presently executing it.

–rw–rwl–––

This example describes a file that is readable and writable only by the user and the group and can be locked during access.

ls -a

This command will print the names of all files in the current directory, including those that begin with a dot (.), which normally do not print.

ls -aisn

This command will provide you with quite a bit of information including **a**ll files, including non-printing ones (**a**), the **i**-number—the memory address of the i-node associated with the file—printed in the left-hand column (**i**); the **s**ize (in blocks) of the files, printed in the column to the right of the i-numbers (**s**); finally, the report is displayed in the **n**umeric version of the long list, printing the **UID** (instead of user name) and **GID** (instead of group name) numbers associated with the files.

When the sizes of the files in a directory are listed, a total count of blocks, including indirect blocks, is printed.

FILES

/etc/passwd	user IDs for **ls −l** and **ls −o**
/etc/group	group IDs for **ls −l** and **ls −g**
/usr/lib/terminfo/?/*	terminal information database

SEE ALSO

chmod(1), find(1).

NOTES

In a Remote File Sharing environment, you may not have the permissions that the output of the **ls −l** command leads you to believe. For more information see the "Mapping Remote Users" section of Chapter 10 of the *System Administrator's Guide*.

BUGS

Unprintable characters in file names may confuse the columnar output options.

NAME

machid: pdp11, u3b, u3b2, u3b5, vax − get processor type truth value

SYNOPSIS

pdp11

u3b

u3b2

u3b5

vax

DESCRIPTION

The following commands will return a true value (exit code of 0) if you are on a processor that the command name indicates.

pdp11 True if you are on a PDP-11/45 or PDP-11/70.

u3b True if you are on a 3B20 computer.

u3b2 True if you are on a 3B2 computer.

u3b5 True if you are on a 3B5 computer.

vax True if you are on a VAX-11/750 or VAX-11/780.

The commands that do not apply will return a false (non-zero) value. These commands are often used within makefiles (see *make*(1)) and shell procedures (see *sh*(1)) to increase portability.

SEE ALSO

sh(1), test(1), true(1).
make(1) in the *Programmer's Reference Manual*.

NAME

mail, rmail – send mail to users or read mail

SYNOPSIS

Sending mail:

mail [**–oswt**] persons

rmail [**–oswt**] persons

Reading mail:

mail [**–ehpqr**] [**–f** file] [**–F** persons]

DESCRIPTION

Sending mail:

The command-line arguments that follow affect SENDING mail:

–o suppresses the address optimization facility.

–s suppresses the addition of a <new-line> at the top of the letter being sent. See WARNINGS below.

–w causes a letter to be sent to a remote user without waiting for the completion of the remote transfer program.

–t causes a **To:** line to be added to the letter, showing the intended recipients.

A *person* is usually a user name recognized by *login*(1). When *persons* are named, *mail* assumes a message is being sent (except in the case of the /-F option). It reads from the standard input up to an end-of-file (control-d), or until it reads a line consisting of just a period. When either of those signals is received, *mail* adds the *letter* to the *mailfile* for each *person*. A *letter* is a *message* preceded by a *postmark*. The message is preceded by the sender's name and a *postmark*. A *postmark* consists of one or more 'From' lines followed by a blank line (unless the –s argument was used).

If a letter is found to be undeliverable, it is returned to the sender with diagnostics that indicate the location and nature of the failure. If *mail* is interrupted during input, the file **dead.letter** is saved to allow editing and resending. **dead.letter** is recreated every time it is needed, erasing any previous contents.

rmail only permits the sending of mail; *uucp*(1C) uses *rmail* as a security precaution.

If the local system has the Basic Networking Utilities installed, mail may be sent to a recipient on a remote system. Prefix *person* by the system name and exclamation point. A series of system names separated by exclamation points can be used to direct a letter through an extended network.

Reading Mail:

The command-line arguments that follow affect READING mail:

–e causes mail not to be printed. An exit value of 0 is returned if the user has mail; otherwise, an exit value of 1 is returned.

–h causes a window of headers to be displayed rather than the latest message. The display is followed by the '**?**' prompt.

−p causes all messages to be printed without prompting for disposition.

−q causes *mail* to terminate after interrupts. Normally an interrupt causes only the termination of the message being printed.

−r causes messages to be printed in first-in, first-out order.

−f*file* causes *mail* to use *file* (e.g., **mbox**) instead of the default *mailfile*.

−F*persons*
entered into an empty *mailbox*, causes all incoming mail to be forwarded to *persons*.

mail, unless otherwise influenced by command-line arguments, prints a user's mail messages in last-in, first-out order. For each message, the user is prompted with a **?**, and a line is read from the standard input. The following commands are available to determine the disposition of the message:

<new-line>, +, or **n**	Go on to next message.
d, or **dp**	Delete message and go on to next message.
d #	Delete message number #. Do not go on to next message.
dq	Delete message and quit *mail*.
h	Display a window of headers around current message.
h #	Display header of message number #.
h a	Display headers of ALL messages in the user's *mailfile*.
h d	Display headers of messages scheduled for deletion.
p	Print current message again.
−	Print previous message.
a	Print message that arrived during the *mail* session.
#	Print message number #.
r [*users* **]**	Reply to the sender, and other *user(s)*, then delete the message.
s [*files*]	Save message in the named *files* (**mbox** is default).
y	Same as save.
u [#]	Undelete message number # (default is last read).
w [*files*]	Save message, without its top-most header, in the named *files* (**mbox** is default).
m [*persons*]	Mail the message to the named *persons*.
q, or **ctl-d**	Put undeleted mail back in the *mailfile* and quit *mail*.
x	Put all mail back in the *mailfile* unchanged and exit *mail*.

!*command*	Escape to the shell to do *command*.
?	Print a command summary.

When a user logs in, the presence of mail, if any, is indicated. Also, notification is made if new mail arrives while using *mail*.

The *mailfile* may be manipulated in two ways to alter the function of *mail*. The *other* permissions of the file may be read-write, read-only, or neither read nor write to allow different levels of privacy. If changed to other than the default, the file will be preserved even when empty to perpetuate the desired permissions. The file may also contain the first line:

Forward to *person*

which will cause all mail sent to the owner of the *mailfile* to be forwarded to *person*. A "Forwarded by..." message is added to the header. This is especially useful in a multi-machine environment to forward all of a person's mail to a single machine, and to keep the recipient informed if the mail has been forwarded. Installation and removal of forwarding is done with the **−F** option.

To forward all of one's mail to systema!user enter:

mail -Fsystema!user

To forward to more than one user enter:

mail -F"user1,systema!user2,systema!systemb!user3"

Note that when more than one user is specified, the whole list should be enclosed in double quotes so that it may all be interpreted as the operand of the **−F** option. The list can be up to 1024 bytes; either commas or white space can be used to separate users.

To remove forwarding enter:

mail −F ""

The pair of double quotes is mandatory to set a NULL argument for the −F option.

In order for forwarding to work properly the *mailfile* should have "mail" as group ID, and the group permission should be read-write.

FILES

/etc/passwd	to identify sender and locate persons
/usr/mail/*user*	incoming mail for *user*; i.e., the *mailfile*
$HOME/mbox	saved mail
$MAIL	variable containing path name of *mailfile*
/tmp/ma*	temporary file
/usr/mail/*.lock	lock for mail directory
dead.letter	unmailable text

SEE ALSO

login(1), mailx(1), write(1).
User's Guide.
System Administrator's Guide.

WARNING

The "Forward to person" feature may result in a loop, if *sys1!userb* forwards to *sys2!userb* and *sys2!userb* forwards to *sys1!userb*. The symptom is a message saying "unbounded...saved mail in dead.letter."

The **−s** option should be used with caution. It allows the text of a message to be interpreted as part of the postmark of the letter, possibly causing confusion to other *mail* programs. To allow compatibility with *mailx*(1), if the first line of the message is "Subject:...", the addition of a <newline> is suppressed whether or not the **−s** option is used.

BUGS

Conditions sometimes result in a failure to remove a lock file.
After an interrupt, the next message may not be printed; printing may be forced by typing a **p**.

NAME

mailx – interactive message processing system

SYNOPSIS

mailx [*options*] [*name...*]

DESCRIPTION

The command *mailx* provides a comfortable, flexible environment for sending and receiving messages electronically. When reading mail, *mailx* provides commands to facilitate saving, deleting, and responding to messages. When sending mail, *mailx* allows editing, reviewing and other modification of the message as it is entered.

Many of the remote features of *mailx* will only work if the Basic Networking Utilities are installed on your system.

Incoming mail is stored in a standard file for each user, called the *mailbox* for that user. When *mailx* is called to read messages, the *mailbox* is the default place to find them. As messages are read, they are marked to be moved to a secondary file for storage, unless specific action is taken, so that the messages need not be seen again. This secondary file is called the *mbox* and is normally located in the user's HOME directory (see "MBOX" (ENVIRONMENT VARIABLES) for a description of this file). Messages can be saved in other secondary files named by the user. Messages remain in a secondary file until forcibly removed.

The user can access a secondary file by using the **–f** option of the *mailx* command. Messages in the secondary file can then be read or otherwise processed using the same COMMANDS as in the primary *mailbox*. This gives rise within these pages to the notion of a current *mailbox*.

On the command line, *options* start with a dash (–) and any other arguments are taken to be destinations (recipients). If no recipients are specified, *mailx* will attempt to read messages from the *mailbox*. Command line options are:

–e	Test for presence of mail. *mailx* prints nothing and exits with a successful return code if there is mail to read.
–f [*filename*]	Read messages from *filename* instead of *mailbox*. If no *filename* is specified, the *mbox* is used.
–F	Record the message in a file named after the first recipient. Overrides the "record" variable, if set (see ENVIRONMENT VARIABLES).
–h *number*	The number of network "hops" made so far. This is provided for network software to avoid infinite delivery loops. (See **addsopt** under ENVIRONMENT VARIABLES)
–H	Print header summary only.
–i	Ignore interrupts. See also "ignore" (ENVIRONMENT VARIABLES).
–n	Do not initialize from the system default *mailx.rc* file.
–N	Do not print initial header summary.
–r *address*	Pass *address* to network delivery software. All tilde commands are disabled. (See **addsopt** under ENVIRONMENT VARIABLES)

−s *subject* Set the Subject header field to *subject*.

−u *user* Read *user's mailbox*. This is only effective if *user's mailbox* is not read protected.

−U Convert *uucp* style addresses to internet standards. Overrides the "conv" environment variable. (See **addsopt** under ENVIRONMENT VARIABLES)

When reading mail, *mailx* is in *command mode*. A header summary of the first several messages is displayed, followed by a prompt indicating *mailx* can accept regular commands (see COMMANDS below). When sending mail, *mailx* is in *input mode*. If no subject is specified on the command line, a prompt for the subject is printed. (A "subject" longer than 1024 characters will cause *mailx* to dump core) As the message is typed, *mailx* will read the message and store it in a temporary file. Commands may be entered by beginning a line with the tilde (~) escape character followed by a single command letter and optional arguments. See TILDE ESCAPES for a summary of these commands.

At any time, the behavior of *mailx* is governed by a set of *environment variables*. These are flags and valued parameters which are set and cleared via the **se**t and **uns**et commands. See ENVIRONMENT VARIABLES below for a summary of these parameters.

Recipients listed on the command line may be of three types: login names, shell commands, or alias groups. Login names may be any network address, including mixed network addressing. If mail is found to to undeliverable, an attempt is made to return it to the sender's *mailbox*. If the recipient name begins with a pipe symbol (|), the rest of the name is taken to be a shell command to pipe the message through. This provides an automatic interface with any program that reads the standard input, such as *lp*(1) for recording outgoing mail on paper. Alias groups are set by the **a**lias command (see COMMANDS below) and are lists of recipients of any type.

Regular commands are of the form

[**command**] [*msglist*] [*arguments*]

If no command is specified in *command mode*, **p**rint is assumed. In *input mode*, commands are recognized by the escape character, and lines not treated as commands are taken as input for the message.

Each message is assigned a sequential number, and there is at any time the notion of a current message, marked by a right angle bracket (>) in the header summary. Many commands take an optional list of messages (*msglist*) to operate on. The default for *msglist* is the current message. A *msglist* is a list of message identifiers separated by spaces, which may include:

n Message number **n**.

. The current message.

^ The first undeleted message.

$ The last message.

***** All messages.

n−m An inclusive range of message numbers.
user All messages from **user**.
/string All messages with **string** in the subject line (case ignored).
:*c* All messages of type *c*, where *c* is one of:

- **d** deleted messages
- **n** new messages
- **o** old messages
- **r** read messages
- **u** unread messages

Note that the context of the command determines whether this type of message specification makes sense.

Other arguments are usually arbitrary strings whose usage depends on the command involved. File names, where expected, are expanded via the normal shell conventions (see *sh*(1)). Special characters are recognized by certain commands and are documented with the commands below.

At start-up time, *mailx* tries to execute commands from the optional system-wide file (**/usr/lib/mailx/mailx.rc**) to initialize certain parameters, then from a private start-up file (**$HOME/.mailrc**) for personalized variables. With the exceptions noted below, regular commands are legal inside start-up files. The most common use of a start-up file is to set up initial display options and alias lists. The following commands are not legal in the start-up file: **!**, **C**opy, **e**dit, **fo**llowup, **F**ollowup, **ho**ld, **m**ail, **pre**serve, **r**eply, **R**eply, **sh**ell, and **v**isual. An error in the start-up file causes the remaining lines in the file to be ignored. The **.mailrc** file is optional, and must be constructed locally.

COMMANDS

The following is a complete list of *mailx* commands:

!*shell-command*
Escape to the shell. See "SHELL" (ENVIRONMENT VARIABLES).

*comment*
Null command (comment). This may be useful in *.mailrc* files.

=
Print the current message number.

?
Prints a summary of commands.

alias *alias name ...*
group *alias name ...*
Declare an alias for the given names. The names will be substituted when *alias* is used as a recipient. Useful in the *.mailrc* file.

alternates *name ...*
Declares a list of alternate names for your login. When responding to a message, these names are removed from the list of recipients for the response. With no arguments, **alt**ernates prints the current list of alternate names. See also "allnet" (ENVIRONMENT VARIABLES).

cd [*directory*]
chdir [*directory*]
Change directory. If *directory* is not specified, $HOME is used.

copy [*filename*]
copy [*msglist*] *filename*
Copy messages to the file without marking the messages as saved. Otherwise equivalent to the **s**ave command.

Copy [*msglist*]
Save the specified messages in a file whose name is derived from the author of the message to be saved, without marking the messages as saved. Otherwise equivalent to the **S**ave command.

delete [*msglist*]
Delete messages from the *mailbox*. If "autoprint" is set, the next message after the last one deleted is printed (see ENVIRONMENT VARIABLES).

discard [*header-field* ...]
ignore [*header-field* ...]
Suppresses printing of the specified header fields when displaying messages on the screen. Examples of header fields to ignore are "status" and "cc." The fields are included when the message is saved. The **P**rint and **T**ype commands override this command.

dp [*msglist*]
dt [*msglist*]
Delete the specified messages from the *mailbox* and print the next message after the last one deleted. Roughly equivalent to a **d**elete command followed by a **p**rint command.

echo *string* ...
Echo the given strings (like *echo*(1)).

edit [*msglist*]
Edit the given messages. The messages are placed in a temporary file and the "EDITOR" variable is used to get the name of the editor (see ENVIRONMENT VARIABLES). Default editor is *ed*(1).

exit
xit
Exit from *mailx*, without changing the *mailbox*. No messages are saved in the *mbox* (see also **q**uit).

file [*filename*]
folder [*filename*]

Quit from the current file of messages and read in the specified file. Several special characters are recognized when used as file names, with the following substitutions:

% the current *mailbox*.

%**user**

the *mailbox* for **user**.

the previous file.

& the current *mbox*.

Default file is the current *mailbox*.

folders

Print the names of the files in the directory set by the "folder" variable (see ENVIRONMENT VARIABLES).

followup [*message*]

Respond to a message, recording the response in a file whose name is derived from the author of the message. Overrides the "record" variable, if set. See also the **F**ollowup, **S**ave, and **C**opy commands and "outfolder" (ENVIRONMENT VARIABLES).

Followup [*msglist*]

Respond to the first message in the *msglist*, sending the message to the author of each message in the *msglist*. The subject line is taken from the first message and the response is recorded in a file whose name is derived from the author of the first message. See also the **fo**llowup, **S**ave, and **C**opy commands and "outfolder" (ENVIRONMENT VARIABLES).

from [*msglist*]

Prints the header summary for the specified messages.

group *alias name ...*
alias *alias name ...*

Declare an alias for the given names. The names will be substituted when *alias* is used as a recipient. Useful in the *.mailrc* file.

headers [*message*]

Prints the page of headers which includes the message specified. The "screen" variable sets the number of headers per page (see ENVIRONMENT VARIABLES). See also the **z** command.

help

Prints a summary of commands.

hold [*msglist*]
preserve [*msglist*]

Holds the specified messages in the *mailbox*.

if *s* | *r*
mail-commands
else
mail-commands
endif

Conditional execution, where *s* will execute following *mail-commands*, up to an **el**se or **en**dif, if the program is in *send* mode, and *r* causes the *mail-commands* to be executed only in *receive* mode. Useful in the *.mailrc* file.

ignore *header-field ...*
discard *header-field ...*

Suppresses printing of the specified header fields when displaying messages on the screen. Examples of header fields to ignore are "status" and "cc." All fields are included when the message is saved. The **P**rint and **T**ype commands override this command.

list

Prints all commands available. No explanation is given.

mail *name ...*

Mail a message to the specified users.

Mail *name*

Mail a message to the specified user and record a copy of it in a file named after that user.

mbox [*msglist*]

Arrange for the given messages to end up in the standard *mbox* save file when *mailx* terminates normally. See "MBOX" (ENVIRONMENT VARIABLES) for a description of this file. See also the **ex**it and **q**uit commands.

next [*message*]

Go to next message matching *message*. A *msglist* may be specified, but in this case the first valid message in the list is the only one used. This is useful for jumping to the next message from a specific user, since the name would be taken as a command in the absence of a real command. See the discussion of *msglists* above for a description of possible message specifications.

pipe [*msglist*] [*shell-command*]
| [*msglist*] [*shell-command*]

Pipe the message through the given *shell-command*. The message is treated as if it were read. If no arguments are given, the current message is piped through the command specified by the value of the "cmd" variable. If the "page" variable is set, a form feed character is inserted after each message (see ENVIRONMENT VARIABLES).

preserve [*msglist*]
hold [*msglist*]
Preserve the specified messages in the *mailbox*.

Print [*msglist*]
Type [*msglist*]
Print the specified messages on the screen, including all header fields. Overrides suppression of fields by the **ig**nore command.

print [*msglist*]
type [*msglist*]
Print the specified messages. If "crt" is set, the messages longer than the number of lines specified by the "crt" variable are paged through the command specified by the "PAGER" variable. The default command is *pg*(1) (see ENVIRONMENT VARIABLES).

quit
Exit from *mailx*, storing messages that were read in *mbox* and unread messages in the *mailbox*. Messages that have been explicitly saved in a file are deleted.

Reply [*msglist*]
Respond [*msglist*]
Send a response to the author of each message in the *msglist*. The subject line is taken from the first message. If "record" is set to a file name, the response is saved at the end of that file (see ENVIRONMENT VARIABLES).

reply [*message*]
respond [*message*]
Reply to the specified message, including all other recipients of the message. If "record" is set to a file name, the response is saved at the end of that file (see ENVIRONMENT VARIABLES).

Save [*msglist*]
Save the specified messages in a file whose name is derived from the author of the first message. The name of the file is taken to be the author's name with all network addressing stripped off. See also the **C**opy, **fo**llowup, and **F**ollowup commands and "outfolder" (ENVIRONMENT VARIABLES).

save [*filename*]
save [*msglist*] *filename*
Save the specified messages in the given file. The file is created if it does not exist. The message is deleted from the *mailbox* when *mailx* terminates unless "keepsave" is set (see also ENVIRONMENT VARIABLES and the **ex**it and **q**uit commands).

set
set *name*
set *name=string*
set *name=number*

Define a variable called *name*. The variable may be given a null, string, or numeric value. **Se**t by itself prints all defined variables and their values. See ENVIRONMENT VARIABLES for detailed descriptions of the *mailx* variables.

shell

Invoke an interactive shell (see also "SHELL" (ENVIRONMENT VARIABLES)).

size [*msglist*]

Print the size in characters of the specified messages.

source *filename*

Read commands from the given file and return to command mode.

top [*msglist*]

Print the top few lines of the specified messages. If the "toplines" variable is set, it is taken as the number of lines to print (see ENVIRONMENT VARIABLES). The default is 5.

touch [*msglist*]

Touch the specified messages. If any message in *msglist* is not specifically saved in a file, it will be placed in the *mbox* upon normal termination. See **ex**it and **q**uit.

Type [*msglist*]
Print [*msglist*]

Print the specified messages on the screen, including all header fields. Overrides suppression of fields by the **ig**nore command.

type [*msglist*]
print [*msglist*]

Print the specified messages. If "crt" is set, the messages longer than the number of lines specified by the "crt" variable are paged through the command specified by the "PAGER" variable. The default command is *pg*(1) (see ENVIRONMENT VARIABLES).

undelete [*msglist*]

Restore the specified deleted messages. Will only restore messages deleted in the current mail session. If "autoprint" is set, the last message of those restored is printed (see ENVIRONMENT VARIABLES).

unset *name* ...
Causes the specified variables to be erased. If the variable was imported from the execution environment (i.e., a shell variable) then it cannot be erased.

version
Prints the current version and release date.

visual [*msglist*]
Edit the given messages with a screen editor. The messages are placed in a temporary file and the "VISUAL" variable is used to get the name of the editor (see ENVIRONMENT VARIABLES).

write [*msglist*] *filename*
Write the given messages on the specified file, minus the header and trailing blank line. Otherwise equivalent to the **s**ave command.

xit
exit
Exit from *mailx,* without changing the *mailbox.* No messages are saved in the *mbox* (see also **q**uit).

z[+ | −]
Scroll the header display forward or backward one screen−full. The number of headers displayed is set by the "screen" variable (see ENVIRONMENT VARIABLES).

TILDE ESCAPES

The following commands may be entered only from *input mode,* by beginning a line with the tilde escape character (~). See "escape" (ENVIRONMENT VARIABLES) for changing this special character.

~! *shell-command*
Escape to the shell.

~.
Simulate end of file (terminate message input).

~: *mail-command*
~_ *mail-command*
Perform the command-level request. Valid only when sending a message while reading mail.

~?
Print a summary of tilde escapes.

~A
Insert the autograph string "Sign" into the message (see ENVIRONMENT VARIABLES).

~a

Insert the autograph string "sign" into the message (see ENVIRONMENT VARIABLES).

~b *name ...*

Add the *names* to the blind carbon copy (Bcc) list.

~c *name ...*

Add the *names* to the carbon copy (Cc) list.

~d

Read in the *dead.letter* file. See "DEAD" (ENVIRONMENT VARIABLES) for a description of this file.

~e

Invoke the editor on the partial message. See also "EDITOR" (ENVIRONMENT VARIABLES).

~f [*msglist*]

Forward the specified messages. The messages are inserted into the message, without alteration.

~h

Prompt for Subject line and To, Cc, and Bcc lists. If the field is displayed with an initial value, it may be edited as if you had just typed it.

~i *string*

Insert the value of the named variable into the text of the message. For example, **~A** is equivalent to '**~i** Sign.'

~m [*msglist*]

Insert the specified messages into the letter, shifting the new text to the right one tab stop. Valid only when sending a message while reading mail.

~p

Print the message being entered.

~q

Quit from input mode by simulating an interrupt. If the body of the message is not null, the partial message is saved in *dead.letter*. See "DEAD" (ENVIRONMENT VARIABLES) for a description of this file.

~**r** *filename*
~~**<** *filename*
~~**<** !*shell-command*

Read in the specified file. If the argument begins with an exclamation point (!), the rest of the string is taken as an arbitrary shell command and is executed, with the standard output inserted into the message.

~**s** *string* ...

Set the subject line to *string*.

~**t** *name* ...

Add the given *names* to the To list.

~**v**

Invoke a preferred screen editor on the partial message. See also "VISUAL" (ENVIRONMENT VARIABLES).

~**w** *filename*

Write the partial message onto the given file, without the header.

~**x**

Exit as with ~**q** except the message is not saved in *dead.letter*.

~| *shell-command*

Pipe the body of the message through the given *shell-command*. If the *shell-command* returns a successful exit status, the output of the command replaces the message.

ENVIRONMENT VARIABLES

The following are environment variables taken from the execution environment and are not alterable within *mailx*.

HOME=*directory*

The user's base of operations.

MAILRC=*filename*

The name of the start-up file. Default is $HOME/.mailrc.

The following variables are internal *mailx* variables. They may be imported from the execution environment or set via the **se**t command at any time. The **uns**et command may be used to erase variables.

addsopt

Enabled by default. If */bin/mail* is not being used as the deliverer, **noaddsopt** should be specified. (See WARNINGS below)

allnet

All network names whose last component (login name) match are treated as identical. This causes the *msglist* message specifications to behave similarly. Default is **noallnet**. See also the **alt**ernates command and the "metoo" variable.

append

Upon termination, append messages to the end of the *mbox* file instead of prepending them. Default is **noappend.**

askcc

Prompt for the Cc list after message is entered. Default is **noaskcc**.

asksub

Prompt for subject if it is not specified on the command line with the **−s** option. Enabled by default.

autoprint

Enable automatic printing of messages after **d**elete and **u**ndelete commands. Default is **noautoprint**.

bang

Enable the special-casing of exclamation points (!) in shell escape command lines as in *vi*(1). Default is **nobang**.

cmd=*shell-command*

Set the default command for the **pi**pe command. No default value.

conv=*conversion*

Convert uucp addresses to the specified address style. The only valid conversion now is *internet*, which requires a mail delivery program conforming to the RFC822 standard for electronic mail addressing. Conversion is disabled by default. See also "sendmail" and the **−U** command line option.

crt=*number*

Pipe messages having more than *number* lines through the command specified by the value of the "PAGER" variable (*pg*(1) by default). Disabled by default.

DEAD=*filename*

The name of the file in which to save partial letters in case of untimely interrupt. Default is $HOME/dead.letter.

debug

Enable verbose diagnostics for debugging. Messages are not delivered. Default is **nodebug**.

dot

Take a period on a line by itself during input from a terminal as end-of-file. Default is **nodot**.

EDITOR=*shell-command*

The command to run when the **e**dit or ~**e** command is used. Default is *ed*(1).

escape=*c*

Substitute *c* for the ~ escape character. Takes effect with next message sent.

folder=*directory*

The directory for saving standard mail files. User-specified file names beginning with a plus (+) are expanded by preceding the file name with this directory name to obtain the real file name. If *directory* does not start with a slash (/), $HOME is prepended to it. In order to use the plus (+) construct on a *mailx* command line, "folder" must be an exported *sh* environment variable. There is no default for the "folder" variable. See also "outfolder" below.

header

Enable printing of the header summary when entering *mailx*. Enabled by default.

hold

Preserve all messages that are read in the *mailbox* instead of putting them in the standard *mbox* save file. Default is **nohold**.

ignore

Ignore interrupts while entering messages. Handy for noisy dial-up lines. Default is **noignore**.

ignoreeof

Ignore end-of-file during message input. Input must be terminated by a period (.) on a line by itself or by the ~. command. Default is **noignoreeof**. See also "dot" above.

keep

When the *mailbox* is empty, truncate it to zero length instead of removing it. Disabled by default.

keepsave

Keep messages that have been saved in other files in the *mailbox* instead of deleting them. Default is **nokeepsave**.

MBOX=*filename*
The name of the file to save messages which have been read. The **x**it command overrides this function, as does saving the message explicitly in another file. Default is $HOME/mbox.

metoo
If your login appears as a recipient, do not delete it from the list. Default is **nometoo**.

LISTER=*shell-command*
The command (and options) to use when listing the contents of the "folder" directory. The default is *ls*(1).

onehop
When responding to a message that was originally sent to several recipients, the other recipient addresses are normally forced to be relative to the originating author's machine for the response. This flag disables alteration of the recipients' addresses, improving efficiency in a network where all machines can send directly to all other machines (i.e., one hop away).

outfolder
Causes the files used to record outgoing messages to be located in the directory specified by the "folder" variable unless the path name is absolute. Default is **nooutfolder**. See "folder" above and the **S**ave, **C**opy, **fo**llowup, and **F**ollowup commands.

page
Used with the **pi**pe command to insert a form feed after each message sent through the pipe. Default is **nopage**.

PAGER=*shell-command*
The command to use as a filter for paginating output. This can also be used to specify the options to be used. Default is *pg*(1).

prompt=*string*
Set the *command mode* prompt to *string*. Default is "? ".

quiet
Refrain from printing the opening message and version when entering *mailx*. Default is **noquiet**.

record=*filename*
Record all outgoing mail in *filename*. Disabled by default. See also "outfolder" above.

save
Enable saving of messages in *dead.letter* on interrupt or delivery error. See "DEAD" for a description of this file. Enabled by default.

screen=*number*
Sets the number of lines in a screen–full of headers for the **h**eaders command.

sendmail=*shell-command*
Alternate command for delivering messages. Default is *mail*(1).

sendwait
Wait for background mailer to finish before returning. Default is **nosendwait**.

SHELL=*shell-command*
The name of a preferred command interpreter. Default is *sh*(1).

showto
When displaying the header summary and the message is from you, print the recipient's name instead of the author's name.

sign=*string*
The variable inserted into the text of a message when the **~a** (autograph) command is given. No default (see also **~i** (TILDE ESCAPES)).

Sign=*string*
The variable inserted into the text of a message when the **~A** command is given. No default (see also **~i** (TILDE ESCAPES)).

toplines=*number*
The number of lines of header to print with the **to**p command. Default is 5.

VISUAL=*shell-command*
The name of a preferred screen editor. Default is *vi*(1).

FILES

$HOME/.mailrc	personal start-up file
$HOME/mbox	secondary storage file
/usr/mail/*	post office directory
/usr/lib/mailx/mailx.help*	help message files
/usr/lib/mailx/mailx.rc	optional global start-up file
/tmp/R[emqsx]*	temporary files

SEE ALSO
ls(1), mail(1), pg(1).

WARNINGS
The **−h**, **−r** and **−U** options can be used only if *mailx* is built with a delivery program other than */bin/mail*.

BUGS

Where *shell-command* is shown as valid, arguments are not always allowed. Experimentation is recommended.

Internal variables imported from the execution environment cannot be **uns**et.

The full internet addressing is not fully supported by *mailx*. The new standards need some time to settle down.

Attempts to send a message having a line consisting only of a "." are treated as the end of the message by *mail*(1) (the standard mail delivery program).

NAME

makekey − generate encryption key

SYNOPSIS

/usr/lib/makekey

DESCRIPTION

makekey improves the usefulness of encryption schemes depending on a key by increasing the amount of time required to search the key space. It reads 10 bytes from its standard input, and writes 13 bytes on its standard output. The output depends on the input in a way intended to be difficult to compute (i.e., to require a substantial fraction of a second).

The first eight input bytes (the *input key*) can be arbitrary ASCII characters. The last two (the *salt*) are best chosen from the set of digits, ., /, and upper- and lower-case letters. The salt characters are repeated as the first two characters of the output. The remaining 11 output characters are chosen from the same set as the salt and constitute the *output key*.

The transformation performed is essentially the following: the salt is used to select one of 4,096 cryptographic machines all based on the National Bureau of Standards DES algorithm, but broken in 4,096 different ways. Using the *input key* as key, a constant string is fed into the machine and recirculated a number of times. The 64 bits that come out are distributed into the 66 *output key* bits in the result.

makekey is intended for programs that perform encryption. Usually, its input and output will be pipes.

SEE ALSO

ed(1), crypt(1), vi(1).
passwd(4) in the *Programmer's Reference Manual.*

WARNING

This command is provided with the Security Administration Utilities, which is only available in the United States.

NAME

mesg − permit or deny messages

SYNOPSIS

mesg [**−n**] [**−y**]

DESCRIPTION

mesg with argument **n** forbids messages via *write*(1) by revoking non-user write permission on the user's terminal. *mesg* with argument **y** reinstates permission. All by itself, *mesg* reports the current state without changing it.

FILES

/dev/tty*

SEE ALSO

write(1).

DIAGNOSTICS

Exit status is 0 if messages are receivable, 1 if not, 2 on error.

NAME

mkdir − make directories

SYNOPSIS

mkdir [**−m** mode] [**−p**] dirname ...

DESCRIPTION

mkdir creates the named directories in mode 777 (possibly altered by *umask*(1)).

Standard entries in a directory (e.g., the files ., for the directory itself, and .., for its parent) are made automatically. *mkdir* cannot create these entries by name. Creation of a directory requires write permission in the parent directory.

The owner ID and group ID of the new directories are set to the process's real user ID and group ID, respectively.

Two options apply to *mkdir*:

−m This option allows users to specify the mode to be used for new directories. Choices for modes can be found in *chmod*(1).

−p With this option, *mkdir* creates *dirname* by creating all the non-existing parent directories first.

EXAMPLE

To create the subdirectory structure **ltr/jd/jan**, type:

```
mkdir -p ltr/jd/jan
```

SEE ALSO

sh(1), rm(1), umask(1).
intro(2), mkdir(2) in the *Programmer's Reference Manual*.

DIAGNOSTICS

mkdir returns exit code 0 if all directories given in the command line were made successfully. Otherwise, it prints a diagnostic and returns non-zero. An error code is stored in *errno*.

NAME

newform − change the format of a text file

SYNOPSIS

newform [−**s**] [−**i**tabspec] [−**o**tabspec] [−**b**n] [−**e**n] [−**p**n] [−**a**n] [−**f**] [−**c**char] [−**l**n] [files]

DESCRIPTION

newform reads lines from the named *files*, or the standard input if no input file is named, and reproduces the lines on the standard output. Lines are reformatted in accordance with command line options in effect.

Except for −**s**, command line options may appear in any order, may be repeated, and may be intermingled with the optional *files*. Command line options are processed in the order specified. This means that option sequences like "−**e**15 −**l**60" will yield results different from "−**l**60 −**e**15". Options are applied to all *files* on the command line.

−**s** Shears off leading characters on each line up to the first tab and places up to 8 of the sheared characters at the end of the line. If more than 8 characters (not counting the first tab) are sheared, the eighth character is replaced by a * and any characters to the right of it are discarded. The first tab is always discarded.

An error message and program exit will occur if this option is used on a file without a tab on each line. The characters sheared off are saved internally until all other options specified are applied to that line. The characters are then added at the end of the processed line.

For example, to convert a file with leading digits, one or more tabs, and text on each line, to a file beginning with the text, all tabs after the first expanded to spaces, padded with spaces out to column 72 (or truncated to column 72), and the leading digits placed starting at column 73, the command would be:

newform −s −i −l −a −e file-name

−**i***tabspec* Input tab specification: expands tabs to spaces, according to the tab specifications given. *Tabspec* recognizes all tab specification forms described in *tabs*(1). In addition, *tabspec* may be −−, in which *newform* assumes that the tab specification is to be found in the first line read from the standard input (see *fspec*(4)). If no *tabspec* is given, *tabspec* defaults to −**8**. A *tabspec* of −**0** expects no tabs; if any are found, they are treated as −**1**.

−**o***tabspec* Output tab specification: replaces spaces by tabs, according to the tab specifications given. The tab specifications are the same as for −**i***tabspec*. If no *tabspec* is given, *tabspec* defaults to −**8**. A *tabspec* of −**0** means that no spaces will be converted to tabs on output.

−**b***n* Truncate *n* characters from the beginning of the line when the line length is greater than the effective line length (see −**l***n*). Default is to truncate the number of characters necessary to obtain the effective line length. The default value is used when −**b** with no *n* is used.

This option can be used to delete the sequence numbers from a COBOL program as follows:
newform −l1 −b7 file-name

−**e***n* Same as −**b***n* except that characters are truncated from the end of the line.

−**p***n* Prefix *n* characters (see −**c***k*) to the beginning of a line when the line length is less than the effective line length. Default is to prefix the number of characters necessary to obtain the effective line length.

−**a***n* Same as −**p***n* except characters are appended to the end of a line.

−**f** Write the tab specification format line on the standard output before any other lines are output. The tab specification format line which is printed will correspond to the format specified in the *last* −**o** option. If no −**o** option is specified, the line which is printed will contain the default specification of −**8**.

−**c***k* Change the prefix/append character to *k*. Default character for *k* is a space.

−**l***n* Set the effective line length to *n* characters. If *n* is not entered, −**l** defaults to 72. The default line length without the −**l** option is 80 characters. Note that tabs and backspaces are considered to be one character (use −**i** to expand tabs to spaces).

The −**l1** must be used to set the effective line length shorter than any existing line in the file so that the −**b** option is activated.

DIAGNOSTICS

All diagnostics are fatal.

usage: ...	*newform* was called with a bad option.
not −s format	There was no tab on one line.
can't open file	Self-explanatory.
internal line too long	A line exceeds 512 characters after being expanded in the internal work buffer.
tabspec in error	A tab specification is incorrectly formatted, or specified tab stops are not ascending.
tabspec indirection illegal	A *tabspec* read from a file (or standard input) may not contain a *tabspec* referencing another file (or standard input).

0 − normal execution
1 − for any error

SEE ALSO

csplit(1), tabs(1).
fspec(4) in the *Programmer's Reference Manual.*

BUGS

newform normally only keeps track of physical characters; however, for the **−i** and **−o** options, *newform* will keep track of backspaces in order to line up tabs in the appropriate logical columns.

newform will not prompt the user if a *tabspec* is to be read from the standard input (by use of **−i**−− or **−o**−−).

If the **−f** option is used, and the last **−o** option specified was **−o**−−, and was preceded by either a **−o**−− or a **−i**−−, the tab specification format line will be incorrect.

NAME

newgrp – log in to a new group

SYNOPSIS

newgrp [–] [group]

DESCRIPTION

newgrp changes a user's group identification. The user remains logged in and the current directory is unchanged, but calculations of access permissions to files are performed with respect to the new real and effective group IDs. The user is always given a new shell, replacing the current shell, by *newgrp*, regardless of whether it terminated successfully or due to an error condition (i.e., unknown group).

Exported variables retain their values after invoking *newgrp*; however, all unexported variables are either reset to their default value or set to null. System variables (such as PS1, PS2, PATH, MAIL, and HOME), unless exported by the system or explicitly exported by the user, are reset to default values. For example, a user has a primary prompt string (PS1) other than **$** (default) and has not exported PS1. After an invocation of *newgrp* , successful or not, their PS1 will now be set to the default prompt string **$**. Note that the shell command *export* (see *sh*(1)) is the method to export variables so that they retain their assigned value when invoking new shells.

With no arguments, *newgrp* changes the group identification back to the group specified in the user's password file entry. This is a way to exit the effect of an earlier *newgrp* command.

If the first argument to *newgrp* is a –, the environment is changed to what would be expected if the user actually logged in again as a member of the new group.

A password is demanded if the group has a password and the user does not, or if the group has a password and the user is not listed in **/etc/group** as being a member of that group.

FILES

/etc/group	system's group file
/etc/passwd	system's password file

SEE ALSO

login(1), sh(1) in the *User's Reference Manual*.
group(4), passwd(4), environ(5) in the *Programmer's Reference Manual*.

BUGS

There is no convenient way to enter a password into **/etc/group**. Use of group passwords is not encouraged, because, by their very nature, they encourage poor security practices. Group passwords may disappear in the future.

NAME

news − print news items

SYNOPSIS

news [**−a**] [**−n**] [**−s**] [items]

DESCRIPTION

news is used to keep the user informed of current events. By convention, these events are described by files in the directory **/usr/news**.

When invoked without arguments, *news* prints the contents of all current files in **/usr/news**, most recent first, with each preceded by an appropriate header. *news* stores the "currency" time as the modification date of a file named **.news_time** in the user's home directory (the identity of this directory is determined by the environment variable **$HOME**); only files more recent than this currency time are considered "current."

−a option causes *news* to print all items, regardless of currency. In this case, the stored time is not changed.

−n option causes *news* to report the names of the current items without printing their contents, and without changing the stored time.

−s option causes *news* to report how many current items exist, without printing their names or contents, and without changing the stored time. It is useful to include such an invocation of *news* in one's **.profile** file, or in the system's **/etc/profile**.

All other arguments are assumed to be specific news items that are to be printed.

If a *delete* is typed during the printing of a news item, printing stops and the next item is started. Another *delete* within one second of the first causes the program to terminate.

FILES

/etc/profile
/usr/news/*
$HOME/.news_time

SEE ALSO

profile(4), environ(5) in the *Programmer's Reference Manual*.

NAME

nice − run a command at low priority

SYNOPSIS

nice [−increment] command [arguments]

DESCRIPTION

nice executes *command* with a lower CPU scheduling priority. If the *increment* argument (in the range 1-19) is given, it is used; if not, an increment of 10 is assumed.

The super-user may run commands with priority higher than normal by using a negative increment, e.g., **−−10**.

SEE ALSO

nohup(1).
nice(2) in the *Programmer's Reference Manual.*

DIAGNOSTICS

nice returns the exit status of the subject command.

BUGS

An *increment* larger than 19 is equivalent to 19.

NAME

nl − line numbering filter

SYNOPSIS

nl [−**h**type] [−**b**type] [−**f**type] [−**v**start#] [−**i**incr] [−**p**] [−**l**num] [−**s**sep] [−**w**width] [−**n**format] [−**d**delim] file

DESCRIPTION

nl reads lines from the named *file* or the standard input if no *file* is named and reproduces the lines on the standard output. Lines are numbered on the left in accordance with the command options in effect.

nl views the text it reads in terms of logical pages. Line numbering is reset at the start of each logical page. A logical page consists of a header, a body, and a footer section. Empty sections are valid. Different line numbering options are independently available for header, body, and footer (e.g., no numbering of header and footer lines while numbering blank lines only in the body).

The start of logical page sections are signaled by input lines containing nothing but the following delimiter character(s):

Line contents	*Start of*
\:\:\:	header
\:\:	body
\:	footer

Unless optioned otherwise, *nl* assumes the text being read is in a single logical page body.

Command options may appear in any order and may be intermingled with an optional file name. Only one file may be named. The options are:

−**b***type* Specifies which logical page body lines are to be numbered. Recognized *types* and their meaning are:

−**h***type* Same as −**b***type* except for header. Default *type* for logical page header is **n** (no lines numbered).

- **a** number all lines
- **t** number lines with printable text only
- **n** no line numbering
- **p***string* number only lines that contain the regular expression specified in *string*.

Default *type* for logical page body is **t** (text lines numbered).

−**f***type* Same as −**b***type* except for footer. Default for logical page footer is **n** (no lines numbered).

−**v***start#* *Start#* is the initial value used to number logical page lines. Default is **1**.

−**i***incr* *Incr* is the increment value used to number logical page lines. Default is **1**.

−p Do not restart numbering at logical page delimiters.

−l*num* *Num* is the number of blank lines to be considered as one. For example, **−l2** results in only the second adjacent blank being numbered (if the appropriate **−ha**, **−ba**, and/or **−fa** option is set). Default is **1**.

−s*sep* *Sep* is the character(s) used in separating the line number and the corresponding text line. Default *sep* is a tab.

−w*width* *Width* is the number of characters to be used for the line number. Default *width* is **6**.

−n*format* *Format* is the line numbering format. Recognized values are: **ln**, left justified, leading zeroes suppressed; **rn**, right justified, leading zeroes supressed; **rz**, right justified, leading zeroes kept. Default *format* is **rn** (right justified).

−d*xx* The delimiter characters specifying the start of a logical page section may be changed from the default characters (\:) to two user-specified characters. If only one character is entered, the second character remains the default character (:). No space should appear between the **−d** and the delimiter characters. To enter a backslash, use two backslashes.

EXAMPLE

The command:

nl −v10 −i10 −d!+ file1

will number file1 starting at line number 10 with an increment of ten. The logical page delimiters are !+.

SEE ALSO

pr(1).

NAME

nohup − run a command immune to hangups and quits

SYNOPSIS

nohup command [arguments]

DESCRIPTION

nohup executes *command* with hangups and quits ignored. If output is not redirected by the user, both standard output and standard error are sent to **nohup.out**. If **nohup.out** is not writable in the current directory, output is redirected to **$HOME/nohup.out**.

EXAMPLE

It is frequently desirable to apply *nohup* to pipelines or lists of commands. This can be done only by placing pipelines and command lists in a single file, called a shell procedure. One can then issue:

```
nohup sh file
```

and the *nohup* applies to everything in *file*. If the shell procedure *file* is to be executed often, then the need to type *sh* can be eliminated by giving *file* execute permission. Add an ampersand and the contents of *file* are run in the background with interrupts also ignored (see *sh*(1)):

```
nohup file &
```

An example of what the contents of *file* could be is:

```
sort ofile > nfile
```

SEE ALSO

chmod(1), nice(1), sh(1),
signal(2) in the *Programmer's Reference Manual*.

WARNINGS

In the case of the following command

```
nohup command1; command2
```

nohup applies only to command1. The command

```
nohup (command1; command2)
```

is syntactically incorrect.

NAME

od − octal dump

SYNOPSIS

od [**−bcdosx**] [file] [[+]offset[**.**][**b**]]

DESCRIPTION

od dumps *file* in one or more formats as selected by the first argument. If the first argument is missing, **−o** is default. The meanings of the format options are:

−b Interpret bytes in octal.

−c Interpret bytes in ASCII. Certain non-graphic characters appear as C escapes: null=**0**, backspace=**b**, form-feed=**f**, new-line=**n**, return=**r**, tab=**t**; others appear as 3-digit octal numbers.

−d Interpret words in unsigned decimal.

−o Interpret words in octal.

−s Interpret 16-bit words in signed decimal.

−x Interpret words in hex.

The *file* argument specifies which file is to be dumped. If no file argument is specified, the standard input is used.

The offset argument specifies the offset in the file where dumping is to commence. This argument is normally interpreted as octal bytes. If **.** is appended, the offset is interpreted in decimal. If **b** is appended, the offset is interpreted in blocks of 512 bytes. If the file argument is omitted, the offset argument must be preceded by +.

Dumping continues until end-of-file.

NAME

pack, pcat, unpack – compress and expand files

SYNOPSIS

pack [–] [–**f**] name ...

pcat name ...

unpack name ...

DESCRIPTION

pack attempts to store the specified files in a compressed form. Wherever possible (and useful), each input file *name* is replaced by a packed file *name*.**z** with the same access modes, access and modified dates, and owner as those of *name*. The **-f** option will force packing of *name*. This is useful for causing an entire directory to be packed even if some of the files will not benefit. If *pack* is successful, *name* will be removed. Packed files can be restored to their original form using *unpack* or *pcat*.

pack uses Huffman (minimum redundancy) codes on a byte-by-byte basis. If the – argument is used, an internal flag is set that causes the number of times each byte is used, its relative frequency, and the code for the byte to be printed on the standard output. Additional occurrences of – in place of *name* will cause the internal flag to be set and reset.

The amount of compression obtained depends on the size of the input file and the character frequency distribution. Because a decoding tree forms the first part of each **.z** file, it is usually not worthwhile to pack files smaller than three blocks, unless the character frequency distribution is very skewed, which may occur with printer plots or pictures.

Typically, text files are reduced to 60-75% of their original size. Load modules, which use a larger character set and have a more uniform distribution of characters, show little compression, the packed versions being about 90% of the original size.

pack returns a value that is the number of files that it failed to compress.

No packing will occur if:

the file appears to be already packed;
the file name has more than 12 characters;
the file has links;
the file is a directory;
the file cannot be opened;
no disk storage blocks will be saved by packing;
a file called *name*.**z** already exists;
the **.z** file cannot be created;
an I/O error occurred during processing.

The last segment of the file name must contain no more than 12 characters to allow space for the appended **.z** extension. Directories cannot be compressed.

Pcat does for packed files what *cat*(1) does for ordinary files, except that *pcat* cannot be used as a filter. The specified files are unpacked and written to the standard output. Thus to view a packed file named *name*.**z** use:

pcat name.z

or just:

pcat name

To make an unpacked copy, say *nnn*, of a packed file named *name*.**z** (without destroying *name*.**z**) use the command:

pcat name >nnn

Pcat returns the number of files it was unable to unpack. Failure may occur if:

the file name (exclusive of the **.z**) has more than 12 characters;
the file cannot be opened;
the file does not appear to be the output of *pack*.

Unpack expands files created by *pack*. For each file *name* specified in the command, a search is made for a file called *name*.**z** (or just *name*, if *name* ends in **.z**). If this file appears to be a packed file, it is replaced by its expanded version. The new file has the **.z** suffix stripped from its name, and has the same access modes, access and modification dates, and owner as those of the packed file.

Unpack returns a value that is the number of files it was unable to unpack. Failure may occur for the same reasons that it may in *pcat*, as well as for the following:

a file with the "unpacked" name already exists;
if the unpacked file cannot be created.

SEE ALSO

cat(1).

NAME

passwd – change login password

SYNOPSIS

passwd [name]

DESCRIPTION

This command changes or installs a password associated with the login *name*.

Ordinary users may change only the password which corresponds to their login *name*.

passwd prompts ordinary users for their old password, if any. It then prompts for the new password twice. The first time the new password is entered *passwd* checks to see if the old password has "aged" sufficiently. Password "aging" is the amount of time (usually a certain number of days) that must elapse between password changes. If "aging" is insufficient the new password is rejected and *passwd* terminates; see *passwd*(4).

Assuming "aging" is sufficient, a check is made to insure that the new password meets construction requirements. When the new password is entered a second time, the two copies of the new password are compared. If the two copies are not identical the cycle of prompting for the new password is repeated for at most two more times.

Passwords must be constructed to meet the following requirements:

> Each password must have at least six characters. Only the first eight characters are significant.
>
> Each password must contain at least two alphabetic characters and at least one numeric or special character. In this case, "alphabetic" means upper and lower case letters.
>
> Each password must differ from the user's login *name* and any reverse or circular shift of that login *name*. For comparison purposes, an upper case letter and its corresponding lower case letter are equivalent.
>
> New passwords must differ from the old by at least three characters. For comparison purposes, an upper case letter and its corresponding lower case letter are equivalent.

One whose effective user ID is zero is called a super-user; see *id*(1), and *su*(1). Super-users may change any password; hence, *passwd* does not prompt super-users for the old password. Super-users are not forced to comply with password aging and password construction requirements. A super-user can create a null password by entering a carriage return in response to the prompt for a new password.

FILES

/etc/passwd

SEE ALSO

login(1).
crypt(3C), passwd(4) in the *Programmer's Reference Manual*.
id(1M), su(1M) in the *System Administrator's Reference Manual*.

NAME

paste − merge same lines of several files or subsequent lines of one file

SYNOPSIS

paste file1 file2 ...
paste −**d**list file1 file2 ...
paste −**s** [−**d**list] file1 file2 ...

DESCRIPTION

In the first two forms, *paste* concatenates corresponding lines of the given input files *file1*, *file2*, etc. It treats each file as a column or columns of a table and pastes them together horizontally (parallel merging). If you will, it is the counterpart of *cat*(1) which concatenates vertically, i.e., one file after the other. In the last form above, *paste* replaces the function of an older command with the same name by combining subsequent lines of the input file (serial merging). In all cases, lines are glued together with the *tab* character, or with characters from an optionally specified *list*. Output is to the standard output, so it can be used as the start of a pipe, or as a filter, if − is used in place of a file name.

The meanings of the options are:

−d Without this option, the new-line characters of each but the last file (or last line in case of the −**s** option) are replaced by a *tab* character. This option allows replacing the *tab* character by one or more alternate characters (see below).

list One or more characters immediately following −**d** replace the default *tab* as the line concatenation character. The list is used circularly, i.e., when exhausted, it is reused. In parallel merging (i.e., no −**s** option), the lines from the last file are always terminated with a new-line character, not from the *list*. The list may contain the special escape sequences: **\n** (new-line), **\t** (tab), \\ (backslash), and **\0** (empty string, not a null character). Quoting may be necessary, if characters have special meaning to the shell (e.g., to get one backslash, use −*d* "\\\\").

−s Merge subsequent lines rather than one from each input file. Use *tab* for concatenation, unless a *list* is specified with −**d** option. Regardless of the *list*, the very last character of the file is forced to be a new-line.

− May be used in place of any file name, to read a line from the standard input. (There is no prompting).

EXAMPLES

ls | paste −d" " −	list directory in one column
ls | paste − − − −	list directory in four columns
paste −s −d"\t\n" file	combine pairs of lines into lines

SEE ALSO

cut(1), grep(1), pr(1).

DIAGNOSTICS

line too long Output lines are restricted to 511 characters.

too many files Except for **−s** option, no more than 12 input files may be specified.

NAME

pg − file perusal filter for CRTs

SYNOPSIS

pg [−*number*] [**−p** *string*] [**−cefns**] [+*linenumber*] [+/*pattern*/] [files...]

DESCRIPTION

The *pg* command is a filter which allows the examination of *files* one screenful at a time on a CRT. (The file name − and/or NULL arguments indicate that *pg* should read from the standard input.) Each screenful is followed by a prompt. If the user types a carriage return, another page is displayed; other possibilities are enumerated below.

This command is different from previous paginators in that it allows you to back up and review something that has already passed. The method for doing this is explained below.

In order to determine terminal attributes, *pg* scans the *terminfo*(4) data base for the terminal type specified by the environment variable **TERM**. If **TERM** is not defined, the terminal type **dumb** is assumed.

The command line options are:

−*number*
: An integer specifying the size (in lines) of the window that *pg* is to use instead of the default. (On a terminal containing 24 lines, the default window size is 23).

−p *string*
: Causes *pg* to use *string* as the prompt. If the prompt string contains a "%d", the first occurrence of "%d" in the prompt will be replaced by the current page number when the prompt is issued. The default prompt string is ":".

−c Home the cursor and clear the screen before displaying each page. This option is ignored if **clear_screen** is not defined for this terminal type in the *terminfo*(4) data base.

−e Causes *pg* *not* to pause at the end of each file.

−f Normally, *pg* splits lines longer than the screen width, but some sequences of characters in the text being displayed (e.g., escape sequences for underlining) generate undesirable results. The −*f* option inhibits *pg* from splitting lines.

−n Normally, commands must be terminated by a <*newline*> character. This option causes an automatic end of command as soon as a command letter is entered.

−s Causes *pg* to print all messages and prompts in standout mode (usually inverse video).

+*linenumber*
: Start up at *linenumber*.

+/*pattern*/
: Start up at the first line containing the regular expression pattern.

The responses that may be typed when *pg* pauses can be divided into three categories: those causing further perusal, those that search, and those that modify the perusal environment.

Commands which cause further perusal normally take a preceding *address*, an optionally signed number indicating the point from which further text should be displayed. This *address* is interpreted in either pages or lines depending on the command. A signed *address* specifies a point relative to the current page or line, and an unsigned *address* specifies an address relative to the beginning of the file. Each command has a default address that is used if none is provided.

The perusal commands and their defaults are as follows:

(+1)<*newline*> or <*blank*>
: This causes one page to be displayed. The address is specified in pages.

(+1) **l** With a relative address this causes *pg* to simulate scrolling the screen, forward or backward, the number of lines specified. With an absolute address this command prints a screenful beginning at the specified line.

(+1) **d** or **^D**
: Simulates scrolling half a screen forward or backward.

The following perusal commands take no *address*.

. or **^L** Typing a single period causes the current page of text to be redisplayed.

$ Displays the last windowful in the file. Use with caution when the input is a pipe.

The following commands are available for searching for text patterns in the text. The regular expressions described in *ed*(1) are available. They must always be terminated by a <*newline*>, even if the *−n* option is specified.

i/pattern/
: Search forward for the *i*th (default *i*=1) occurrence of *pattern*. Searching begins immediately after the current page and continues to the end of the current file, without wrap-around.

*i^pattern^*
i?pattern?
: Search backwards for the *i*th (default *i*=1) occurrence of *pattern*. Searching begins immediately before the current page and continues to the beginning of the current file, without wrap-around. The ^ notation is useful for Adds 100 terminals which will not properly handle the ?.

After searching, *pg* will normally display the line found at the top of the screen. This can be modified by appending **m** or **b** to the search command to leave the line found in the middle or at the bottom of the window from now on. The suffix **t** can be used to restore the original situation.

The user of *pg* can modify the environment of perusal with the following commands:

*i***n** Begin perusing the *i*th next file in the command line. The *i* is an unsigned number, default value is 1.

*i***p** Begin perusing the *i*th previous file in the command line. *i* is an unsigned number, default is 1.

*i***w** Display another window of text. If *i* is present, set the window size to *i*.

s *filename*
Save the input in the named file. Only the current file being perused is saved. The white space between the **s** and *filename* is optional. This command must always be terminated by a <*newline*>, even if the −*n* option is specified.

h Help by displaying an abbreviated summary of available commands.

q or **Q** Quit *pg*.

!*command*
Command is passed to the shell, whose name is taken from the **SHELL** environment variable. If this is not available, the default shell is used. This command must always be terminated by a <*newline*>, even if the −*n* option is specified.

At any time when output is being sent to the terminal, the user can hit the quit key (normally control-\) or the interrupt (break) key. This causes *pg* to stop sending output, and display the prompt. The user may then enter one of the above commands in the normal manner. Unfortunately, some output is lost when this is done, due to the fact that any characters waiting in the terminal's output queue are flushed when the quit signal occurs.

If the standard output is not a terminal, then *pg* acts just like *cat*(1), except that a header is printed before each file (if there is more than one).

EXAMPLE

A sample usage of *pg* in reading system news would be

```
news | pg -p "(Page %d):"
```

NOTES

While waiting for terminal input, *pg* responds to **BREAK**, **DEL**, and ^ by terminating execution. Between prompts, however, these signals interrupt *pg*'s current task and place the user in prompt mode. These should be used with caution when input is being read from a pipe, since an interrupt is likely to terminate the other commands in the pipeline.

Users of Berkeley's *more* will find that the z and f commands are available, and that the terminal /, ^, or ? may be omitted from the searching commands.

FILES

/usr/lib/terminfo/?/*	terminal information database
/tmp/pg*	temporary file when input is from a pipe

SEE ALSO

ed(1), grep(1).
terminfo(4) in the *Programmer's Reference Manual* .

BUGS

If terminal tabs are not set every eight positions, undesirable results may occur.

When using *pg* as a filter with another command that changes the terminal I/O options terminal settings may not be restored correctly.

NAME

pr − print files

SYNOPSIS

pr [[−column] [−**w**width] [−**a**]] [−**e**ck] [−**i**ck] [−**drtfp**] [+page] [−**n**ck] [−**o**offset] [−**l**length] [−**s**separator] [−**h** header] [file ...]

pr [[−**m**] [−**w**width]] [−**e**ck] [−**i**ck] [−**drtfp**] [+page] [−**n**ck] [−**o**offset] [−**l**length] [−**s**separator] [−**h** header] file1 file2 ...

DESCRIPTION

pr is used to format and print the contents of a file. If *file* is −, or if no files are specified, *pr* assumes standard input. *pr* prints the named files on standard output.

By default, the listing is separated into pages, each headed by the page number, a date and time, and the name of the file. Page length is 66 lines which includes 10 lines of header and trailer output. The header is composed of 2 blank lines, 1 line of text (can be altered with −**h**), and 2 blank lines; the trailer is 5 blank lines. For single column output, line width may not be set and is unlimited. For multicolumn output, line width may be set and the default is 72 columns. Diagnostic reports (failed options) are reported at the end of standard output associated with a terminal, rather than interspersed in the output. Pages are separated by series of line feeds rather than form feed characters.

By default, columns are of equal width, separated by at least one space; lines which do not fit are truncated. If the −**s** option is used, lines are not truncated and columns are separated by the *separator* character.

Either −*column* or −**m** should be used to produce multi-column output. −**a** should only be used with −*column* and not −**m**.

Command line options are

+*page* Begin printing with page numbered *page* (default is 1).

−*column*
: Print *column* columns of output (default is 1). Output appears as if −**e** and −**i** are turned on for multi-column output. May not use with **-m**.

−**a** Print multi-column output across the page one line per column. *columns* must be greater than one. If a line is too long to fit in a column, it is truncated.

−**m** Merge and print all files simultaneously, one per column. The maximum number of files that may be specifed is eight. If a line is too long to fit in a column, it is truncated. May not use with −*column*.

−**d** Double-space the output. Blank lines that result from double-spacing are dropped when they occur at the top of a page.

−**e***ck* Expand input tabs to character positions *k*+1, 2∗*k*+1, 3∗*k*+1, etc. If *k* is 0 or is omitted, default tab settings at every eighth position are assumed. Tab characters in the input are expanded into the appropriate number of spaces. If *c* (any non-digit character) is given, it is treated as the input tab character (default for *c* is the tab character).

−i*ck* In output, replace white space wherever possible by inserting tabs to character positions *k*+1, 2∗*k*+1, 3∗*k*+1, etc. If *k* is 0 or is omitted, default tab settings at every eighth position are assumed. If *c* (any non-digit character) is given, it is treated as the output tab character (default for *c* is the tab character).

−n*ck* Provide *k*-digit line numbering (default for *k* is 5). The number occupies the first *k*+1 character positions of each column of single column output or each line of **−m** output. If *c* (any non-digit character) is given, it is appended to the line number to separate it from whatever follows (default for *c* is a tab).

−w*width*
Set the width of a line to *width* character positions (default is 72). This is effective only for multi-column output (*-column* and **-m**). There is no line limit for single column output.

−o*offset*
Offset each line by *offset* character positions (default is 0). The number of character positions per line is the sum of the width and offset.

−l*length*
Set the length of a page to *length* lines (default is 66). **−l0** is reset to **−l66**. When the value of *length* is 10 or less, **−t** appears to be in effect since headers and trailers are suppressed. By default, output contains 5 lines of header and 5 lines of trailer leaving 56 lines for user-supplied text. When **−l***length* is used and *length* exceeds 10, then *length*-10 lines are left per page for user supplied text. When *length* is 10 or less, header and trailer output is omitted to make room for user supplied text.

−h *header*
Use *header* as the text line of the header to be printed instead of the file name. **−h** is ignored when **−t** is specified or **−l***length* is specified and the value of *length* is 10 or less. (**−h is the only** *pr* option requiring space between the option and argument.)

−p Pause before beginning each page if the output is directed to a terminal (*pr* will ring the bell at the terminal and wait for a carriage return).

−f Use single form-feed character for new pages (default is to use a sequence of line-feeds). Pause before beginning the first page if the standard output is associated with a terminal.

−r Print no diagnostic reports on files that will not open.

−t Print neither the five-line identifying header nor the five-line trailer normally supplied for each page. Quit printing after the last line of each file without spacing to the end of the page. Use of **−t** overrides the **−h** option.

−s*separator*
Separate columns by the single character *separator* instead of by the appropriate number of spaces (default for *separator* is a tab). Prevents truncation of lines on multicolumn output unless **-w** is specified.

EXAMPLES

Print **file1** and **file2** as a double-spaced, three-column listing headed by "file list":

```
pr −3dh "file list" file1 file2
```

Copy **file1** to **file2**, expanding tabs to columns 10, 19, 28, 37, ... :

```
pr −e9 −t <file1 >file2
```

Print **file1** and **file2** simultaneously in a two-column listing with no header or trailer where both columns have line numbers:

```
pr −t -n file1 | pr -t -m -n file2 -
```

FILES

/dev/tty* to delay messages enabling them to print at the bottom of files rather than interspersed throughout printed output.

SEE ALSO

cat(1), pg(1).

NAME

ps − report process status

SYNOPSIS

ps [options]

DESCRIPTION

ps prints certain information about active processes. Without *options,* information is printed about processes associated with the controlling terminal. The output consists of a short listing containing only the process ID, terminal identifier, cumulative execution time, and the command name. Otherwise, the information that is displayed is controlled by the selection of *options.*

Options accept names or lists as arguments. Arguments can be either separated from one another by commas or enclosed in double quotes and separated from one another by commas or spaces. Values for *proclist* and *grplist* must be numeric.

The *options* are given in descending order according to volume and range of information provided:

−e Print information about **e**very process now running.

−d Print information about all processes except process group leaders.

−a Print information about **a**ll processes most frequently requested: all those except process group leaders and processes not associated with a terminal.

−f Generate a **f**ull listing. (See below for significance of columns in a full listing.)

−l Generate a **l**ong listing. (See below.)

−n *name* Take argument signifying an alternate system *name* in place of **/unix**.

−t *termlist* List only process data associated with the terminal given in *termlist*. Terminal identifiers may be specified in one of two forms: the device's file name (e.g., **tty04**) or, if the device's file name starts with **tty**, just the digit identifier (e.g., **04**).

−p *proclist* List only process data whose process ID numbers are given in *proclist*.

−u *uidlist* List only process data whose user ID number or login name is given in *uidlist*. In the listing, the numerical user ID will be printed unless you give the **−f** option, which prints the login name.

−g *grplist* List only process data whose process group leader's ID number(s) appears in *grplist*. (A group leader is a process whose process ID number is identical to its process group ID number. A login shell is a common example of a process group leader.)

Under the **−f** option, *ps* tries to determine the command name and arguments given when the process was created by examining the user block. Failing this, the command name is printed, as it would have appeared without the **−f** option, in square brackets.

The column headings and the meaning of the columns in a *ps* listing are given below; the letters **f** and **l** indicate the option (**f**ull or **l**ong, respectively) that causes the corresponding heading to appear; **all** means that the heading always appears. Note that these two options determine only what information is provided for a process; they do not determine which processes will be listed.

F (l) Flags (hexadecimal and additive) associated with the process

3B2 COMPUTER

- 00 Process has terminated: process table entry now available.
- 01 A system process: always in primary memory.
- 02 Parent is tracing process.
- 04 Tracing parent's signal has stopped process: parent is waiting [*ptrace*(2)].
- 08 Process is currently in primary memory.
- 10 Process currently in primary memory: locked until an event completes.

VAX PROCESSOR

- 00 Process has terminated: process table entry now available.
- 01 Process currently in primary memory.
- 02 A system process: always in primary memory.
- 04 Process is currently in primary memory: locked until an event completes.
- 08 Should not occur on this system.
- 10 Parent is tracing process.
- 20 Tracing parent's signal has stopped process: parent is waiting [*ptrace*(2)].

S (l) The state of the process:

- O 3B2 Computer: Process is running on a processor. VAX processor: Should not occur on this system.
- S Sleeping: process is waiting for an event to complete.
- R Runnable: process is on run queue.
- I Idle: process is being created.
- Z Zombie state: process terminated and parent not waiting.
- T Traced: process stopped by a signal because parent is tracing it.
- X SXBRK state: process is waiting for more primary memory.

UID (f,l) The user ID number of the process owner (the login name is printed under the **−f** option).

PID (all) The process ID of the process (this datum is necessary in order to kill a process).

PPID (f,l) The process ID of the parent process.

C (f,l) Processor utilization for scheduling.

PRI	(l)	The priority of the process (higher numbers mean lower priority).
NI	(l)	Nice value, used in priority computation.
ADDR	(l)	The memory address of the process.
SZ	(l)	The size (in pages or clicks) of the swappable process's image in main memory.
WCHAN	(l)	The address of an event for which the process is sleeping, or in SXBRK state, (if blank, the process is running).
STIME	(f)	The starting time of the process, given in hours, minutes, and seconds. (A process begun more than twenty-four hours before the *ps* inquiry is executed is given in months and days.)
TTY	(all)	The controlling terminal for the process (the message, **?**, is printed when there is no controlling terminal).
TIME	(all)	The cumulative execution time for the process.
COMMAND	(all)	The command name (the full command name and its arguments are printed under the **−f** option).

A process that has exited and has a parent, but has not yet been waited for by the parent, is marked **<defunct>**.

FILES

/dev	
/dev/sxt/*	
/dev/tty*	
/dev/xt/*	terminal ("tty") names searcher files
/dev/kmem	kernel virtual memory
/dev/swap	the default swap device
/dev/mem	memory
/etc/passwd	UID information supplier
/etc/ps_data	internal data structure
/unix	system namelist

SEE ALSO

kill(1), nice(1).
getty(1M) in the *System Administrator's Reference Manual.*

WARNING

Things can change while *ps* is running; the snap-shot it gives is only true for a split-second, and it may not be accurate by the time you see it. Some data printed for defunct processes is irrelevant.

If no *termlist, proclist, uidlist,* or *grplist* is specified, *ps* checks *stdin, stdout,* and *stderr* in that order, looking for the controlling terminal and will attempt to report on processes associated with the controlling terminal. In this situation, if *stdin, stdout,* and *stderr* are all redirected, *ps* will not find a controlling terminal, so there will be no report.

On a heavily loaded system, *ps* may report an *lseek(2)* error and exit. *ps* may seek to an invalid user area address: having got the address of a process' user area, *ps* may not be able to seek to that address before the process exits and the address becomes invalid.

ps −ef may not report the actual start of a tty login session, but rather an earlier time, when a getty was last respawned on the tty line.

NAME

pwd – working directory name

SYNOPSIS

pwd

DESCRIPTION

pwd prints the path name of the working (current) directory.

SEE ALSO

cd(1).

DIAGNOSTICS

"Cannot open .." and "Read error in .." indicate possible file system trouble and should be referred to a UNIX system administrator.

NAME

relogin – rename login entry to show current layer

SYNOPSIS

/usr/lib/layersys/relogin [–s] [line]

DESCRIPTION

The *relogin* command changes the terminal *line* field of a user's *utmp*(4) entry to the name of the windowing terminal layer attached to standard input. *write*(1) messages sent to this user are directed to this layer. In addition, the *who*(1) command will show the user associated with this layer. *relogin* may only be invoked under *layers*(1).

relogin is invoked automatically by *layers*(1) to set the *utmp*(4) entry to the terminal line of the first layer created upon startup, and to reset the *utmp*(4) entry to the real line on termination. It may be invoked by a user to designate a different layer to receive *write*(1) messages.

–s Suppress error messages.

line Specifies which *utmp*(4) entry to change. The *utmp*(4) file is searched for an entry with the specified *line* field. That field is changed to the line associated with the standard input. (To learn what lines are associated with a given user, say **jdoe**, type **ps -f -u jdoe** and note the values shown in the **TTY** field (see *ps*(1))).

FILES

/etc/utmp database of users versus terminals

EXIT STATUS

Returns **0** upon successful completion, **1** otherwise.

SEE ALSO

utmp(4) in the *Programmer's Reference Manual.*
layers(1), mesg(1), ps(1), who(1), write(1) in the *User's Reference Manual.*

NOTES

If *line* does not belong to the user issuing the *relogin* command or standard input is not associated with a terminal, *relogin* will fail.

NAME

rm, rmdir − remove files or directories

SYNOPSIS

rm [**−f**] [**−i**] file ...

rm −r [**−f**] [**−i**] dirname ... [file ...]

rmdir [**−p**] [**−s**] dirname ...

DESCRIPTION

rm removes the entries for one or more files from a directory. If an entry was the last link to the file, the file is destroyed. Removal of a file requires write permission in its directory, but neither read nor write permission on the file itself.

If a file has no write permission and the standard input is a terminal, the full set of permissions (in octal) for the file are printed followed by a question mark. This is a prompt for confirmation. If the answer begins with **y** (for yes), the file is deleted, otherwise the file remains.

Note that if the standard input is not a terminal, the command will operate as if the **−f** option is in effect.

rmdir removes the named directories, which must be empty.

Three options apply to *rm*:

−f This option causes the removal of all files (whether write-protected or not) in a directory without prompting the user. In a write-protected directory, however, files are never removed (whatever their permissions are), but no messages are displayed. If the removal of a write-protected directory was attempted, this option cannot suppress an error message.

−r This option causes the recursive removal of any directories and subdirectories in the argument list. The directory will be emptied of files and removed. Note that the user is normally prompted for removal of any write-protected files which the directory contains. The write-protected files are removed without prompting, however, if the **−f** option is used, or if the standard input is not a terminal and the **−i** option is not used.

If the removal of a non-empty, write-protected directory was attempted, the command will always fail (even if the **−f** option is used), resulting in an error message.

−i With this option, confirmation of removal of any write-protected file occurs interactively. It overrides the **−f** option and remains in effect even if the standard input is not a terminal.

Two options apply to *rmdir*:

−p This option allows users to remove the directory *dirname* and its parent directories which become empty. A message is printed on standard output as to whether the whole path is removed or part of the path remains for some reason.

−s This option is used to suppress the message printed on standard error when **−p** is in effect.

DIAGNOSTICS

All messages are generally self-explanatory.
It is forbidden to remove the files "." and ".." in order to avoid the consequences of inadvertently doing something like the following:

rm −r .*

Both *rm* and *rmdir* return exit codes of 0 if all the specified directories are removed successfully. Otherwise, they return a non-zero exit code.

SEE ALSO

unlink(2), rmdir(2) in the *Programmer's Reference Manual*.

NAME

sag − system activity graph

SYNOPSIS

sag [options]

DESCRIPTION

sag graphically displays the system activity data stored in a binary data file by a previous *sar*(1) run. Any of the *sar* data items may be plotted singly, or in combination; as cross plots, or versus time. Simple arithmetic combinations of data may be specified. *sag* invokes *sar* and finds the desired data by string-matching the data column header (run *sar* to see what is available). These *options* are passed through to *sar*:

−s *time* Select data later than *time* in the form hh[:mm]. Default is 08:00.

−e *time* Select data up to *time*. Default is 18:00.

−i *sec* Select data at intervals as close as possible to *sec* seconds.

−f *file* Use *file* as the data source for *sar*. Default is the current daily data file **/usr/adm/sa/sa***dd*.

Other *options*:

−T *term* Produce output suitable for terminal *term*. See *tplot*(1G) for known terminals. Default for *term* is **$TERM**.

−x *spec* x axis specification with *spec* in the form:
"name[op name]...[lo hi]"

−y *spec* y axis specification with *spec* in the same form as above.

Name is either a string that will match a column header in the *sar* report, with an optional device name in square brackets, e.g., **r+w/s[dsk−1]**, or an integer value. *Op* is + − * or / surrounded by blanks. Up to five names may be specified. Parentheses are not recognized. Contrary to custom, + and − have precedence over * and /. Evaluation is left to right. Thus A / A + B * 100 is evaluated (A/(A+B))*100, and A + B / C + D is (A+B)/(C+D). *Lo* and *hi* are optional numeric scale limits. If unspecified, they are deduced from the data.

A single *spec* is permitted for the x axis. If unspecified, *time* is used. Up to 5 *spec*'s separated by **;** may be given for **−y**. Enclose the **−x** and **−y** arguments in "" if blanks or \<CR> are included. The **−y** default is:

−y "%usr 0 100; %usr + %sys 0 100; %usr + %sys + %wio 0 100"

EXAMPLES

To see today's CPU utilization:

```
sag
```

To see activity over 15 minutes of all disk drives:

```
TS=date +%H:%M
sar −o tempfile 60 15
TE=date +%H:%M
sag −f tempfile −s $TS −e $TE −y "r+w/s[dsk]"
```

FILES

/usr/adm/sa/sa*dd* daily data file for day *dd*.

SEE ALSO

sar(1), tplot(1G)

NAME

sar – system activity reporter

SYNOPSIS

sar [**–ubdycwaqvmprDSA**] [**–o** file] t [n]

sar [**–ubdycwaqvmprDSA**] [**–s** time] [**–e** time] [**–i** sec] [**–f** file]

DESCRIPTION

sar, in the first instance, samples cumulative activity counters in the operating system at *n* intervals of *t* seconds, where *t* should be 5 or greater. If the **–o** option is specified, it saves the samples in *file* in binary format. The default value of *n* is 1. In the second instance, with no sampling interval specified, **sar** extracts data from a previously recorded *file,* either the one specified by **–f** option or, by default, the standard system activity daily data file **/usr/adm/sa/sa***dd* for the current day *dd.* The starting and ending times of the report can be bounded via the **–s** and **–e** *time* arguments of the form *hh*[:*mm*[:*ss*]]. The **–i** option selects records at *sec* second intervals. Otherwise, all intervals found in the data file are reported.

In either case, subsets of data to be printed are specified by option:

–u Report CPU utilization (the default):
%usr, %sys, %wio, %idle – portion of time running in user mode, running in system mode, idle with some process waiting for block I/O, and otherwise idle. When used with **–D**, %sys is split into percent of time servicing requests from remote machines (%sys remote) and all other system time (%sys local).

–b Report buffer activity:
bread/s, bwrit/s – transfers per second of data between system buffers and disk or other block devices;
lread/s, lwrit/s – accesses of system buffers;
%rcache, %wcache – cache hit ratios, i. e., (1–bread/lread) as a percentage;
pread/s, pwrit/s – transfers via raw (physical) device mechanism.

–d Report activity for each block device, e. g., disk or tape drive. When data is displayed, the device specification *dsk-* is generally used to represent a disk drive. The device specification used to represent a tape drive is machine dependent. The activity data reported is:
%busy, avque – portion of time device was busy servicing a transfer request, average number of requests outstanding during that time;
r+w/s, blks/s – number of data transfers from or to device, number of bytes transferred in 512-byte units;
avwait, avserv – average time in ms. that transfer requests wait idly on queue, and average time to be serviced (which for disks includes seek, rotational latency and data transfer times).

–y Report TTY device activity:
rawch/s, canch/s, outch/s – input character rate, input character rate processed by canon, output character rate;
rcvin/s, xmtin/s, mdmin/s – receive, transmit and modem interrupt rates.

−c Report system calls:
scall/s − system calls of all types;
sread/s, swrit/s, fork/s, exec/s − specific system calls;
rchar/s, wchar/s − characters transferred by read and write system calls. When used with **−D**, the system calls are split into incoming, outgoing, and strictly local calls.

−w Report system swapping and switching activity:
swpin/s, swpot/s, bswin/s, bswot/s − number of transfers and number of 512-byte units transferred for swapins and swapouts (including initial loading of some programs);
pswch/s − process switches.

−a Report use of file access system routines:
iget/s, namei/s, dirblk/s.

−q Report average queue length while occupied, and % of time occupied:
runq-sz, %runocc − run queue of processes in memory and runnable;
swpq-sz, %swpocc − swap queue of processes swapped out but ready to run.

−v Report status of process, i-node, file tables:
text-sz, proc-sz, inod-sz, file-sz, lock-sz − entries/size for each table, evaluated once at sampling point;
ov − overflows that occur between sampling points for each table.

−m Report message and semaphore activities:
msg/s, sema/s − primitives per second.

−p Report paging activities:
vflt/s − address translation page faults (valid page not in memory);
pflt/s − page faults from protection errors (illegal access to page) or "copy-on-writes";
pgfil/s − vflt/s satisfied by page-in from file system;
rclm/s − valid pages reclaimed for free list.

−r Report unused memory pages and disk blocks:
freemem − average pages available to user processes;
freeswap − disk blocks available for process swapping.

−D Report Remote File Sharing activity:
When used in combination with **−u** or **−c**, it causes **sar** to produce the remote file sharing version of the corresponding report. **−u** is assumed when neither **−u** or **−c** is specified.

−S Report server and request queue status:
Average number of Remote File Sharing servers on the system (serv/lo-hi), % of time receive descriptors are on the request queue (request %busy), average number of receive descriptors waiting for service when queue is occupied (request avg lgth), % of time there are idle servers (server %avail), average number of idle servers when idle ones exist (server avg avail).

−A Report all data. Equivalent to **−udqbwcayvmprSD**.

EXAMPLES

To see today's CPU activity so far:

```
sar
```

To watch CPU activity evolve for 10 minutes and save data:

```
sar −o temp 60 10
```

To later review disk and tape activity from that period:

```
sar −d −f temp
```

FILES

/usr/adm/sa/sa*dd*
: daily data file, where *dd* are digits representing the day of the month.

SEE ALSO

sag(1G).
sar(1M) in the *System Administrator's Reference Manual.*

NAME

sdiff − side-by-side difference program

SYNOPSIS

sdiff [options ...] file1 file2

DESCRIPTION

sdiff uses the output of *diff*(1) to produce a side-by-side listing of two files indicating those lines that are different. Each line of the two files is printed with a blank gutter between them if the lines are identical, a < in the gutter if the line only exists in *file1*, a > in the gutter if the line only exists in *file2*, and a | for lines that are different.

For example:

```
x   |   y
a       a
b   <
c   <
d       d
    >   c
```

The following options exist:

−w *n* Use the next argument, *n*, as the width of the output line. The default line length is 130 characters.

−l Only print the left side of any lines that are identical.

−s Do not print identical lines.

−o *output* Use the next argument, *output*, as the name of a third file that is created as a user-controlled merging of *file1* and *file2*. Identical lines of *file1* and *file2* are copied to *output*. Sets of differences, as produced by *diff*(1), are printed; where a set of differences share a common gutter character. After printing each set of differences, *sdiff* prompts the user with a % and waits for one of the following user-typed commands:

- **l** append the left column to the output file
- **r** append the right column to the output file
- **s** turn on silent mode; do not print identical lines
- **v** turn off silent mode
- **e l** call the editor with the left column
- **e r** call the editor with the right column
- **e b** call the editor with the concatenation of left and right
- **e** call the editor with a zero length file
- **q** exit from the program

On exit from the editor, the resulting file is concatenated on the end of the *output* file.

SEE ALSO

diff(1), ed(1).

NAME

sed − stream editor

SYNOPSIS

sed [**−n**] [**−e** script] [**−f** sfile] [files]

DESCRIPTION

sed copies the named *files* (standard input default) to the standard output, edited according to a script of commands. The **−f** option causes the script to be taken from file *sfile;* these options accumulate. If there is just one **−e** option and no **−f** options, the flag **−e** may be omitted. The **−n** option suppresses the default output. A script consists of editing commands, one per line, of the following form:

[address [, address]] function [arguments]

In normal operation, *sed* cyclically copies a line of input into a *pattern space* (unless there is something left after a **D** command), applies in sequence all commands whose *addresses* select that pattern space, and at the end of the script copies the pattern space to the standard output (except under **−n**) and deletes the pattern space.

Some of the commands use a *hold space* to save all or part of the *pattern space* for subsequent retrieval.

An *address* is either a decimal number that counts input lines cumulatively across files, a **$** that addresses the last line of input, or a context address, i.e., a */regular expression/* in the style of *ed*(1) modified thus:

In a context address, the construction *\?regular expression?*, where *?* is any character, is identical to */regular expression/*. Note that in the context address **\xabc\xdefx**, the second **x** stands for itself, so that the regular expression is **abcxdef**.

The escape sequence **\n** matches a new-line *embedded* in the pattern space.

A period **.** matches any character except the *terminal* new-line of the pattern space.

A command line with no addresses selects every pattern space.

A command line with one address selects each pattern space that matches the address.

A command line with two addresses selects the inclusive range from the first pattern space that matches the first address through the next pattern space that matches the second. (If the second address is a number less than or equal to the line number first selected, only one line is selected.) Thereafter the process is repeated, looking again for the first address.

Editing commands can be applied only to non-selected pattern spaces by use of the negation function **!** (below).

In the following list of functions the maximum number of permissible addresses for each function is indicated in parentheses.

The *text* argument consists of one or more lines, all but the last of which end with \ to hide the new-line. Backslashes in text are treated like backslashes in the replacement string of an **s** command, and may be used to protect initial blanks and tabs against the stripping that is done on every script line. The *rfile* or *wfile* argument must terminate the command line and must be preceded by exactly one blank. Each *wfile* is created before processing begins. There can be at most 10 distinct *wfile* arguments.

(1)**a**\
text Append. Place *text* on the output before reading the next input line.

(2)**b** *label* Branch to the **:** command bearing the *label*. If *label* is empty, branch to the end of the script.

(2)**c**\
text Change. Delete the pattern space. With 0 or 1 address or at the end of a 2-address range, place *text* on the output. Start the next cycle.

(2)**d** Delete the pattern space. Start the next cycle.

(2)**D** Delete the initial segment of the pattern space through the first new-line. Start the next cycle.

(2)**g** Replace the contents of the pattern space by the contents of the hold space.

(2)**G** Append the contents of the hold space to the pattern space.

(2)**h** Replace the contents of the hold space by the contents of the pattern space.

(2)**H** Append the contents of the pattern space to the hold space.

(1)**i**\
text Insert. Place *text* on the standard output.

(2)**l** List the pattern space on the standard output in an unambiguous form. Non-printing characters are spelled in two-digit ASCII and long lines are folded.

(2)**n** Copy the pattern space to the standard output. Replace the pattern space with the next line of input.

(2)**N** Append the next line of input to the pattern space with an embedded new-line. (The current line number changes.)

(2)**p** Print. Copy the pattern space to the standard output.

(2)**P** Copy the initial segment of the pattern space through the first new-line to the standard output.

(1)**q** Quit. Branch to the end of the script. Do not start a new cycle.

(2)**r** *rfile* Read the contents of *rfile*. Place them on the output before reading the next input line.

(2)**s**/*regular expression*/*replacement*/*flags*

Substitute the *replacement* string for instances of the *regular expression* in the pattern space. Any character may be used instead of **/**. For a fuller description see *ed*(1). *Flags* is zero or more of:

- **n** n= 1 - 512. Substitute for just the n th occurrence of the *regular expression.*
- **g** Global. Substitute for all nonoverlapping instances of the *regular expression* rather than just the first one.
- **p** Print the pattern space if a replacement was made.

w *wfile*

Write. Append the pattern space to *wfile* if a replacement was made.

(2)**t** *label* Test. Branch to the **:** command bearing the *label* if any substitutions have been made since the most recent reading of an input line or execution of a **t**. If *label* is empty, branch to the end of the script.

(2)**w** *wfile* Write. Append the pattern space to *wfile*.

(2)**x** Exchange the contents of the pattern and hold spaces.

(2)**y**/*string1*/*string2*/

Transform. Replace all occurrences of characters in *string1* with the corresponding character in *string2*. The lengths of *string1* and *string2* must be equal.

(2)**!** *function*

Don't. Apply the *function* (or group, if *function* is {) only to lines *not* selected by the address(es).

(0)**:** *label* This command does nothing; it bears a *label* for **b** and **t** commands to branch to.

(1)**=** Place the current line number on the standard output as a line.

(2)**{** Execute the following commands through a matching } only when the pattern space is selected.

(0) An empty command is ignored.

(0)**#** If a **#** appears as the first character on the first line of a script file, then that entire line is treated as a comment, with one exception. If the character after the **#** is an 'n', then the default output will be suppressed. The rest of the line after **#**n is also ignored. A script file must contain at least one non-comment line.

SEE ALSO

awk(1), ed(1), grep(1).

NAME

setup – initialize system for first user

SYNOPSIS

setup

DESCRIPTION

The *setup* command, which is also accessible as a login by the same name, allows the first user to be established as the "owner" of the machine.

The user is permitted to add the first logins to the system, usually starting with his or her own.

The user can then protect the system from unauthorized modification of the machine configuration and software by giving passwords to the administrative and maintenance functions. Normally, the first user of the machine enters this command through the setup login, which initially has no password, and then gives passwords to the various functions in the system. Any that the user leaves without password protection can be exercised by anyone.

The user can then give passwords to system logins such as "root", "bin", etc. (*provided they do not already have passwords*). Once given a password, each login can only be changed by that login or "root".

The user can then set the date, time and time zone of the machine.

The user can then set the node name of the machine.

SEE ALSO

passwd(1).

DIAGNOSTICS

The *passwd*(1) command complains if the password provided does not meet its standards.

WARNING

If the setup login is not under password control, anyone can put passwords on the other functions.

NAME

sh, rsh – shell, the standard/restricted command programming language

SYNOPSIS

sh [**−acefhiknrstuvx**] [args]
rsh [**−acefhiknrstuvx**] [args]

DESCRIPTION

sh is a command programming language that executes commands read from a terminal or a file. *rsh* is a restricted version of the standard command interpreter *sh;* it is used to set up login names and execution environments whose capabilities are more controlled than those of the standard shell. See "Invocation" below for the meaning of arguments to the shell.

Definitions

A *blank* is a tab or a space. A *name* is a sequence of letters, digits, or underscores beginning with a letter or underscore. A *parameter* is a name, a digit, or any of the characters *****, **@**, **#**, **?**, **−**, **$**, and **!**.

Commands

A *simple-command* is a sequence of non-blank *words* separated by *blanks*. The first word specifies the name of the command to be executed. Except as specified below, the remaining words are passed as arguments to the invoked command. The command name is passed as argument 0 (see *exec*(2)). The *value* of a *simple-command* is its exit status if it terminates normally, or (octal) 200+*status* if it terminates abnormally (see *signal*(2) for a list of status values).

A *pipeline* is a sequence of one or more *commands* separated by **|**. The standard output of each command but the last is connected by a *pipe*(2) to the standard input of the next command. Each command is run as a separate process; the shell waits for the last command to terminate. The exit status of a pipeline is the exit status of the last command.

A *list* is a sequence of one or more pipelines separated by **;**, **&**, **&&**, or **||**, and optionally terminated by **;** or **&**. Of these four symbols, **;** and **&** have equal precedence, which is lower than that of **&&** and **||**. The symbols **&&** and **||** also have equal precedence. A semicolon (**;**) causes sequential execution of the preceding pipeline; an ampersand (**&**) causes asynchronous execution of the preceding pipeline (i.e., the shell does *not* wait for that pipeline to finish). The symbol **&&** (**||**) causes the *list* following it to be executed only if the preceding pipeline returns a zero (non-zero) exit status. An arbitrary number of new-lines may appear in a *list*, instead of semicolons, to delimit commands.

A *command* is either a *simple-command* or one of the following. Unless otherwise stated, the value returned by a command is that of the last *simple-command* executed in the command.

for *name* [**in** *word* ...] **do** *list* **done**

Each time a **for** command is executed, *name* is set to the next *word* taken from the **in** *word* list. If **in** *word* ... is omitted, then the **for** command executes the **do** *list* once for each positional parameter that is set (see *Parameter Substitution* below). Execution ends when there are no more words in the list.

case *word* **in** [*pattern* [**|** *pattern*] ... **)** *list* **;;**] ... **esac**

A **case** command executes the *list* associated with the first *pattern* that matches *word*. The form of the patterns is the same as that used for file-name generation (see "File Name Generation") except that a slash, a leading dot, or a dot immediately following a slash need not be matched explicitly.

if *list* **then** *list* [**elif** *list* **then** *list*] ... [**else** *list*] **fi**

The *list* following **if** is executed and, if it returns a zero exit status, the *list* following the first **then** is executed. Otherwise, the *list* following **elif** is executed and, if its value is zero, the *list* following the next **then** is executed. Failing that, the **else** *list* is executed. If no **else** *list* or **then** *list* is executed, then the **if** command returns a zero exit status.

while *list* **do** *list* **done**

A **while** command repeatedly executes the **while** *list* and, if the exit status of the last command in the list is zero, executes the **do** *list*; otherwise the loop terminates. If no commands in the **do** *list* are executed, then the **while** command returns a zero exit status; **until** may be used in place of **while** to negate the loop termination test.

(*list***)**

Execute *list* in a sub-shell.

{*list*;}

list is executed in the current (that is, parent) shell.

name **()** {*list*;}

Define a function which is referenced by *name*. The body of the function is the *list* of commands between { and }. Execution of functions is described below (see *Execution*).

The following words are only recognized as the first word of a command and when not quoted:

if then else elif fi case esac for while until do done { }

Comments

A word beginning with **#** causes that word and all the following characters up to a new-line to be ignored.

Command Substitution

The shell reads commands from the string between two grave accents (**\`\`**) and the standard output from these commands may be used as all or part of a word. Trailing new-lines from the standard output are removed.

No interpretation is done on the string before the string is read, except to remove backslashes (\) used to escape other characters. Backslashes may be used to escape a grave accent (**\`**) or another backslash (\) and are removed before the command string is read. Escaping grave accents allows nested command substitution. If the command substitution lies within a pair of double quotes (" ...\` ...\` ... "), a backslash used to escape a double quote (\") will be removed; otherwise, it will be left intact.

If a backslash is used to escape a new-line character (**new-line**), both the backslash and the new-line are removed (see the later section on "Quoting"). In addition, backslashes used to escape dollar signs (**$**) are removed. Since no interpretation is done on the command string before it is read, inserting a backslash to escape a dollar sign has no effect. Backslashes that precede characters other than \, `, ", **new-line**, and **$** are left intact when the command string is read.

Parameter Substitution

The character **$** is used to introduce substitutable *parameters*. There are two types of parameters, positional and keyword. If *parameter* is a digit, it is a positional parameter. Positional parameters may be assigned values by **set**. Keyword parameters (also known as variables) may be assigned values by writing:

name=value [*name=value*] ...

Pattern-matching is not performed on *value*. There cannot be a function and a variable with the same *name*.

${*parameter*}
The value, if any, of the parameter is substituted. The braces are required only when *parameter* is followed by a letter, digit, or underscore that is not to be interpreted as part of its name. If *parameter* is * or **@**, all the positional parameters, starting with **$1**, are substituted (separated by spaces). Parameter **$0** is set from argument zero when the shell is invoked.

${*parameter*:–*word*}
If *parameter* is set and is non-null, substitute its value; otherwise substitute *word*.

${*parameter*:=*word*}
If *parameter* is not set or is null set it to *word*; the value of the parameter is substituted. Positional parameters may not be assigned to in this way.

${*parameter*:?*word*}
If *parameter* is set and is non-null, substitute its value; otherwise, print *word* and exit from the shell. If *word* is omitted, the message "parameter null or not set" is printed.

${*parameter*:+*word*}
If *parameter* is set and is non-null, substitute *word*; otherwise substitute nothing.

In the above, *word* is not evaluated unless it is to be used as the substituted string, so that, in the following example, **pwd** is executed only if **d** is not set or is null:

echo ${d:–`pwd`}

If the colon (:) is omitted from the above expressions, the shell only checks whether *parameter* is set or not.

The following parameters are automatically set by the shell:

- **#** The number of positional parameters in decimal.
- **–** Flags supplied to the shell on invocation or by the **set** command.
- **?** The decimal value returned by the last synchronously executed command.

$ The process number of this shell.

! The process number of the last background command invoked.

The following parameters are used by the shell:

HOME The default argument (home directory) for the *cd* command.

PATH The search path for commands (see *Execution* below). The user may not change **PATH** if executing under *rsh*.

CDPATH
The search path for the *cd* command.

MAIL If this parameter is set to the name of a mail file *and* the **MAILPATH** parameter is not set, the shell informs the user of the arrival of mail in the specified file.

MAILCHECK
This parameter specifies how often (in seconds) the shell will check for the arrival of mail in the files specified by the **MAILPATH** or **MAIL** parameters. The default value is 600 seconds (10 minutes). If set to 0, the shell will check before each prompt.

MAILPATH
A colon (:) separated list of file names. If this parameter is set, the shell informs the user of the arrival of mail in any of the specified files. Each file name can be followed by % and a message that will be printed when the modification time changes. The default message is *you have mail*.

PS1 Primary prompt string, by default "**$** ".

PS2 Secondary prompt string, by default "> ".

IFS Internal field separators, normally **space**, **tab**, and **new-line**.

SHACCT
If this parameter is set to the name of a file writable by the user, the shell will write an accounting record in the file for each shell procedure executed.

SHELL When the shell is invoked, it scans the environment (see "Environment" below) for this name. If it is found and 'rsh' is the file name part of its value, the shell becomes a restricted shell.

The shell gives default values to **PATH**, **PS1**, **PS2**, **MAILCHECK** and **IFS**. **HOME** and **MAIL** are set by *login*(1).

Blank Interpretation

After parameter and command substitution, the results of substitution are scanned for internal field separator characters (those found in **IFS**) and split into distinct arguments where such characters are found. Explicit null arguments ("" or '') are retained. Implicit null arguments (those resulting from *parameters* that have no values) are removed.

Input/Output

A command's input and output may be redirected using a special notation interpreted by the shell. The following may appear anywhere in a *simple-command* or may precede or follow a *command* and are *not* passed on as arguments to the invoked command. Note that parameter and command substitution occurs before *word* or *digit* is used.

<word Use file *word* as standard input (file descriptor 0).

>word Use file *word* as standard output (file descriptor 1). If the file does not exist it is created; otherwise, it is truncated to zero length.

>>word Use file *word* as standard output. If the file exists output is appended to it (by first seeking to the end-of-file); otherwise, the file is created.

<<[−]**word** After parameter and command substitution is done on *word*, the shell input is read up to the first line that literally matches the resulting *word*, or to an end-of-file. If, however, − is appended to <<:

1) leading tabs are stripped from *word* before the shell input is read (but after parameter and command substitution is done on *word*),
2) leading tabs are stripped from the shell input as it is read and before each line is compared with *word*, and
3) shell input is read up to the first line that literally matches the resulting *word*, or to an end-of-file.

If any character of *word* is quoted (see "Quoting," later), no additional processing is done to the shell input. If no characters of *word* are quoted:

1) parameter and command substitution occurs,
2) (escaped) **new-line** is ignored, and
3) \ must be used to quote the characters \, **$**, and **`**.

The resulting document becomes the standard input.

<&digit Use the file associated with file descriptor *digit* as standard input. Similarly for the standard output using **>&digit**.

<&− The standard input is closed. Similarly for the standard output using **>&−**.

If any of the above is preceded by a digit, the file descriptor which will be associated with the file is that specified by the digit (instead of the default 0 or 1). For example:

```
... 2>&1
```

associates file descriptor 2 with the file currently associated with file descriptor 1.

The order in which redirections are specified is significant. The shell evaluates redirections left-to-right. For example:

... 1>*xxx* 2>&1

first associates file descriptor 1 with file *xxx*. It associates file descriptor 2 with the file associated with file descriptor 1 (i.e., *xxx*). If the order of redirections were reversed, file descriptor 2 would be associated with the terminal (assuming file descriptor 1 had been) and file descriptor 1 would be associated with file *xxx*.

Using the terminology introduced on the first page, under "Commands," if a *command* is composed of several *simple commands*, redirection will be evaluated for the entire *command* before it is evaluated for each *simple command*. That is, the shell evaluates redirection for the entire *list*, then each *pipeline* within the *list*, then each *command* within each *pipeline*, then each *list* within each *command*.

If a command is followed by **&** the default standard input for the command is the empty file **/dev/null**. Otherwise, the environment for the execution of a command contains the file descriptors of the invoking shell as modified by input/output specifications.

Redirection of output is not allowed in the restricted shell.

File Name Generation

Before a command is executed, each command *word* is scanned for the characters *, ?, and [. If one of these characters appears the word is regarded as a *pattern*. The word is replaced with alphabetically sorted file names that match the pattern. If no file name is found that matches the pattern, the word is left unchanged. The character . at the start of a file name or immediately following a /, as well as the character / itself, must be matched explicitly.

- ***** Matches any string, including the null string.
- **?** Matches any single character.
- **[...]** Matches any one of the enclosed characters. A pair of characters separated by − matches any character lexically between the pair, inclusive. If the first character following the opening "[" is a "!" any character not enclosed is matched.

Quoting

The following characters have a special meaning to the shell and cause termination of a word unless quoted:

; & ( ) | ^ < > new-line space tab

A character may be *quoted* (i.e., made to stand for itself) by preceding it with a backslash (\) or inserting it between a pair of quote marks (′′ or ""). During processing, the shell may quote certain characters to prevent them from taking on a special meaning. Backslashes used to quote a single character are removed from the word before the command is executed. The pair **\new-line** is removed from a word before command and parameter substitution.

All characters enclosed between a pair of single quote marks (′′), except a single quote, are quoted by the shell. Backslash has no special meaning inside a pair of single quotes. A single quote may be quoted inside a pair of double quote marks (for example, "′").

Inside a pair of double quote marks (""), parameter and command substitution occurs and the shell quotes the results to avoid blank interpretation and file name generation. If **$*** is within a pair of double quotes, the positional parameters are substituted and quoted, separated by quoted spaces ("**$1 $2** ..."); however, if **$@** is within a pair of double quotes, the positional parameters are substituted and quoted, separated by unquoted spaces ("**$1**" "**$2**" ...). \ quotes the characters \, `, ", and **$**. The pair **\new-line** is removed before parameter and command substitution. If a backslash precedes characters other than \, `, ", **$**, and new-line, then the backslash itself is quoted by the shell.

Prompting

When used interactively, the shell prompts with the value of **PS1** before reading a command. If at any time a new-line is typed and further input is needed to complete a command, the secondary prompt (i.e., the value of **PS2**) is issued.

Environment

The *environment* (see *environ*(5)) is a list of name-value pairs that is passed to an executed program in the same way as a normal argument list. The shell interacts with the environment in several ways. On invocation, the shell scans the environment and creates a parameter for each name found, giving it the corresponding value. If the user modifies the value of any of these parameters or creates new parameters, none of these affects the environment unless the **export** command is used to bind the shell's parameter to the environment (see also **set -a**). A parameter may be removed from the environment with the **unset** command. The environment seen by any executed command is thus composed of any unmodified name-value pairs originally inherited by the shell, minus any pairs removed by **unset**, plus any modifications or additions, all of which must be noted in **export** commands.

The environment for any *simple-command* may be augmented by prefixing it with one or more assignments to parameters. Thus:

```
TERM=450 cmd                          and
(export TERM; TERM=450; cmd)
```

are equivalent (as far as the execution of *cmd* is concerned).

If the **−k** flag is set, *all* keyword arguments are placed in the environment, even if they occur after the command name. The following first prints **a=b c** and **c**:

```
echo a=b c
set −k
echo a=b c
```

Signals

The INTERRUPT and QUIT signals for an invoked command are ignored if the command is followed by **&**; otherwise signals have the values inherited by the shell from its parent, with the exception of signal 11 (but see also the **trap** command below).

Execution

Each time a command is executed, the above substitutions are carried out. If the command name matches one of the *Special Commands* listed below, it is executed in the shell process. If the command name does not match a *Special Command*, but matches the name of a defined function, the function is executed in the shell process (note how this differs from the execution of shell procedures). The positional parameters **$1**, **$2**, ... are set to the arguments of the function. If the command name matches neither a *Special Command* nor the name of a defined function, a new process is created and an attempt is made to execute the command via *exec*(2).

The shell parameter **PATH** defines the search path for the directory containing the command. Alternative directory names are separated by a colon (:). The default path is **:/bin:/usr/bin** (specifying the current directory, **/bin**, and **/usr/bin**, in that order). Note that the current directory is specified by a null path name, which can appear immediately after the equal sign, between two colon delimiters anywhere in the path list, or at the end of the path list. If the command name contains a / the search path is not used; such commands will not be executed by the restricted shell. Otherwise, each directory in the path is searched for an executable file. If the file has execute permission but is not an **a.out** file, it is assumed to be a file containing shell commands. A sub-shell is spawned to read it. A parenthesized command is also executed in a sub-shell.

The location in the search path where a command was found is remembered by the shell (to help avoid unnecessary *execs* later). If the command was found in a relative directory, its location must be re-determined whenever the current directory changes. The shell forgets all remembered locations whenever the **PATH** variable is changed or the **hash -r** command is executed (see below).

Special Commands

Input/output redirection is now permitted for these commands. File descriptor 1 is the default output location.

: No effect; the command does nothing. A zero exit code is returned.

. *file* Read and execute commands from *file* and return. The search path specified by **PATH** is used to find the directory containing *file*.

break [*n*]
Exit from the enclosing **for** or **while** loop, if any. If *n* is specified break *n* levels.

continue [*n*]
Resume the next iteration of the enclosing **for** or **while** loop. If *n* is specified resume at the *n*-th enclosing loop.

cd [*arg*]
Change the current directory to *arg*. The shell parameter **HOME** is the default *arg*. The shell parameter **CDPATH** defines the search path for the directory containing *arg*. Alternative directory names are separated by a colon (:). The default path is **<null>** (specifying the current directory). Note that the current directory is specified by a null path name, which can appear immediately after the equal sign or between the colon delimiters anywhere else in the path list. If *arg* begins with a / the search path is not used. Otherwise, each directory in the path is searched for *arg*. The *cd* command may not be executed by *rsh*.

echo [*arg* ...]
Echo arguments. See *echo*(1) for usage and description.

eval [*arg* ...]
The arguments are read as input to the shell and the resulting command(s) executed.

exec [*arg* ...]
The command specified by the arguments is executed in place of this shell without creating a new process. Input/output arguments may appear and, if no other arguments are given, cause the shell input/output to be modified.

exit [*n*]
Causes a shell to exit with the exit status specified by *n*. If *n* is omitted the exit status is that of the last command executed (an end-of-file will also cause the shell to exit.)

export [*name* ...]
The given *names* are marked for automatic export to the *environment* of subsequently-executed commands. If no arguments are given, variable names that have been marked for export during the current shell's execution are listed. (Variable names exported from a parent shell are listed only if they have been exported again during the current shell's execution.) Function names are *not* exported.

getopts
Use in shell scripts to support command syntax standards (see *intro*(1)); it parses positional parameters and checks for legal options. See *getopts*(1) for usage and description.

hash [**−r**] [*name* ...]
For each *name*, the location in the search path of the command specified by *name* is determined and remembered by the shell. The **-r** option causes the shell to forget all remembered locations. If no arguments are given, information about remembered commands is presented. *Hits* is the number of times a command has been invoked by the shell process. *Cost* is a measure of the work required to locate a command in the search path. If a command is found in a "relative" directory in the search path, after changing to that directory, the stored location of that command is recalculated. Commands for which this will be done are indicated by an asterisk (*) adjacent to the *hits* information. *Cost* will be incremented when the recalculation is done.

newgrp [*arg* ...]
Equivalent to **exec newgrp** *arg* .... See *newgrp*(1) for usage and description.

pwd Print the current working directory. See *pwd*(1) for usage and description.

read [*name* ...]
One line is read from the standard input and, using the internal field separator, **IFS** (normally space or tab), to delimit word boundaries, the first word is assigned to the first *name*, the second word to the second *name*, etc., with leftover words assigned to the last *name*. Lines can be

continued using **\new-line**. Characters other than **new-line** can be quoted by preceding them with a backslash. These backslashes are removed before words are assigned to *names*, and no interpretation is done on the character that follows the backslash. The return code is 0 unless an end-of-file is encountered.

readonly [*name* ...]
: The given *names* are marked *readonly* and the values of the these *names* may not be changed by subsequent assignment. If no arguments are given, a list of all *readonly* names is printed.

return [*n*]
: Causes a function to exit with the return value specified by *n*. If *n* is omitted, the return status is that of the last command executed.

set [**−−aefhkntuvx** [*arg* ...]]

- **−a** Mark variables which are modified or created for export.
- **−e** Exit immediately if a command exits with a non-zero exit status.
- **−f** Disable file name generation
- **−h** Locate and remember function commands as functions are defined (function commands are normally located when the function is executed).
- **−k** All keyword arguments are placed in the environment for a command, not just those that precede the command name.
- **−n** Read commands but do not execute them.
- **−t** Exit after reading and executing one command.
- **−u** Treat unset variables as an error when substituting.
- **−v** Print shell input lines as they are read.
- **−x** Print commands and their arguments as they are executed.
- **−−** Do not change any of the flags; useful in setting **$1** to −.

Using + rather than − causes these flags to be turned off. These flags can also be used upon invocation of the shell. The current set of flags may be found in **$−**. The remaining arguments are positional parameters and are assigned, in order, to **$1**, **$2**, ... If no arguments are given the values of all names are printed.

shift [*n*]
: The positional parameters from **$n+1** ... are renamed **$1** .... If *n* is not given, it is assumed to be 1.

test
: Evaluate conditional expressions. See *test*(1) for usage and description.

times
: Print the accumulated user and system times for processes run from the shell.

trap [*arg*] [*n*] ...
: The command *arg* is to be read and executed when the shell receives signal(s) *n*. (Note that *arg* is scanned once when the trap is set and once when the trap is taken.) Trap commands are executed in order of signal number. Any attempt to set a trap on a signal that was ignored on

entry to the current shell is ineffective. An attempt to trap on signal 11 (memory fault) produces an error. If *arg* is absent all trap(s) *n* are reset to their original values. If *arg* is the null string this signal is ignored by the shell and by the commands it invokes. If *n* is 0 the command *arg* is executed on exit from the shell. The **trap** command with no arguments prints a list of commands associated with each signal number.

type [*name* ...]
For each *name*, indicate how it would be interpreted if used as a command name.

ulimit [*n*]
Impose a size limit of *n* blocks on files written by the shell and its child processes (files of any size may be read). If *n* is omitted, the current limit is printed. You may lower your own ulimit, but only a super-user (see *su*(1M)) can raise a ulimit.

umask [*nnn*]
The user file-creation mask is set to *nnn* (see *umask*(1)). If *nnn* is omitted, the current value of the mask is printed.

unset [*name* ...]
For each *name*, remove the corresponding variable or function. The variables **PATH**, **PS1**, **PS2**, **MAILCHECK** and **IFS** cannot be unset.

wait [*n*]
Wait for your background process whose process id is *n* and report its termination status. If *n* is omitted, all your shell's currently active background processes are waited for and the return code will be zero.

Invocation

If the shell is invoked through *exec*(2) and the first character of argument zero is −, commands are initially read from */etc/profile* and from *$HOME/.profile*, if such files exist. Thereafter, commands are read as described below, which is also the case when the shell is invoked as */bin/sh*. The flags below are interpreted by the shell on invocation only; Note that unless the **−c** or **−s** flag is specified, the first argument is assumed to be the name of a file containing commands, and the remaining arguments are passed as positional parameters to that command file:

−c *string* If the **−c** flag is present commands are read from *string*.

−s If the **−s** flag is present or if no arguments remain commands are read from the standard input. Any remaining arguments specify the positional parameters. Shell output (except for *Special Commands*) is written to file descriptor 2.

−i If the **−i** flag is present or if the shell input and output are attached to a terminal, this shell is *interactive*. In this case TERMINATE is ignored (so that **kill 0** does not kill an interactive shell) and INTERRUPT is caught and ignored (so that **wait** is interruptible). In all cases, QUIT is ignored by the shell.

−r If the **−r** flag is present the shell is a restricted shell.

The remaining flags and arguments are described under the **set** command above.

rsh Only

rsh is used to set up login names and execution environments whose capabilities are more controlled than those of the standard shell. The actions of *rsh* are identical to those of *sh*, except that the following are disallowed:

changing directory (see *cd*(1)),
setting the value of **$PATH,**
specifying path or command names containing /,
redirecting output (> and >>).

The restrictions above are enforced after *.profile* is interpreted.

A restricted shell can be invoked in one of the following ways: (1) *rsh* is the file name part of the last entry in the */etc/passwd* file (see *passwd*(4)); (2) the environment variable **SHELL** exists and *rsh* is the file name part of its value; (3) the shell is invoked and *rsh* is the file name part of argument 0; (4) the shell is invoke with the **−r** option.

When a command to be executed is found to be a shell procedure, *rsh* invokes *sh* to execute it. Thus, it is possible to provide to the end-user shell procedures that have access to the full power of the standard shell, while imposing a limited menu of commands; this scheme assumes that the end-user does not have write and execute permissions in the same directory.

The net effect of these rules is that the writer of the *.profile* (see *profile*(4)) has complete control over user actions by performing guaranteed setup actions and leaving the user in an appropriate directory (probably *not* the login directory).

The system administrator often sets up a directory of commands (i.e., **/usr/rbin**) that can be safely invoked by a restricted shell. Some systems also provide a restricted editor, *red*.

EXIT STATUS

Errors detected by the shell, such as syntax errors, cause the shell to return a non-zero exit status. If the shell is being used non-interactively execution of the shell file is abandoned. Otherwise, the shell returns the exit status of the last command executed (see also the **exit** command above).

FILES

/etc/profile
$HOME/.profile
/tmp/sh*
/dev/null

SEE ALSO

cd(1), echo(1), env(1), getopts(1), intro(1), login(1), newgrp(1), pwd(1), test(1), umask(1), wait(1).
dup(2), exec(2), fork(2), pipe(2), profile(4), signal(2), ulimit(2) in the *Programmer's Reference Manual.*

CAVEATS

Words used for filenames in input/output redirection are not interpreted for filename generation (see "File Name Generation," above). For example, **cat file1 >a*** will create a file named **a***.

Because commands in pipelines are run as separate processes, variables set in a pipeline have no effect on the parent shell.

If you get the error message *cannot fork, too many processes*, try using the *wait*(1) command to clean up your background processes. If this doesn't help, the system process table is probably full or you have too many active foreground processes. (There is a limit to the number of process ids associated with your login, and to the number the system can keep track of.)

BUGS

If a command is executed, and a command with the same name is installed in a directory in the search path before the directory where the original command was found, the shell will continue to *exec* the original command. Use the **hash** command to correct this situation.

If you move the current directory or one above it, **pwd** may not give the correct response. Use the **cd** command with a full path name to correct this situation.

Not all the processes of a 3- or more-stage pipeline are children of the shell, and thus cannot be waited for.

For *wait n*, if *n* is not an active process id, all your shell's currently active background processes are waited for and the return code will be zero.

NAME

shl − shell layer manager

SYNOPSIS

shl

DESCRIPTION

shl allows a user to interact with more than one shell from a single terminal. The user controls these shells, known as *layers*, using the commands described below.

The *current layer* is the layer which can receive input from the keyboard. Other layers attempting to read from the keyboard are blocked. Output from multiple layers is multiplexed onto the terminal. To have the output of a layer blocked when it is not current, the *stty* option **loblk** may be set within the layer.

The *stty* character **swtch** (set to ^Z if NUL) is used to switch control to *shl* from a layer. *shl* has its own prompt, >>>, to help distinguish it from a layer.

A *layer* is a shell which has been bound to a virtual tty device (**/dev/sxt???**). The virtual device can be manipulated like a real tty device using *stty*(1) and *ioctl*(2). Each layer has its own process group id.

Definitions

A *name* is a sequence of characters delimited by a blank, tab or new-line. Only the first eight characters are significant. The *names* **(1)** through **(7)** cannot be used when creating a layer. They are used by *shl* when no name is supplied. They may be abbreviated to just the digit.

Commands

The following commands may be issued from the *shl* prompt level. Any unique prefix is accepted.

create [*name*]
: Create a layer called *name* and make it the current layer. If no argument is given, a layer will be created with a name of the form *(#)* where # is the last digit of the virtual device bound to the layer. The shell prompt variable **PS1** is set to the name of the layer followed by a space. A maximum of seven layers can be created.

block *name* [*name* ...]
: For each *name*, block the output of the corresponding layer when it is not the current layer. This is equivalent to setting the *stty* option **−loblk** within the layer.

delete *name* [*name* ...]
: For each *name*, delete the corresponding layer. All processes in the process group of the layer are sent the SIGHUP signal (see *signal*(2)).

help (or **?**)
: Print the syntax of the *shl* commands.

layers [**−l**] [*name* ...]
: For each *name*, list the layer name and its process group. The **−l** option produces a *ps*(1)-like listing. If no arguments are given, information is presented for all existing layers.

resume [*name*]
Make the layer referenced by *name* the current layer. If no argument is given, the last existing current layer will be resumed.

toggle Resume the layer that was current before the last current layer.

unblock *name* [*name* ...]
For each *name,* do not block the output of the corresponding layer when it is not the current layer. This is equivalent to setting the *stty* option **−loblk** within the layer.

quit Exit *shl*. All layers are sent the SIGHUP signal.

name Make the layer referenced by *name* the current layer.

FILES

/dev/sxt???	Virtual tty devices
$SHELL	Variable containing path name of the shell to use (default is /bin/sh).

SEE ALSO

sh(1), stty(1).
ioctl(2), signal(2) in the *Programmer's Reference Manual.*
sxt(7) in the *System Administrator's Reference Manual.*

NAME

sleep – suspend execution for an interval

SYNOPSIS

sleep time

DESCRIPTION

sleep suspends execution for *time* seconds. It is used to execute a command after a certain amount of time, as in:

```
(sleep 105; command)&
```

or to execute a command every so often, as in:

```
while true
do
        command
        sleep 37
done
```

SEE ALSO

alarm(2), sleep(3C) in the *Programmer's Reference Manual.*

NAME

sort − sort and/or merge files

SYNOPSIS

sort [**−cmu**] [**−o**output] [**−y**kmem] [**−z**recsz] [**−dfiMnr**] [**−bt**x] [+pos1 [−pos2]] [files]

DESCRIPTION

sort sorts lines of all the named files together and writes the result on the standard output. The standard input is read if − is used as a file name or no input files are named.

Comparisons are based on one or more sort keys extracted from each line of input. By default, there is one sort key, the entire input line, and ordering is lexicographic by bytes in machine collating sequence.

The following options alter the default behavior:

−c Check that the input file is sorted according to the ordering rules; give no output unless the file is out of sort.

−m Merge only, the input files are already sorted.

−u Unique: suppress all but one in each set of lines having equal keys.

−o*output*
The argument given is the name of an output file to use instead of the standard output. This file may be the same as one of the inputs. There may be optional blanks between **−o** and *output.*

−y*kmem*
The amount of main memory used by the sort has a large impact on its performance. Sorting a small file in a large amount of memory is a waste. If this option is omitted, *sort* begins using a system default memory size, and continues to use more space as needed. If this option is presented with a value, *kmem, sort* will start using that number of kilobytes of memory, unless the administrative minimum or maximum is violated, in which case the corresponding extremum will be used. Thus, **−y**0 is guaranteed to start with minimum memory. By convention, **−y** (with no argument) starts with maximum memory.

−z*recsz*
The size of the longest line read is recorded in the sort phase so buffers can be allocated during the merge phase. If the sort phase is omitted via the **−c** or **−m** options, a popular system default size will be used. Lines longer than the buffer size will cause *sort* to terminate abnormally. Supplying the actual number of bytes in the longest line to be merged (or some larger value) will prevent abnormal termination.

The following options override the default ordering rules.

−d "Dictionary" order: only letters, digits and blanks (spaces and tabs) are significant in comparisons.

−f Fold lower case letters into upper case.

−i Ignore characters outside the ASCII range 040-0176 in non-numeric comparisons.

−M Compare as months. The first three non-blank characters of the field are folded to upper case and compared so that "JAN" < "FEB" < ... < "DEC". Invalid fields compare low to "JAN". The **−M** option implies the **−b** option (see below).

−n An initial numeric string, consisting of optional blanks, optional minus sign, and zero or more digits with optional decimal point, is sorted by arithmetic value. The **−n** option implies the **−b** option (see below). Note that the **−b** option is only effective when restricted sort key specifications are in effect.

−r Reverse the sense of comparisons.

When ordering options appear before restricted sort key specifications, the requested ordering rules are applied globally to all sort keys. When attached to a specific sort key (described below), the specified ordering options override all global ordering options for that key.

The notation *+pos1 −pos2* restricts a sort key to one beginning at *pos1* and ending just before *pos2*. The characters at position *pos1* and just before *pos2* are included in the sort key (provided that *pos2* does not precede *pos1*). A missing *−pos2* means the end of the line.

Specifying *pos1* and *pos2* involves the notion of a field, a minimal sequence of characters followed by a field separator or a new-line. By default, the first blank (space or tab) of a sequence of blanks acts as the field separator. All blanks in a sequence of blanks are considered to be part of the next field; for example, all blanks at the beginning of a line are considered to be part of the first field. The treatment of field separators can be altered using the options:

−b Ignore leading blanks when determining the starting and ending positions of a restricted sort key. If the **−b** option is specified before the first *+pos1* argument, it will be applied to all *+pos1* arguments. Otherwise, the **b** flag may be attached independently to each *+pos1* or *−pos2* argument (see below).

−t*x* Use *x* as the field separator character; *x* is not considered to be part of a field (although it may be included in a sort key). Each occurrence of *x* is significant (for example, *xx* delimits an empty field).

Pos1 and *pos2* each have the form *m.n* optionally followed by one or more of the flags **bdfinr**. A starting position specified by *+m.n* is interpreted to mean the *n*+1st character in the *m*+1st field. A missing *.n* means .0, indicating the first character of the *m*+1st field. If the **b** flag is in effect *n* is counted from the first non-blank in the *m*+1st field; *+m*.0**b** refers to the first non-blank character in the *m*+1st field.

A last position specified by *−m.n* is interpreted to mean the *n*th character (including separators) after the last character of the *m th* field. A missing *.n* means .0, indicating the last character of the *m*th field. If the **b** flag is in effect *n* is counted from the last leading blank in the *m*+1st field; *−m*.1**b** refers to the first non-blank in the *m*+1st field.

When there are multiple sort keys, later keys are compared only after all earlier keys compare equal. Lines that otherwise compare equal are ordered with all bytes significant.

EXAMPLES

Sort the contents of *infile* with the second field as the sort key:

sort +1 −2 infile

Sort, in reverse order, the contents of *infile1* and *infile2*, placing the output in *outfile* and using the first character of the second field as the sort key:

sort −r −o outfile +1.0 −1.2 infile1 infile2

Sort, in reverse order, the contents of *infile1* and *infile2* using the first non-blank character of the second field as the sort key:

sort −r +1.0b −1.1b infile1 infile2

Print the password file (*passwd*(4)) sorted by the numeric user ID (the third colon-separated field):

sort −t: +2n −3 /etc/passwd

Print the lines of the already sorted file *infile*, suppressing all but the first occurrence of lines having the same third field (the options **−um** with just one input file make the choice of a unique representative from a set of equal lines predictable):

sort −um +2 −3 infile

FILES

/usr/tmp/stm???

SEE ALSO

comm(1), join(1), uniq(1).

WARNINGS

Comments and exits with non-zero status for various trouble conditions (for example, when input lines are too long), and for disorder discovered under the **−c** option. When the last line of an input file is missing a **new-line** character, *sort* appends one, prints a warning message, and continues.

sort does not guarantee preservation of relative line ordering on equal keys.

NAME

spell, hashmake, spellin, hashcheck – find spelling errors

SYNOPSIS

spell [**−v**] [**−b**] [**−x**] [**−l**] [+local_file] [files]

/usr/lib/spell/hashmake

/usr/lib/spell/spellin n

/usr/lib/spell/hashcheck spelling_list

DESCRIPTION

spell collects words from the named *files* and looks them up in a spelling list. Words that neither occur among nor are derivable (by applying certain inflections, prefixes, and/or suffixes) from words in the spelling list are printed on the standard output. If no *files* are named, words are collected from the standard input.

spell ignores most *troff*(1), *tbl*(1), and *eqn*(1) constructions.

Under the **−v** option, all words not literally in the spelling list are printed, and plausible derivations from the words in the spelling list are indicated.

Under the **−b** option, British spelling is checked. Besides preferring *centre, colour, programme, speciality, travelled*, etc., this option insists upon *-ise* in words like *standardise*, Fowler and the OED to the contrary notwithstanding.

Under the **−x** option, every plausible stem is printed with = for each word.

By default, *spell* (like *deroff*(1)) follows chains of included files (**.so** and **.nx** *troff*(1) requests), *unless* the names of such included files begin with **/usr/lib**. Under the **−l** option, *spell* will follow the chains of *all* included files.

Under the *+local_file* option, words found in *local_file* are removed from *spell*'s output. *Local_file* is the name of a user-provided file that contains a sorted list of words, one per line. With this option, the user can specify a set of words that are correct spellings (in addition to *spell*'s own spelling list) for each job.

The spelling list is based on many sources, and while more haphazard than an ordinary dictionary, is also more effective with respect to proper names and popular technical words. Coverage of the specialized vocabularies of biology, medicine, and chemistry is light.

Pertinent auxiliary files may be specified by name arguments, indicated below with their default settings (see *FILES*). Copies of all output are accumulated in the history file. The stop list filters out misspellings (e.g., thier=thy−y+ier) that would otherwise pass.

Three routines help maintain and check the hash lists used by *spell*:

hashmake Reads a list of words from the standard input and writes the corresponding nine-digit hash code on the standard output.

spellin Reads *n* hash codes from the standard input and writes a compressed spelling list on the standard output.

hashcheck Reads a compressed *spelling_list* and recreates the nine-digit hash codes for all the words in it; it writes these codes on the standard output.

FILES

D_SPELL=/usr/lib/spell/hlist[ab]	hashed spelling lists, American & British
S_SPELL=/usr/lib/spell/hstop	hashed stop list
H_SPELL=/usr/lib/spell/spellhist	history file
/usr/lib/spell/spellprog	program

SEE ALSO

deroff(1), sed(1), sort(1), tee(1).
eqn(1), tbl(1), troff(1) in the *DOCUMENTER'S WORKBENCH Software 2.0 Technical Discussion and Reference Manual.*

BUGS

The spelling list's coverage is uneven; new installations will probably wish to monitor the output for several months to gather local additions; typically, these are kept in a separate local file that is added to the hashed *spelling_list* via *spellin*.

NAME

spline − interpolate smooth curve

SYNOPSIS

spline [options]

DESCRIPTION

spline takes pairs of numbers from the standard input as abscissas and ordinates of a function. It produces a similar set, which is approximately equally spaced and includes the input set, on the standard output. The cubic spline output has two continuous derivatives, and sufficiently many points to look smooth when plotted, for example by *graph*(1G).

The following *options* are recognized, each as a separate argument:

−a Supply abscissas automatically (they are missing from the input); spacing is given by the next argument, or is assumed to be 1 if next argument is not a number.

−k The constant k used in the boundary value computation:

$$y_0'' = ky_1'', \quad y_n'' = ky_{n-1}''$$

is set by the next argument (default $k = 0$).

−n Space output points so that approximately n intervals occur between the lower and upper x limits (default $n = 100$).

−p Make output periodic, i.e., match derivatives at ends. First and last input values should normally agree.

−x Next 1 (or 2) arguments are lower (and upper) x limits. Normally, these limits are calculated from the data. Automatic abscissas start at lower limit (default 0).

SEE ALSO

graph(1G).

DIAGNOSTICS

When data is not strictly monotone in x, *spline* reproduces the input without interpolating extra points.

BUGS

A limit of 1,000 input points is enforced silently.

NAME

split − split a file into pieces

SYNOPSIS

split [−*n*] [file [name]]

DESCRIPTION

split reads *file* and writes it in *n*-line pieces (default 1000 lines) onto a set of output files. The name of the first output file is *name* with **aa** appended, and so on lexicographically, up to **zz** (a maximum of 676 files). *Name* cannot be longer than 12 characters. If no output name is given, **x** is default.

If no input file is given, or if − is given in its stead, then the standard input file is used.

SEE ALSO

bfs(1), csplit(1).

NAME

starter – information about the UNIX system for beginning users

SYNOPSIS

[**help**] **starter**

DESCRIPTION

The UNIX system Help Facility command *starter* provides five categories of information about the UNIX system to assist new users.

The five categories are:

- commands a new user should learn first
- UNIX system documents important for beginners
- education centers offering UNIX system courses
- local environment information
- on-line teaching aids installed on the UNIX system

The user may choose one of the above categories by entering its corresponding letter (given in the menu), or may exit to the shell by typing q (for "quit"). When a category is chosen, the user will receive one or more pages of information pertaining to it.

From any screen in the Help Facility, a user may execute a command via the shell (*sh*(1)) by typing a ! and the command to be executed. The screen will be redrawn if the command that was executed was entered at a first level prompt. If entered at any other prompt level, only the prompt will be redrawn.

By default, the Help Facility scrolls the data that is presented to the user. If you prefer to have the screen clear before printing the data (non-scrolling), the shell variable **SCROLL** must be set to **no** and exported so it will become part of your environment. This is done by adding the following line to your *.profile* file (see *profile*(4)): "`export SCROLL ; SCROLL=no`". If you later decide that scrolling is desired, **SCROLL** must be set to **yes**.

Information on each of the Help Facility commands (*starter, locate, usage, glossary,* and *help*) is located on their respective manual pages.

SEE ALSO

glossary(1), help(1), locate(1), sh(1), usage(1).
term(5) in the *Programmer's Reference Manual.*

WARNINGS

If the shell variable **TERM** (see *sh*(1)) is not set in the user's *.profile* file, then **TERM** will default to the terminal value type 450 (a hard-copy terminal). For a list of valid terminal types, refer to *term*(5).

NAME

stat − statistical network useful with graphical commands

SYNOPSIS

node-name [options] [files]

DESCRIPTION

stat is a collection of command level functions (nodes) that can be interconnected using *sh*(1) to form a statistical network. The nodes reside in **/usr/bin/graf** (see *graphics*(1G)). Data is passed through the network as sequences of numbers (vectors), where a number is of the form:

[sign](digits)(.digits)[**e**[sign]digits]

evaluated in the usual way. Brackets and parentheses surround fields. All fields are optional, but at least one of the fields surrounded by parentheses must be present. Any character input to a node that is not part of a number is taken as a delimiter.

stat nodes are divided into four classes.

Transformers,	which map input vector elements into output vector elements;
Summarizers,	which calculate statistics of a vector;
Translators,	which convert among formats; and
Generators,	which are sources of definable vectors.

Below is a list of synopses for *stat* nodes. Most nodes accept options indicated by a leading minus (−). In general, an option is specified by a character followed by a value, such as **c5**. This is interpreted as **c** := 5 (**c** is assigned 5). The following keys are used to designate the expected type of the value:

c	characters,
i	integer,
f	floating point or integer,
file	file name, and
string	string of characters, surrounded by quotes to include a *shell* argument delimiter.

Options without keys are flags. All nodes except *generators* accept files as input, hence it is not indicated in the synopses.

Transformers:

abs	[−**c***i*] − absolute value **c**olumns (similarly for −**c** options that follow)
af	[−**c***i* **t** **v**] − arithmetic function **t**itled output, **v**erbose
ceil	[−**c***i*] − round up to next integer
cusum	[−**c***i*] − cumulative sum

exp [−c*i*] − exponential

floor [−c*i*] − round down to next integer

gamma [−c*i*] − gamma

list [−c*i* d*string*] − list vector elements
delimiter(s)

log [−c*i* b*f*] − logarithm
base

mod [−c*i* m*f*] − modulus
modulus

pair [−c*i* F*file* x*i*] − pair elements
File containing base vector, **x** group size

power [−c*i* p*f*] − raise to a power
power

root [−c*i* r*f*] − take a root
root

round [−c*i* p*i* s*i*] − round to nearest integer, .5 rounds to 1
places after decimal point, **s**ignificant digits

siline [−c*i* i*f* n*i* s*f*] − generate a line given slope and intercept
intercept, **n**umber of positive integers, **s**lope

sin [−c*i*] − sine

subset [−a*f* b*f* c*i* F*file* i*i* l*f* nl np p*f* s*i* t*i*] − generate a subset
above, **b**elow, **F**ile with master vector, **i**nterval, **l**eave, master contains element **n**umbers to **l**eave, master contains element **n**umbers to **p**ick, **p**ick, **s**tart, **t**erminate

Summarizers:

bucket [−a*i* c*i* F*file* h*f* i*i* l*f* n*i*] − break into buckets
average size, **F**ile containing bucket boundaries, **h**igh, **i**nterval, **l**ow, **n**umber
Input data should be sorted

cor [−F*file*] − correlation coefficient
File containing base vector

hilo [− **h l o ox oy**]− find high and low values
high only, **l**ow only, **o**ption form, **o**ption form with **x** prepended, **o**ption form with **y** prepended

lreg [−F*file* **i o s**] − linear regression
File containing base vector, **i**ntercept only, **o**ption form for *siline*, **s**lope only

mean [−f*f* n*i* p*f*] − (trimmed) arithmetic mean
fraction, **n**umber, **p**ercent

point [−f*f* n*i* p*f* **s**] − point from empirical cumulative density function
fraction, **n**umber, **p**ercent, **s**orted input

prod – internal product

qsort [−c*i*] – quick sort

rank – vector rank

total – sum total

var – variance

Translators:

bar [−**a b f g r***i* **w***i* **x***f* **xa y***f* **ya yl***f* **yh***f*] – build a bar chart
suppress **a**xes, **b**old, suppress **f**rame, suppress **g**rid, **r**egion, **w**idth in percent, **x** origin, suppress **x**-**a**xis label, **y** origin, suppress **y**-**a**xis label, **y**-axis **l**ower bound, **y**-axis **h**igh bound
Data is rounded off to integers.

hist [−**a b f g r***i* **x***f* **xa y***f* **ya yl***f* **yh***f*] – build a histogram
suppress **a**xes, **b**old, suppress **f**rame, suppress **g**rid, **r**egion, **x** origin, suppress **x**-**a**xis label, **y** origin, suppress **y**-**a**xis label, **y**-axis **l**ower bound, **y**-axis **h**igh bound

label [−**b c F***file* **h p r***i* **x xu y yr**] – label the axis of a GPS file
bar chart input, retain **c**ase, label **F**ile, **h**istogram input, **p**lot input, **r**otation, **x**-axis, **u**pper **x**-axis, **y**-axis, **r**ight **y**-axis

pie [−**b o p pn***i* **pp***i* **r***i* **v x***i* **y***i*] – build a pie chart
bold, values **o**utside pie, value as **p**ercentage(:=100), value as **p**ercentage(:=i), draw **p**ercent of **p**ie, **r**egion, no **v**alues, **x** origin, **y** origin
Unlike other nodes, input is lines of the form

[< **i e f c***c* >] value [label]
ignore (do not draw) slice, **e**xplode slice, **f**ill slice, **c**olor slice *c*=(**b**lack, **r**ed, **g**reen, bl**u**e)

plot [−**a b c***string* **d f F***file* **g m r***i* **x***f* **xa xi***f* **xh***f* **xl***f* **xn***i* **xt y***f* **ya yi***f* **yh***f* **yl***f* **yn***i* **yt**] – plot a graph
suppress **a**xes, **b**old, plotting **c**haracters, **d**isconnected, suppress **f**rame, **F**ile containing x vector, suppress **g**rid, **m**ark points, **r**egion, **x** origin, suppress **x**-**a**xis label, **x** **i**nterval, **x** **h**igh bound, **x** **l**ow bound, **n**umber of ticks on **x**-axis, suppress **x**-axis **t**itle, **y** origin, suppress **y**-**a**xis label, **y** **i**nterval, **y** **h**igh bound, **y** **l**ow bound, **n**umber of ticks on **y**-axis, suppress **y**-axis **t**itle

title [−**b c l***string* **v***string* **u***string*] – title a vector or a GPS
title **b**old, retain **c**ase, **l**ower title, **u**pper title, **v**ector title

Generators:

gas [−c*i* **i***f* **n***i* **s***f* **t***f*] – generate additive sequence
interval, **n**umber, **s**tart, **t**erminate

prime [-c*i* **h***i* **l***i* **n***i*] – generate prime numbers
high, **l**ow, **n**umber

rand [−c*i* **h***f* **l***f* **m***f* **n***i* **s***i*] – generate random sequence
high, **l**ow, **m**ultiplier, **n**umber, **s**eed

RESTRICTIONS

Some nodes have a limit on the size of the input vector.

SEE ALSO

graphics(1G).
gps(4) in the *Programmer's Reference Manual.*

NAME

stty – set the options for a terminal

SYNOPSIS

stty [**−a**] [**−g**] [options]

DESCRIPTION

stty sets certain terminal I/O options for the device that is the current standard input; without arguments, it reports the settings of certain options.

In this report, if a character is preceded by a caret (^), then the value of that option is the corresponding CTRL character (e.g., "**^h**" is **CTRL-h ;** in this case, recall that **CTRL-h** is the same as the "back-space" key.) The sequence "^`" means that an option has a null value. For example, normally **stty −a** will report that the value of **swtch** is "^`"; however, if **shl (1)** or **layers (1)** has been invoked, **stty −a** will have the value "**^z**".

−a reports all of the option settings;

−g reports current settings in a form that can be used as an argument to another *stty* command.

Options in the last group are implemented using options in the previous groups. Note that many combinations of options make no sense, but no sanity checking is performed. The options are selected from the following:

Control Modes

parenb (−parenb) enable (disable) parity generation and detection.
parodd (−parodd) select odd (even) parity.
cs5 cs6 cs7 cs8 select character size (see *termio*(7)).
0 hang up phone line immediately.
110 300 600 1200 1800 2400 4800 9600 19200 38400
Set terminal baud rate to the number given, if possible. (All speeds are not supported by all hardware interfaces.)
hupcl (−hupcl) hang up (do not hang up) Dataphone connection on last close.
hup (−hup) same as **hupcl (−hupcl)**.
cstopb (−cstopb) use two (one) stop bits per character.
cread (−cread) enable (disable) the receiver.
clocal (−clocal) n assume a line without (with) modem control.
loblk (−loblk) block (do not block) output from a non-current layer.

Input Modes

ignbrk (−ignbrk) ignore (do not ignore) break on input.
brkint (−brkint) signal (do not signal) INTR on break.
ignpar (−ignpar) ignore (do not ignore) parity errors.
parmrk (−parmrk) mark (do not mark) parity errors (see *termio*(7)).
inpck (−inpck) enable (disable) input parity checking.
istrip (−istrip) strip (do not strip) input characters to seven bits.
inlcr (−inlcr) map (do not map) NL to CR on input.
igncr (−igncr) ignore (do not ignore) CR on input.
icrnl (−icrnl) map (do not map) CR to NL on input.

iuclc (−iuclc) map (do not map) upper-case alphabetics to lower case on input.

ixon (−ixon) enable (disable) START/STOP output control. Output is stopped by sending an ASCII DC3 and started by sending an ASCII DC1.

ixany (−ixany) allow any character (only DC1) to restart output.

ixoff (−ixoff) request that the system send (not send) START/STOP characters when the input queue is nearly empty/full.

Output Modes

opost (−opost) post-process output (do not post-process output; ignore all other output modes).

olcuc (−olcuc) map (do not map) lower-case alphabetics to upper case on output.

onlcr (−onlcr) map (do not map) NL to CR-NL on output.

ocrnl (−ocrnl) map (do not map) CR to NL on output.

onocr (−onocr) do not (do) output CRs at column zero.

onlret (−onlret) on the terminal NL performs (does not perform) the CR function.

ofill (−ofill) use fill characters (use timing) for delays.

ofdel (−ofdel) fill characters are DELs (NULs).

cr0 cr1 cr2 cr3 select style of delay for carriage returns (see *termio*(7)).

nl0 nl1 select style of delay for line-feeds (see *termio*(7)).

tab0 tab1 tab2 tab3 select style of delay for horizontal tabs (see *termio*(7)).

bs0 bs1 select style of delay for backspaces (see *termio*(7)).

ff0 ff1 select style of delay for form-feeds (see *termio*(7)).

vt0 vt1 select style of delay for vertical tabs (see *termio*(7)).

Local Modes

isig (−isig) enable (disable) the checking of characters against the special control characters INTR, QUIT, and SWTCH.

icanon (−icanon) enable (disable) canonical input (ERASE and KILL processing).

xcase (−xcase) canonical (unprocessed) upper/lower-case presentation.

echo (−echo) echo back (do not echo back) every character typed.

echoe (−echoe) echo (do not echo) ERASE character as a backspace-space-backspace string. Note: this mode will erase the ERASEed character on many CRT terminals; however, it does *not* keep track of column position and, as a result, may be confusing on escaped characters, tabs, and backspaces.

echok (−echok) echo (do not echo) NL after KILL character.

lfkc (−lfkc) the same as **echok (−echok)**; obsolete.

echonl (−echonl) echo (do not echo) NL.

noflsh (−noflsh) disable (enable) flush after INTR, QUIT, or SWTCH.

stwrap (−stwrap) disable (enable) truncation of lines longer than 79 characters on a synchronous line. (Does not apply to the 3B2.)

stflush (−stflush) enable (disable) flush on a synchronous line after every *write*(2).*(Does*not*apply*to

stappl (−**stappl**) use application mode (use line mode) on a synchronous line. (Does not apply to the 3B2.)

Control Assignments

control-character c set *control-character* to *c*, where *control-character* is **erase**, **kill**, **intr**, **quit**, **swtch**, **eof**, **ctab**, **min**, or **time** (**ctab** is used with −**stappl**; **min** and **time** are used with −**icanon**; see *termio*(7)). If *c* is preceded by an (escaped from the shell) caret (^), then the value used is the corresponding CTRL character (e.g., "^**d**" is a **CTRL-d**); "^**?**" is interpreted as DEL and "^−" is interpreted as undefined.

line *i* set line discipline to *i* (0 < *i* < 127).

Combination Modes

evenp or **parity** enable **parenb** and **cs7**.

oddp enable **parenb**, **cs7**, and **parodd**.

−**parity**, −**evenp**, or −**oddp**
disable **parenb**, and set **cs8**.

raw (−**raw** or **cooked**)
enable (disable) raw input and output (no ERASE, KILL, INTR, QUIT, SWTCH, EOT, or output post processing).

nl (−**nl**) unset (set) **icrnl**, **onlcr**. In addition −**nl** unsets **inlcr**, **igncr**, **ocrnl**, and **onlret**.

lcase (−**lcase**) set (unset) **xcase**, **iuclc**, and **olcuc**.

LCASE (−LCASE) same as **lcase** (−**lcase**).

tabs (−**tabs** or **tab3**) preserve (expand to spaces) tabs when printing.

ek reset ERASE and KILL characters back to normal # and @.

sane resets all modes to some reasonable values.

term set all modes suitable for the terminal type *term*, where *term* is one of **tty33**, **tty37**, **vt05**, **tn300**, **ti700**, or **tek**.

SEE ALSO

tabs(1).
ioctl(2) in the *Programmer's Reference Manual*.
termio(7) in the *System Administrator's Reference Manual*.

NAME

su — become super-user or another user

SYNOPSIS

su [−] [name [arg ...]]

DESCRIPTION

su allows one to become another user without logging off. The default user *name* is **root** (i.e., super-user).

To use *su*, the appropriate password must be supplied (unless one is already **root**). If the password is correct, *su* will execute a new shell with the real and effective user ID set to that of the specified user. The new shell will be the optional program named in the shell field of the specified user's password file entry (see *passwd*(4)), or **/bin/sh** if none is specified (see *sh*(1)). To restore normal user ID privileges, type an **EOF** (*cntrl-d*) to the new shell.

Any additional arguments given on the command line are passed to the program invoked as the shell. When using programs like *sh*(1), an *arg* of the form **−c** *string* executes *string* via the shell and an arg of **−r** will give the user a restricted shell.

The following statements are true only if the optional program named in the shell field of the specified user's password file entry is like *sh*(1). If the first argument to *su* is a −, the environment will be changed to what would be expected if the user actually logged in as the specified user. This is done by invoking the program used as the shell with an *arg0* value whose first character is −, thus causing first the system's profile (**/etc/profile**) and then the specified user's profile (**.profile** in the new HOME directory) to be executed. Otherwise, the environment is passed along with the possible exception of **$PATH**, which is set to **/bin:/etc:/usr/bin** for **root**. Note that if the optional program used as the shell is **/bin/sh**, the user's **.profile** can check *arg0* for **−sh** or **−su** to determine if it was invoked by *login*(1) or *su*(1), respectively. If the user's program is other than **/bin/sh**, then **.profile** is invoked with an *arg0* of *-program* by both *login*(1) and *su*(1).

All attempts to become another user using *su* are logged in the log file **/usr/adm/sulog**.

EXAMPLES

To become user **bin** while retaining your previously exported environment, execute:

```
su bin
```

To become user **bin** but change the environment to what would be expected if **bin** had originally logged in, execute:

```
su - bin
```

To execute *command* with the temporary environment and permissions of user **bin**, type:

su - bin -c "*command args*"

FILES

/etc/passwd	system's password file
/etc/profile	system's profile
$HOME/.profile	user's profile
/usr/adm/sulog	log file

SEE ALSO

env(1), login(1), sh(1) in the *User's Reference Manual*.
passwd(4), profile(4), environ(5) in the *Programmer's Reference Manual*.

NAME

sum − print checksum and block count of a file

SYNOPSIS

sum [**−r**] file

DESCRIPTION

sum calculates and prints a 16-bit checksum for the named file, and also prints the number of blocks in the file. It is typically used to look for bad spots, or to validate a file communicated over some transmission line. The option **−r** causes an alternate algorithm to be used in computing the checksum.

SEE ALSO

wc(1).

DIAGNOSTICS

"Read error" is indistinguishable from end of file on most devices; check the block count.

NAME

sync — update the super block

SYNOPSIS

sync

DESCRIPTION

sync executes the *sync* system primitive. If the system is to be stopped, *sync* must be called to insure file system integrity. It will flush all previously unwritten system buffers out to disk, thus assuring that all file modifications up to that point will be saved. See *sync*(2) for details.

NOTE

If you have done a write to a file on a remote machine in a Remote File Sharing environment, you cannot use *sync* to force buffers to be written out to disk on the remote machine. *sync* will only write local buffers to local disks.

SEE ALSO

sync(2) in the *Programmer's Reference Manual*.

NAME

sysadm – menu interface to do system administration

SYNOPSIS

sysadm [*sub-command*]

DESCRIPTION

This command, when invoked without an argument, presents a menu of system administration sub-commands, from which the user selects. If the optional argument is presented, the named sub-command is run or the named sub-menu is presented.

The *sysadm* command may be given a password. See **admpasswd** in the SUB-COMMANDS section.

SUB-COMMANDS

The following menus of sub-commands are available. (The number of bullets (•) in front of each item indicates the level of the menu or subcommand.)

• diagnostics

system diagnostics menu

These subcommands look for and sometimes repair problems in the system. Those subcommands that issue reports allow you to determine if there are detectable problems. Commands that attempt repair are for repair people only. You must know what you are doing!

• • diskrepair

advice on repair of built-in disk errors

This subcommand advises you on how to go about repairing errors that occur on built-in disks.

WARNING: Because this is a repair function, it should only be performed by qualified service personnel.
NOTE: Reports of disk errors most probably result in the loss of files and/or damage to data. It will be necessary to restore the repaired disk from backup copies.

• • diskreport

report on built-in disk errors

This subcommand shows you if the system has collected any information indicating that there have been errors while reading the built-in disks. You can request either summary or full reports. The summary report provides sufficient information about disk errors to determine if repair should be attempted. If the message no errors logged is part of the report, then there is probably no damage. If a number of errors is reported, there is damage and you should call for service. The full report gives additional detail for the expert repair person trouble shooting complicated problems.

NOTE: Reports of disk errors most probably result in the loss of files and/or damage to data. It will be necessary to restore the repaired disk from backup copies.

• diskmgmt
disk management menu

The subcommands in this menu provide functions for using removable disks. The subcommands include the ability to format disks, copy disks, and to use disks as mountable file systems. It also contains a menu of subcommands for handling non-removable media.

• • checkfsys
check a removable disk file system for errors

Checkfsys checks a file system on a removable disk for errors. If there are errors, this procedure attempts to repair them.

• • cpdisk
make exact copies of a removable disk

This procedure copies the contents of a removable disk into the machine and then allows the user to make exact copies of it. These copies are identical to the original in every way. The copies are made by first reading the original removable disk entirely into the machine and then writing it out onto duplicate disks. The procedure will fail if there is not enough space in the system to hold the original disk.

• • erase
erase data from removable disk

This procedure erases a removable disk by overwriting it with null bytes. The main purpose is to remove data that the user does not want seen. Once performed, this operation is irreversible.

• • format
format new removable disks

Format prepares new removable disks for use. Once formatted, programs and data can be written on the disks.

• • harddisk
hard disk management menu

The subcommands in this menu provide functions for using hard disks. For each hard disk, the disk can be partitioned with default partitioning or the current disk partitioning can be displayed.

• • • display
display hard disk partitioning

Display will allow the user to display the hard disk partitioning. This will inform the user of current disk partitioning information.

• • • partitioning
partition a hard disk

Partitioning configures hard disks. This will allow you to partition a hard disk according to the default partitioning.

• • • rmdisk
remove a hard disk

Removes a hard disk from the system configuration. It may then be physically disconnected (once the machine has been turned off) or freshly partitioned (after the machine has been restarted).

• • makefsys
create a new file system on a removable disk

Makefsys creates a new file system on a removable disk which can then store data which the user does not wish to keep on the hard disk. When "mounted", the file system has all the properties of a file kept on the hard disk, except that it is smaller.

• • mountfsys
mount a removable disk file system

Mountfsys mounts a file system, found on a removable disk, making it available to the user. The file system is unmounted with the "umountfsys" command. THE DISK MUST NOT BE REMOVED WHILE THE FILE SYSTEM IS STILL MOUNTED.
IF THE FILE SYSTEM HAS BEEN MOUNTED WITH THE **mountfsys** COMMAND, IT MUST BE UNMOUNTED WITH **umountfsys**.

• • umountfsys
unmount a removable disk file system

Umountfsys unmounts a file system, allowing the user to remove the disk. THE DISK MUST NOT BE REMOVED UNTIL THE FILE SYSTEM IS UNMOUNTED.
umountfsys MAY ONLY BE USED TO UNMOUNT FILE SYSTEMS MOUNTED WITH THE **mountfsys** COMMAND.

• filemgmt
file management menu

The subcommands in this menu allow the user to protect files on the hard disk file systems by copying them onto diskettes and later restoring them to the hard disk by copying them back. Subcommands are also provided to determine which files might be best kept on diskette based on age or size.

• • backup

backup files from integral hard disk to removable disk or tape

Backup saves copies of files from the integral hard disk file systems to removable disk or tape. There are two kinds of backups:

COMPLETE — copies all files (useful in case of serious file system damage)

INCREMENTAL — copies files changed since the last backup

The normal usage is to do a complete backup of each file system and then periodically do incremental backups. Two cycles are recommended (one set of complete backups and several incrementals to each cycle). Files backed up with "backup" are restored using "restore".

• • bupsched

backup reminder scheduling menu

Backup scheduling is used to schedule backup reminder messages and backup reminder checks. Backup reminder messages are sent to the console to remind the administrator to backup particular file systems when the machine is shutdown or a reminder check has been run during the specified time period.

Backup reminder checks specify particular times at which the system will check to see if any backup reminder messages have been scheduled.

• • • schedcheck

schedule backup reminder checks

Backup reminder checks are run at specific times to check to see if any reminders are scheduled. The user specifies the times at which the check is to be run. Checks are run for the reminder messages scheduled by *schedmsg*.

• • • schedmsg

schedule backup reminder message

Backup reminder messages are sent to the console if the machine is shutdown or a reminder check has been scheduled. The user specifies the times at which it is appropriate to send a message and the file systems to be included in the message.

• • diskuse

display how much of the hard disk is being used

Diskuse lets the user know what percentage of the hard disk is currently occupied by files. The list is organized by file system names.

• • fileage

list files older than a particular date

Fileage prints the names of all files older than the date specified by the user. If no date is entered, all files older than 90 days will be listed. If no directory is specified to look in, the **/usr/admin** directory will be used.

• • filesize

list the largest files in a particular directory

Filesize prints the names of the largest files in a specific directory. If no directory is specified, the **/usr/admin** directory will be used. If the user does not specify how many large files to list, 10 files will be listed.

• • restore

restore files from "backup" and "store" media to integral hard disk

Restore copies files from disks and tapes made by "backup" and "store" back onto the hard disk. You can restore individual files, directories of files, or the entire contents of a disk or tape. The user can restore from both "incremental" and "complete" media. The user can also list the names of files stored on the disk or tape.

• • store

store files and directories of files onto disk or tape

Store copies files from the integral hard disk to disk or tape and allows the user to optionally verify that they worked and to optionally remove them when done. Typically, these would be files that the user wants to archive or restrict access to. The user can store single files and directories of files. Use the "restore" command to put stored files back on the integral hard disk and to list the files stored.

• machinemgmt

machine management menu

Machine management functions are tools used to operate the machine, e.g., turn it off, reboot, or go to the firmware monitor.

• • autold

set automatic boot device, default manual boot program

This procedure specifies the default manual program to boot from firmware and/or the device to be used when automatically rebooting.

• • firmware

stop all running programs then enter firmware mode

This procedure will stop all running programs, close any open files, write out information to the disk (such as directory information), then enter the firmware mode. (Machine diagnostics and other special functions that are not available on the UNIX system.)

• • floppykey

create a "floppy key" removable disk

The "floppy key" removable disk allows the user to enter firmware mode if the firmware password has been changed and then forgotten. Thus the "floppy key" is just that, the "key" to the system and should be protected as such.

• • powerdown

stop all running programs, then turn off the machine

Powerdown will stop all running programs, close any open files, write out information to disk (such as directory information), then turn the machine power off.

• • reboot

stop all running programs then reboot the machine

Reboot will stop all running programs, close any open files, write out information to disk (such as directory information), then reboot the machine. This can be used to get out of some types of system trouble, such as when a process cannot be killed.

• • whoson

print list of users currently logged onto the system

Whoson prints the login ID, terminal device number, and sign-on time of all users who are currently using the computer.

• packagemgmt

package management

These submenus and subcommands manage various software and hardware packages that you install on your machine. Not all optional packages add subcommands here.

• softwaremgmt
software management menu

These subcommands permit the user to install new software, remove software, and run software directly from the removable disk it is delivered on. The "remove" and "run" capabilities are dependent on the particular software packages. See the instructions delivered with each package.

• • installpkg
install new software package onto integral hard disk

Install copies files from removable disk onto the integral hard disk and performs additional work if necessary so that the software can be run. From then on, the user will have access to those commands.

• • listpkg
list packages already installed

This subcommand show you a list of currently installed optional software packages.

• • removepkg
remove previously installed package from integral hard disk

This subcommand displays a list of currently installed optional software packages. Actions necessary to remove the software packages specified by the user will then be performed. The removable disk used to "installpkg" the software is needed to remove it.

• • runpkg
run software package without installing it

This package allows the user to run software from a removable disk without installing it permanently on the system. This is useful if the user does not use the software often or does not have enough room on the system. WARNING: Not all software packages have the ability to run their contents this way. See the instructions that come with the software package.

• syssetup
system setup menu

System setup routines allow the user to tell the computer what its environment looks like: what the date, time, and time zone is, what administration and system capabilities are to be under password control, what the machine's name is, etc. The first-time setup sequence is also here.

• • admpasswd

assign or change administrative passwords

Admpasswd lets you set or make changes to passwords for administrative commands and logins such as setup and sysadm.

• • datetime

set the date, time, time zone, and daylight savings time

Datetime tells the computer the date, time, time zone, and whether you observe Daylight Savings Time (DST). It is normally run once when the machine is first set up. If you observe DST, the computer will automatically start to observe it in the spring and return to Standard Time in the fall. The machine has to be turned off and turned back on again to guarantee that ALL times will be reported correctly. Most are correct the next time the user logs in.

• • nodename

set the node name of this machine

This allows you to change the node name of this machine. The node name is used by various communications networks to identify this machine.

• • setup

set up your machine the very first time

Setup allows the user to define the first login, to set the passwords on the user-definable administration logins and to set the time zone for your location.

• • syspasswd

assign system passwords

Syspasswd lets the user set system passwords normally reserved for the very knowledgeable user. For this reason, this procedure may assign those passwords, but may not change or clear them. Once set, they may only be changed by the specific login or the "root" login.

• ttymgmt

terminal management

This procedure allows the user to manage the computer's terminal functions.

• • lineset

show tty line settings and hunt sequences

The tty line settings are often hunt sequences where, if the first line setting does not work, the line "hunts" to the next line setting until one that does work comes by. This subcommand shows the various sequences with only specific line settings in them. It also shows each line setting in detail.

• • mklineset

create new tyy line settings and hunt sequences

This subcommand helps you to create tty line setting entries. You might want to add line settings that are not in the current set or create hunt sequences with only specific line settings in them. The created hunt sequences are circular; stepping past the last setting puts you on the first.

• • modtty

show and optionally modify characteristics of tty lines

This subcommand reports and allows you to change the characteristics of tty lines (also called "ports").

• usermgmt

user management menu

These subcommands allow you to add, modify and delete the list of users that have access to your machine. You can also place them in separate groups so that they can share access to files within the group but protect themselves from other groups.

• • addgroup

add a group to the system

Addgroup adds a new group name or ID to the computer. Group names and IDs are used to identify groups of users who desire common access to a set of files and directories.

• • adduser

add a user to the system

Adduser installs a new login ID on the machine. You are asked a series of questions about the user and then the new entry is made. You can enter more than one user at a time. Once this procedure is finished, the new login ID is available.

• • delgroup

delete a group from the system

Delgroup allows you to remove groups from the computer. The deleted group is no longer identified by name. However, files may still be identified with the group ID number.

• • deluser

delete a user from the system

Deluser allows you to remove users from the computer. The deleted user's files are removed from the hard disk and their logins are removed from the **/etc/passwd** file.

• • lsgroup
list groups in the system

Lsgroup will list all the groups that have been entered into the computer. This list is updated automatically by "addgroup" and "delgroup"

• • lsuser
list users in the system

Lsuser will list all the users that have been entered into the computer. This list is updated automatically by "adduser" and "deluser".

• • modadduser
modify defaults used by adduser

Modadduser allows the user to change some of the defaults used when adduser creates a new login. Changing the defaults does not effect any existing logins, only logins made from this point on.

• • modgroup
make changes to a group on the system

Modgroup allows the user to change the name of a group that the user enters when "addgroup" is run to set up new groups.

• • moduser
menu of commands to modify a user's login

This menu contains commands that modify the various aspects of a user's login.

• • • chgloginid
change a user's login ID

This procedure allows the user to change a user's login ID. Administrative and system logins cannot be changed.

• • • chgpasswd
change a user's passwd

This proceudure allows removal or change of a suer's password. Administrative and system login passwords channot be changed. To change administrative and system login passwords, see the system setup menu: sysadm syssetup.

• • • chgshell
change a user's login shell

This procedure allows the user to change the command run when a user logs in. The login shell of the administrative and system logins cannot be changed by this procedure.

EXAMPLES

sysadm adduser

FILES

The files that support *sysadm* are found in **/usr/admin**.

The menu starts in directory **/usr/admin/menu**.

NAME

tabs – set tabs on a terminal

SYNOPSIS

tabs [tabspec] [–**T**type] [+**m**n]

DESCRIPTION

tabs sets the tab stops on the user's terminal according to the tab specification *tabspec*, after clearing any previous settings. The user's terminal must have remotely-settable hardware tabs.

tabspec Four types of tab specification are accepted for *tabspec*. They are described below: canned (–*code*), repetitive (–*n*), arbitrary (*n1,n2,...*), and file (––*file*). If no *tabspec* is given, the default value is **–8**, i.e., UNIX system "standard" tabs. The lowest column number is 1. Note that for *tabs*, column 1 always refers to the leftmost column on a terminal, even one whose column markers begin at 0, e.g., the DASI 300, DASI 300s, and DASI 450.

–*code* Use one of the codes listed below to select a *canned* set of tabs. The legal codes and their meanings are as follows:

–a 1,10,16,36,72
Assembler, IBM S/370, first format

–a2 1,10,16,40,72
Assembler, IBM S/370, second format

–c 1,8,12,16,20,55
COBOL, normal format

–c2 1,6,10,14,49
COBOL compact format (columns 1-6 omitted). Using this code, the first typed character corresponds to card column 7, one space gets you to column 8, and a tab reaches column 12. Files using this tab setup should include a format specification as follows (see *fspec*(4)):

<:t–c2 m6 s66 d:>

–c3 1,6,10,14,18,22,26,30,34,38,42,46,50,54,58,62,67
COBOL compact format (columns 1-6 omitted), with more tabs than **–c2.** This is the recommended format for COBOL. The appropriate format specification is (see *fspec*(4)):

<:t–c3 m6 s66 d:>

–f 1,7,11,15,19,23
FORTRAN

–p 1,5,9,13,17,21,25,29,33,37,41,45,49,53,57,61
PL/I

–s 1,10,55
SNOBOL

–u 1,12,20,44
UNIVAC 1100 Assembler

−*n* A *repetitive* specification requests tabs at columns 1+*n*, 1+2**n*, etc. Of particular importance is the value **8**: this represents the UNIX system "standard" tab setting, and is the most likely tab setting to be found at a terminal. Another special case is the value **0**, implying no tabs at all.

n1,n2,... The *arbitrary* format permits the user to type any chosen set of numbers, separated by commas, in ascending order. Up to 40 numbers are allowed. If any number (except the first one) is preceded by a plus sign, it is taken as an increment to be added to the previous value. Thus, the formats **1,10,20,30**, and **1,10,+10,+10** are considered identical.

−−*file* If the name of a *file* is given, *tabs* reads the first line of the file, searching for a format specification (see *fspec*(4)). If it finds one there, it sets the tab stops according to it, otherwise it sets them as **−8**. This type of specification may be used to make sure that a tabbed file is printed with correct tab settings, and would be used with the *pr*(1) command:

tabs −− file; **pr** file

Any of the following also may be used; if a given flag occurs more than once, the last value given takes effect:

−T*type* *tabs* usually needs to know the type of terminal in order to set tabs and always needs to know the type to set margins. *type* is a name listed in *term*(5). If no **−T** flag is supplied, *tabs* uses the value of the environment variable **TERM**. If **TERM** is not defined in the *environment* (see *environ*(5)), *tabs* tries a sequence that will work for many terminals.

+m*n* The margin argument may be used for some terminals. It causes all tabs to be moved over *n* columns by making column *n+1* the left margin. If **+m** is given without a value of *n*, the value assumed is **10**. For a TermiNet, the first value in the tab list should be **1**, or the margin will move even further to the right. The normal (leftmost) margin on most terminals is obtained by **+m0**. The margin for most terminals is reset only when the **+m** flag is given explicitly.

Tab and margin setting is performed via the standard output.

EXAMPLES

tabs −a example using −*code* (*canned* specification) to set tabs to the settings required by the IBM assembler: columns 1, 10, 16, 36, 72.

tabs −8 example of using −*n* (*repetitive* specification), where *n* is **8**, causes tabs to be set every eighth position:
1+(1*8), 1+(2*8), ... which evaluate to columns 9, 17, ...

tabs 1,8,36 example of using *n1,n2,...* (*arbitrary* specification) to set tabs at columns 1, 8, and 36.

tabs −−$HOME/fspec.list/att4425
example of using −−*file* (*file* specification) to indicate that tabs should be set according to the first line of *$HOME/fspec.list/att4425* (see *fspec*(4)).

DIAGNOSTICS

illegal tabs	when arbitrary tabs are ordered incorrectly
illegal increment	when a zero or missing increment is found in an arbitrary specification
unknown tab code	when a *canned* code cannot be found
can't open	if −−*file* option used, and file can't be opened
file indirection	if −−*file* option used and the specification in that file points to yet another file. Indirection of this form is not permitted

SEE ALSO

newform(1), pr(1), tput(1).
fspec(4), terminfo(4), environ(5), term(5) in the *Programmer's Reference Manual.*

NOTE

There is no consistency among different terminals regarding ways of clearing tabs and setting the left margin.

tabs clears only 20 tabs (on terminals requiring a long sequence), but is willing to set 64.

WARNING

The *tabspec* used with the *tabs* command is different from the one used with the *newform*(1) command. For example, **tabs −8** sets every eighth position; whereas **newform −i−8** indicates that tabs are set every eighth position.

NAME

tail − deliver the last part of a file

SYNOPSIS

tail [±[number][**lbc**[**f**]]] [file]

DESCRIPTION

tail copies the named file to the standard output beginning at a designated place. If no file is named, the standard input is used.

Copying begins at distance *+number* from the beginning, or *−number* from the end of the input (if *number* is null, the value 10 is assumed). *Number* is counted in units of lines, blocks, or characters, according to the appended option **l**, **b**, or **c**. When no units are specified, counting is by lines.

With the **−f** ("follow") option, if the input file is not a pipe, the program will not terminate after the line of the input file has been copied, but will enter an endless loop, wherein it sleeps for a second and then attempts to read and copy further records from the input file. Thus it may be used to monitor the growth of a file that is being written by some other process. For example, the command:

```
tail −f fred
```

will print the last ten lines of the file **fred**, followed by any lines that are appended to **fred** between the time *tail* is initiated and killed. As another example, the command:

```
tail −15cf fred
```

will print the last 15 characters of the file **fred**, followed by any lines that are appended to **fred** between the time *tail* is initiated and killed.

SEE ALSO

dd(1M).

BUGS

Tails relative to the end of the file are stored in a buffer, and thus are limited in length. Various kinds of anomalous behavior may happen with character special files.

WARNING

The *tail* command will only tail the last 4096 bytes of a file regardless of its line count.

NAME

tar − tape file archiver

SYNOPSIS

/etc/tar −c[vwfb[#*s*]] *device block files ...*
/etc/tar −r[vwb[#*s*]] *device block [files ...]*
/etc/tar −t[vf[#*s*] *device*
/etc/tar −u[vwb[#*s*]] *device block [files ...]*
/etc/tar −x[lmovwf[#*s*]] *device [files ...]*

DESCRIPTION

tar saves and restores files on magnetic tape. Its actions are controlled by the *key* argument. The *key* is a string of characters containing one function letter (c, r, t, u, or x) and possibly followed by one or more function modifiers (v, w, f, b, and #). Other arguments to the command are *files* (or directory names) specifying which files are to be dumped or restored. In all cases, appearance of a directory name refers to the files and (recursively) subdirectories of that directory.

The function portion of the key is specified by one of the following letters:

r Replace. The named *files* are written on the end of the tape. The **c** function implies this function.

x Extract. The named *files* are extracted from the tape. If a named file matches a directory whose contents had been written onto the tape, this directory is (recursively) extracted. Use the file or directory's relative path when appropriate, or *tar* will not find a match. The owner, modification time, and mode are restored (if possible). If no *files* argument is given, the entire content of the tape is extracted. Note that if several files with the same name are on the tape, the last one overwrites all earlier ones.

t Table. The names and other information for the specified files are listed each time that they occur on the tape. The listing is similar to the format produced by the *ls -l* command. If no *files* argument is given, all the names on the tape are listed.

u Update. The named *files* are added to the tape if they are not already there, or have been modified since last written on that tape. This key implies the **r** key.

c Create a new tape; writing begins at the beginning of the tape, instead of after the last file. This key implies the **r** key.

The characters below may be used in addition to the letter that selects the desired function. Use them in the order shown in the synopsis. **Note**: the only applicable device information for the 3B 2 Computer is as follows:

/dev/mt/ctape [12...]

#s This modifier determines the drive on which the tape is mounted (replace # with the drive number) and the speed of the drive (replace **s** with **l**, **m**, or **h** for low, medium or high). The modifier tells *tar* to use a drive other than the default drive, or the drive specified with the -f option. For example, with the **5h** modifier, *tar* would use /dev/mt/5h or /dev/mt0 instead of the default drives /dev/mt/0m or /dev/mt0,

respectively. However, if for example, "-f /dev/rmt0 5h" appeared on the command line, *tar* would use /dev/rmt5h or /devmt0. The default entry is **0m**.

v Verbose. Normally, *tar* does its work silently. The **v** (verbose) option causes it to type the name of each file it treats, preceded by the function letter. With the **t** function, **v** gives more information about the tape entries than just the name.

w What. This causes *tar* to print the action to be taken, followed by the name of the file, and then wait for the user's confirmation. If a word beginning with **y** is given, the action is performed. Any other input means "no". This is not valid with the **t** key.

f File. This causes *tar* to use the *device* argument as the name of the archive instead of /dev/mt/0m or /dev/mt0. If the name of the file is –, *tar* writes to the standard output or reads from the standard input, whichever is appropriate. Thus, *tar* can be used as the head or tail of a pipeline. *tar* can also be used to move hierarchies with the command:

```
cd fromdir; tar cf - . | (cd todir; tar xf -)
```

b Blocking Factor. This causes *tar* to use the *block* argument as the blocking factor for tape records. The default is 1, the maximum is 20. This function should not be supplied when operating on regular archives or block special devices. It is mandatory however, when reading archives on raw magnetic tape archives (see **f** above). The block size is determined automatically when reading tapes created on block special devices (key letters **x** and **t**).

l Link. This tells *tar* to complain if it cannot resolve all of the links to the files being dumped. If **l** is not specified, no error messages are printed.

m Modify. This tells *tar* to not restore the modification times. The modification time of the file will be the time of extraction.

o Ownership. This causes extracted files to take on the user and group identifier of the user running the program, rather than those on tape. This is only valid with the **x** key.

FILES

/dev/mt/*
/dev/mt*
/tmp/tar*
/dev/mt/ctape
/dev/mt/0m
/dev/rmt/0m

SEE ALSO

ar(1), cpio(1), ls(1).

DIAGNOSTICS

Complaints about bad key characters and tape read/write errors.
Complaints if enough memory is not available to hold the link tables.

BUGS

There is no way to ask for the *n*-th occurrence of a file.
Tape errors are handled ungracefully.
The **u** option can be slow.
The **b** option should not be used with archives that are going to be updated. The current magnetic tape driver cannot backspace raw magnetic tape. If the archive is on a disk file, the **b** option should not be used at all, because updating an archive stored on disk can destroy it.
The current limit on file name length is 100 characters.
tar doesn't copy empty directories or special files.

NAME

tee – pipe fitting

SYNOPSIS

tee [**–i**] [**–a**] [file] ...

DESCRIPTION

tee transcribes the standard input to the standard output and makes copies in the *files*. The

–i ignore interrupts;

–a causes the output to be appended to the *files* rather than overwriting them.

NAME

test — condition evaluation command

SYNOPSIS

test expr

[expr **]**

DESCRIPTION

test evaluates the expression *expr* and, if its value is true, sets a zero (true) exit status; otherwise, a non-zero (false) exit status is set; *test* also sets a non-zero exit status if there are no arguments. When permissions are tested, the effective user ID of the process is used.

All operators, flags, and brackets (brackets used as shown in the second SYNOPSIS line) must be separate arguments to the *test* command; normally these items are separated by spaces.

The following primitives are used to construct *expr*:

−r *file* true if *file* exists and is readable.

−w *file* true if *file* exists and is writable.

−x *file* true if *file* exists and is executable.

−f *file* true if *file* exists and is a regular file.

−d *file* true if *file* exists and is a directory.

−c *file* true if *file* exists and is a character special file.

−b *file* true if *file* exists and is a block special file.

−p *file* true if *file* exists and is a named pipe (fifo).

−u *file* true if *file* exists and its set-user-ID bit is set.

−g *file* true if *file* exists and its set-group-ID bit is set.

−k *file* true if *file* exists and its sticky bit is set.

−s *file* true if *file* exists and has a size greater than zero.

−t [*fildes*] true if the open file whose file descriptor number is *fildes* (1 by default) is associated with a terminal device.

−z *s1* true if the length of string *s1* is zero.

−n *s1* true if the length of the string *s1* is non-zero.

s1 **=** *s2* true if strings *s1* and *s2* are identical.

s1 **!=** *s2* true if strings *s1* and *s2* are *not* identical.

s1 true if *s1* is *not* the null string.

n1 **−eq** *n2* true if the integers *n1* and *n2* are algebraically equal. Any of the comparisons **−ne**, **−gt**, **−ge**, **−lt**, and **−le** may be used in place of **−eq**.

These primaries may be combined with the following operators:

! unary negation operator.

−a binary *and* operator.

−o binary *or* operator (**−a** has higher precedence than **−o**).

(expr **)** parentheses for grouping. Notice also that parentheses are meaningful to the shell and, therefore, must be quoted.

SEE ALSO

find(1), sh(1).

WARNING

If you test a file you own (the *-r*, *-w*, or *-x* tests), but the permission tested does not have the *owner* bit set, a non-zero (false) exit status will be returned even though the file may have the *group* or *other* bit set for that permission. The correct exit status will be set if you are super-user.

The = and **!=** operators have a higher precedence than the **−r** through **−n** operators, and = and **!=** always expect arguments; therefore, = and **!=** cannot be used with the **−r** through **−n** operators.

If more than one argument follows the **−r** through **−n** operators, only the first argument is examined; the others are ignored, unless a **−a** or a **−o** is the second argument.

NAME

time − time a command

SYNOPSIS

time command

DESCRIPTION

The *command* is executed; after it is complete, *time* prints the elapsed time during the command, the time spent in the system, and the time spent in execution of the command. Times are reported in seconds.

The times are printed on standard error.

SEE ALSO

times(2) in the *Programmer's Reference Manual.*

NAME

timex – time a command; report process data and system activity

SYNOPSIS

timex [options] command

DESCRIPTION

The given *command* is executed; the elapsed time, user time and system time spent in execution are reported in seconds. Optionally, process accounting data for the *command* and all its children can be listed or summarized, and total system activity during the execution interval can be reported.

The output of *timex* is written on standard error.

Options are:

–p List process accounting records for *command* and all its children. Suboptions **f, h, k, m, r,** and **t** modify the data items reported. The options are as follows:

- **–f** Print the *fork/exec* flag and system exit status columns in the output.
- **–h** Instead of mean memory size, show the fraction of total available CPU time consumed by the process during its execution. This "hog factor" is computed as:
  (total CPU time)/(elapsed time).
- **–k** Instead of memory size, show total kcore-minutes.
- **–m** Show mean core size (the default).
- **–r** Show CPU factor (user time/(system-time + user-time).
- **–t** Show separate system and user CPU times. The number of blocks read or written and the number of characters transferred are always reported.

–o Report the total number of blocks read or written and total characters transferred by *command* and all its children.

–s Report total system activity (not just that due to *command*) that occurred during the execution interval of *command*. All the data items listed in *sar*(1) are reported.

SEE ALSO

sar(1).

WARNING

Process records associated with *command* are selected from the accounting file **/usr/adm/pacct** by inference, since process genealogy is not available. Background processes having the same user-id, terminal-id, and execution time window will be spuriously included.

EXAMPLES

A simple example:

```
timex −ops sleep 60
```

A terminal session of arbitrary complexity can be measured by timing a sub-shell:

```
timex −opskmt sh
        session commands
EOT
```

NAME

toc: dtoc, ttoc, vtoc − graphical table of contents routines

SYNOPSIS

dtoc [directory]
ttoc mm-file
vtoc [−**cdhnimsv**n] [TTOC file]

DESCRIPTION

All of the commands listed below reside in **/usr/bin/graf** (see *graphics*(1G)).

dtoc Dtoc makes a textual table of contents, TTOC, of all subdirectories beginning at *directory* (*directory* defaults to **.**). The list has one entry per directory. The entry fields from left to right are level number, directory name, and the number of ordinary readable files in the directory. *Dtoc* is useful in making a visual display of all or parts of a file system. The following will make a visual display of all the readable directories under **/**:

dtoc / | vtoc | td

ttoc Output is the table of contents generated by the .TC macro of *mm*(1) translated to TTOC format. The input is assumed to be an *mm* file that uses the .H family of macros for section headers (see the DOCUMENTER'S WORKBENCH Software). If no *file* is given, the standard input is assumed.

vtoc *Vtoc* produces a GPS describing a hierarchy chart from a TTOC. The output drawing consists of boxes containing text connected in a tree structure. If no *file* is given, the standard input is assumed. Each TTOC entry describes one box and has the form:

id [*line-weight,line-style*] "*text*" [*mark*]

where:

id is an alternating sequence of numbers and dots. The *id* specifies the position of the entry in the hierarchy. The *id* **0.** is the root of the tree.

line-weight is either:

n, normal-weight; or
m, medium-weight; or
b, bold-weight.

line-style is either:

so, solid-line;
do, dotted-line;
dd, dot-dash line;
da, dashed-line; or
ld, long-dashed

text is a character string surrounded by quotes. The characters between the quotes become the contents of the box. To include a quote within a box it must be escaped (\").

mark is a character string (surrounded by quotes if it contains spaces), with included dots being escaped. The string is put above the top right corner of the box. To include either a quote or a dot within a *mark* it must be escaped.

Entry example: 1.1 b,da "ABC" DEF
Entries may span more than one line by escaping the new-line (**new-line**).

Comments are surrounded by the /*,*/ pair. They may appear anywhere in a TTOC.

Options:

c Use text as entered (default is all upper case).

d Connect the boxes with diagonal lines.

h*n* Horizontal interbox space is *n*% of box width.

i Suppress the box *id*.

m Suppress the box *mark*.

s Do not compact boxes horizontally.

v*n* Vertical interbox space is *n*% of box height.

SEE ALSO

graphics(1G).
gps(4) in the *Programmer's Reference Manual.*
mm(1) in the *DOCUMENTER'S WORKBENCH Software Release 2.0 Technical Discussion and Reference Manual.*

NAME

touch − update access and modification times of a file

SYNOPSIS

touch [**−amc**] [mmddhhmm[yy]] files

DESCRIPTION

touch causes the access and modification times of each argument to be updated. The file name is created if it does not exist. If no time is specified (see *date*(1)) the current time is used. The **−a** and **−m** options cause touch to update only the access or modification times respectively (default is **−am**). The **−c** option silently prevents *touch* from creating the file if it did not previously exist.

The return code from *touch* is the number of files for which the times could not be successfully modified (including files that did not exist and were not created).

SEE ALSO

date(1).
utime(2) in the *Programmer's Reference Manual*.

NAME

tplot − graphics filters

SYNOPSIS

tplot [−**T**terminal [−**e** raster]]

DESCRIPTION

These commands read plotting instructions (see *plot*(4)) from the standard input and in general produce, on the standard output, plotting instructions suitable for a particular *terminal*. If no *terminal* is specified, the environment parameter **$TERM** (see *environ*(5)) is used. Known *terminal*s are:

300	DASI 300.
300S	DASI 300s.
450	DASI 450.
4014	Tektronix 4014.
ver	Versatec D1200A. This version of *plot* places a scan-converted image in **/usr/tmp/raster$$** and sends the result directly to the plotter device, rather than to the standard output. The −**e** option causes a previously scan-converted file *raster* to be sent to the plotter.

FILES

/usr/lib/t300
/usr/lib/t300s
/usr/lib/t450
/usr/lib/t4014
/usr/lib/vplot
/usr/tmp/raster$$

SEE ALSO

plot(3X), plot(4), term(5) in the *Programmer's Reference Manual.*

NAME

tput – initialize a terminal or query terminfo database

SYNOPSIS

tput [–Ttype] capname [parms ...]

tput [–Ttype] **init**

tput [–Ttype] **reset**

tput [–Ttype] **longname**

DESCRIPTION

tput uses the *terminfo*(4) database to make the values of terminal-dependent capabilities and information available to the shell (see *sh*(1)), to initialize or reset the terminal, or return the long name of the requested terminal type. *tput* outputs a string if the attribute (*cap*ability *name*) is of type string, or an integer if the attribute is of type integer. If the attribute is of type boolean, *tput* simply sets the exit code (**0** for TRUE if the terminal has the capability, **1** for FALSE if it does not), and produces no output. Before using a value returned on standard output, the user should test the exit code ($?, see *sh*(1)) to be sure it is **0**. (See **EXIT CODES** and **DIAGNOSTICS** below.) For a complete list of capabilities and the *capname* associated with each, see *terminfo*(4).

–T*type* indicates the *type* of terminal. Normally this option is unnecessary, because the default is taken from the environment variable **TERM.** If **–T** is specified, then the shell variables **LINES** and **COLUMNS** and the layer size (see *layers*(1)) will not be referenced.

capname indicates the attribute from the *terminfo*(4) database.

parms If the attribute is a string that takes parameters, the arguments *parms* will be instantiated into the string. An all numeric argument will be passed to the attribute as a number.

init If the *terminfo*(4) database is present and an entry for the user's terminal exists (see –T*type*, above), the following will occur: (1) if present, the terminal's initialization strings will be output (**is1**, **is2**, **is3**, **if**, **iprog**), (2) any delays (e.g., newline) specified in the entry will be set in the tty driver, (3) tabs expansion will be turned on or off according to the specification in the entry, and (4) if tabs are not expanded, standard tabs will be set (every 8 spaces). If an entry does not contain the information needed for any of the four above activities, that activity will silently be skipped.

reset Instead of putting out initialization strings, the terminal's reset strings will be output if present (**rs1**, **rs2**, **rs3**, **rf**). If the reset strings are not present, but initialization strings are, the initialization strings will be output. Otherwise, **reset** acts identically to **init**.

longname If the *terminfo*(4) database is present and an entry for the user's terminal exists (see −T*type* above), then the long name of the terminal will be put out. The long name is the last name in the first line of the terminal's description in the *terminfo*(4) database (see *term*(5)).

EXAMPLES

tput init Initialize the terminal according to the type of terminal in the environmental variable **TERM**. This command should be included in everyone's .profile after the environmental variable **TERM** has been exported, as illustrated on the *profile*(4) manual page.

tput −T5620 reset Reset an AT&T 5620 terminal, overriding the type of terminal in the environmental variable **TERM**.

tput cup 0 0 Send the sequence to move the cursor to row **0**, column **0** (the upper left corner of the screen, usually known as the "home" cursor position).

tput clear Echo the clear-screen sequence for the current terminal.

tput cols Print the number of columns for the current terminal.

tput -T450 cols Print the number of columns for the 450 terminal.

bold='tput smso'

offbold='tput rmso'

Set the shell variables **bold**, to begin stand-out mode sequence, and **offbold**, to end standout mode sequence, for the current terminal. This might be followed by a prompt:
echo "${bold}Please type in your name: ${offbold}\c"

tput hc Set exit code to indicate if the current terminal is a hardcopy terminal.

tput cup 23 4 Send the sequence to move the cursor to row 23, column 4.

tput longname Print the long name from the *terminfo*(4) database for the type of terminal specified in the environmental variable **TERM**.

FILES

/usr/lib/terminfo/?/*	compiled terminal description database
/usr/include/curses.h	*curses*(3X) header file
/usr/include/term.h	*terminfo*(4) header file
/usr/lib/tabset/*	tab settings for some terminals, in a format appropriate to be output to the terminal (escape sequences that set margins and tabs); for more information, see the "Tabs and Initialization" section of *terminfo*(4)

SEE ALSO

stty (1), tabs (1).
profile(4), terminfo(4) in the *Programmer's Reference Manual*.
Chapter 10 of the *Programmer's Guide*.

EXIT CODES

If *capname* is of type boolean, a value of **0** is set for TRUE and **1** for FALSE.

If *capname* is of type string, a value of **0** is set if the *capname* is defined for this terminal *type* (the value of *capname* is returned on standard output); a value of **1** is set if *capname* is not defined for this terminal *type* (a null value is returned on standard output).

If *capname* is of type integer, a value of **0** is always set, whether or not *capname* is defined for this terminal *type*. To determine if *capname* is defined for this terminal *type*, the user must test the value of standard output. A value of **−1** means that *capname* is not defined for this terminal *type*.

Any other exit code indicates an error; see **DIAGNOSTICS**, below.

DIAGNOSTICS

tput prints the following error messages and sets the corresponding exit codes.

exit code	error message
0	−1 (*capname* is a numeric variable that is not specified in the *terminfo*(4) database for this terminal type, e.g. **tput −T450 lines** and **tput −T2621 xmc**)
1	no error message is printed, see **EXIT CODES**, above.
2	usage error
3	unknown terminal *type* or no *terminfo*(4) database
4	unknown *terminfo*(4) capability *capname*

NAME

tr − translate characters

SYNOPSIS

tr [**−cds**] [string1 [string2]]

DESCRIPTION

tr copies the standard input to the standard output with substitution or deletion of selected characters. Input characters found in *string1* are mapped into the corresponding characters of *string2*. Any combination of the options **−cds** may be used:

−c Complements the set of characters in *string1* with respect to the universe of characters whose ASCII codes are 001 through 377 octal.

−d Deletes all input characters in *string1*.

−s Squeezes all strings of repeated output characters that are in *string2* to single characters.

The following abbreviation conventions may be used to introduce ranges of characters or repeated characters into the strings:

[a−z] Stands for the string of characters whose ASCII codes run from character **a** to character **z**, inclusive.

[a*n] Stands for *n* repetitions of **a**. If the first digit of *n* is **0**, *n* is considered octal; otherwise, *n* is taken to be decimal. A zero or missing *n* is taken to be huge; this facility is useful for padding *string2*.

The escape character \ may be used as in the shell to remove special meaning from any character in a string. In addition, \ followed by 1, 2, or 3 octal digits stands for the character whose ASCII code is given by those digits.

EXAMPLE

The following example creates a list of all the words in *file1* one per line in *file2*, where a word is taken to be a maximal string of alphabetics. The strings are quoted to protect the special characters from interpretation by the shell; 012 is the ASCII code for newline.

```
tr −cs "[A−Z][a−z]" "[\012*]" <file1 >file2
```

SEE ALSO

ed(1), sh(1).
ascii(5) in the *Programmer's Reference Manual*.

BUGS

Will not handle ASCII **NUL** in *string1* or *string2*; always deletes **NUL** from input.

NAME

true, false – provide truth values

SYNOPSIS

true

false

DESCRIPTION

true does nothing, successfully. *False* does nothing, unsuccessfully. They are typically used in input to *sh*(1) such as:

```
while true
do
        command
done
```

SEE ALSO

sh(1).

DIAGNOSTICS

true has exit status zero, *false* nonzero.

NAME

tty – get the name of the terminal

SYNOPSIS

tty [**–l**] [**–s**]

DESCRIPTION

tty prints the path name of the user's terminal.

–l prints the synchronous line number to which the user's terminal is connected, if it is on an active synchronous line.

–s inhibits printing of the terminal path name, allowing one to test just the exit code.

EXIT CODES

2 if invalid options were specified,
0 if standard input is a terminal,
1 otherwise.

DIAGNOSTICS

"not on an active synchronous line" if the standard input is not a synchronous terminal and **–l** is specified.
"not a tty" if the standard input is not a terminal and **–s** is not specified.

NAME

umask – set file-creation mode mask

SYNOPSIS

umask [ooo]

DESCRIPTION

The user file-creation mode mask is set to *ooo*. The three octal digits refer to read/write/execute permissions for *owner*, *group*, and *others*, respectively (see *chmod*(2) and *umask*(2)). The value of each specified digit is subtracted from the corresponding "digit" specified by the system for the creation of a file (see *creat*(2)). For example, **umask 022** removes *group* and *others* write permission (files normally created with mode **777** become mode **755**; files created with mode **666** become mode **644**).

If *ooo* is omitted, the current value of the mask is printed.

umask is recognized and executed by the shell.

umask can be included in the user's **.profile** (see *profile*(4)) and invoked at login to automatically set the user's permissions on files or directories created.

SEE ALSO

chmod(1), sh(1).
chmod(2), creat(2), umask(2), profile(4) in the *Programmer's Reference Manual.*

NAME

uname − print name of current UNIX system

SYNOPSIS

uname [**−snrvma**]
uname [**−S** system name]

DESCRIPTION

uname prints the current system name of the UNIX system on the standard output file. It is mainly useful to determine which system one is using. The options cause selected information returned by *uname*(2) to be printed:

−s print the system name (default).

−n print the nodename (the nodename is the name by which the system is known to a communications network).

−r print the operating system release.

−v print the operating system version.

−m print the machine hardware name.

−a print all the above information.

On the 3B2 computer, the system name and the nodename may be changed by specifying a system name argument to the **−S** option. The system name argument is restricted to 8 characters. Only the super-user is allowed this capability.

SEE ALSO

uname(2) in the *Programmer's Reference Manual.*

NAME

uniq − report repeated lines in a file

SYNOPSIS

uniq [**−udc** [+n] [−n]] [input [output]]

DESCRIPTION

uniq reads the input file comparing adjacent lines. In the normal case, the second and succeeding copies of repeated lines are removed; the remainder is written on the output file. *Input* and *output* should always be different. Note that repeated lines must be adjacent in order to be found; see *sort*(1). If the **−u** flag is used, just the lines that are not repeated in the original file are output. The **−d** option specifies that one copy of just the repeated lines is to be written. The normal mode output is the union of the **−u** and **−d** mode outputs.

The **−c** option supersedes **−u** and **−d** and generates an output report in default style but with each line preceded by a count of the number of times it occurred.

The *n* arguments specify skipping an initial portion of each line in the comparison:

−*n* The first *n* fields together with any blanks before each are ignored. A field is defined as a string of non-space, non-tab characters separated by tabs and spaces from its neighbors.

+*n* The first *n* characters are ignored. Fields are skipped before characters.

SEE ALSO

comm(1), sort(1).

NAME

units − conversion program

SYNOPSIS

units

DESCRIPTION

units converts quantities expressed in various standard scales to their equivalents in other scales. It works interactively in this fashion:

```
You have: inch
You want: cm
        * 2.540000e+00
        / 3.937008e−01
```

A quantity is specified as a multiplicative combination of units optionally preceded by a numeric multiplier. Powers are indicated by suffixed positive integers, division by the usual sign:

```
You have: 15 lbs force/in2
You want: atm
        * 1.020689e+00
        / 9.797299e−01
```

units only does multiplicative scale changes; thus it can convert Kelvin to Rankine, but not Celsius to Fahrenheit. Most familiar units, abbreviations, and metric prefixes are recognized, together with a generous leavening of exotica and a few constants of nature including:

pi	ratio of circumference to diameter,
c	speed of light,
e	charge on an electron,
g	acceleration of gravity,
force	same as **g**,
mole	Avogadro's number,
water	pressure head per unit height of water,
au	astronomical unit.

Pound is not recognized as a unit of mass; **lb** is. Compound names are run together, (e.g., **lightyear**). British units that differ from their U.S. counterparts are prefixed thus: **brgallon**. For a complete list of units, type:

```
cat /usr/lib/unittab
```

FILES

/usr/lib/unittab

NAME

usage – retrieve a command description and usage examples

SYNOPSIS

[**help**] **usage** [**−d**] [**−e**] [**−o**] [command_name]

DESCRIPTION

The UNIX system Help Facility command *usage* retrieves information about UNIX system commands. With no argument, *usage* displays a menu screen prompting the user for the name of a command, or allows the user to retrieve a list of commands supported by *usage*. The user may also exit to the shell by typing q (for "quit).

After a command is selected, the user is asked to choose among a description of the command, examples of typical usage of the command, or descriptions of the command's options. Then, based on the user's request, the appropriate information will be printed.

A command name may also be entered at shell level as an argument to *usage*. To receive information on the command's description, examples, or options, the user may use the **−d**, **−e**, or **−o** options respectively. (The default option is **−d**.)

From any screen in the Help Facility, a user may execute a command via the shell (*sh*(1)) by typing a ! and the command to be executed. The screen will be redrawn if the command that was executed was entered at a first level prompt. If entered at any other prompt level, only the prompt will be redrawn.

By default, the Help Facility scrolls the data that is presented to the user. If you prefer to have the screen clear before printing the data (non-scrolling), the shell variable **SCROLL** must be set to **no** and exported so it will become part of your environment. This is done by adding the following line to your *.profile* file (see *profile*(4)): "`export SCROLL ; SCROLL=no`". If you later decide that scrolling is desired, **SCROLL** must be set to **yes**.

Information on each of the Help Facility commands (*starter, locate, usage, glossary*, and *help*) is located on their respective manual pages.

SEE ALSO

glossary(1), help(1), locate(1), sh(1), starter(1).
term(5) in the *Programmer's Reference Manual*.

WARNINGS

If the shell variable **TERM** (see *sh*(1)) is not set in the user's *.profile* file, then **TERM** will default to the terminal value type 450 (a hard-copy terminal). For a list of valid terminal types, refer to *term*(5).

NAME

uucp, uulog, uuname − UNIX-to-UNIX system copy

SYNOPSIS

uucp [options] source-files destination-file
uulog [options] **−s**system
uulog [options] system
uulog [options] **−f**system
uuname [**−l**] [**−c**]

DESCRIPTION

uucp

uucp copies files named by the *source-file* arguments to the *destination-file* argument. A file name may be a path name on your machine, or may have the form:

system-name!path-name

where *system-name* is taken from a list of system names that *uucp* knows about. The *system-name* may also be a list of names such as

system-name!system-name!...!system-name!path-name

in which case an attempt is made to send the file via the specified route, to the destination. See WARNINGS and BUGS below for restrictions. Care should be taken to ensure that intermediate nodes in the route are willing to foward information (see WARNINGS below for restrictions).

The shell metacharacters **?**, * and **[...]** appearing in *path-name* will be expanded on the appropriate system.

Path names may be one of:

(1) a full path name;

(2) a path name preceded by *~user* where *user* is a login name on the specified system and is replaced by that user's login directory;

(3) a path name preceded by *~/destination* where *destination* is appended to **/usr/spool/uucppublic**; (NOTE: This destination will be treated as a file name unless more than one file is being transfered by this request or the destination is already a directory. To ensure that it is a directory, follow the destination with a '/'. For example ~/dan/ as the destination will make the directory /usr/spool/uucppublic/dan if it does not exist and put the requested file(s) in that directory).

(4) anything else is prefixed by the current directory.

If the result is an erroneous path name for the remote system the copy will fail. If the *destination-file* is a directory, the last part of the *source-file* name is used.

uucp preserves execute permissions across the transmission and gives 0666 read and write permissions (see *chmod*(2)).

The following options are interpreted by *uucp*:

−c Do not copy local file to the spool directory for transfer to the remote machine (default).

−C Force the copy of local files to the spool directory for transfer.

−d Make all necessary directories for the file copy (default).

−f Do not make intermediate directories for the file copy.

−g*grade* *Grade* is a single letter/number; lower ascii sequence characters will cause the job to be transmitted earlier during a particular conversation.

−j Output the job identification ASCII string on the standard output. This job identification can be used by *uustat* to obtain the status or terminate a job.

−m Send mail to the requester when the copy is completed.

−n*user* Notify *user* on the remote system that a file was sent.

−r Do not start the file transfer, just queue the job.

−s*file* Report status of the transfer to *file*. Note that the *file* must be a full path name.

−x*debug_level*
Produce debugging output on standard output. The *debug_level* is a number between 0 and 9; higher numbers give more detailed information. (Debugging will not be available if **uucp** was compiles with -DSMALL.)

uulog

uulog queries a log file of *uucp* or *uuxqt* transactions in a file **/usr/spool/uucp/.Log/uucico/** *system*, or **/usr/spool/uucp/.Log/uuxqt/** *system*.

The options cause *uulog* to print logging information:

−s*sys* Print information about file transfer work involving system *sys*.

−f*system* Does a "tail **−f**" of the file transfer log for *system*. (You must hit BREAK to exit this function.) Other options used in conjunction with the above:

−x Look in the *uuxqt* log file for the given system.

−number Indicates that a "tail" command of *number* lines should be executed.

uuname

uuname lists the names of systems known to *uucp*. The **−c** option returns the names of systems known to *cu*. (The two lists are the same, unless your machine is using different *Systems* files for *cu* and *uucp*. See the *Sysfiles* file.) The **−l** option returns the local system name.

FILES

/usr/spool/uucp	spool directories
/usr/spool/uucppublic/*	public directory for receiving and sending (**/usr/spool/uucppublic**)
/usr/lib/uucp/*	other data and program files

SEE ALSO

mail(1), uustat(1C), uux(1C), uuxqt(1M).
chmod(2) in the *Programmer's Reference Manual.*

WARNINGS

The domain of remotely accessible files can (and for obvious security reasons, usually should) be severely restricted. You will very likely not be able to fetch files by path name; ask a responsible person on the remote system to send them to you. For the same reasons you will probably not be able to send files to arbitrary path names. As distributed, the remotely accessible files are those whose names begin **/usr/spool/uucppublic** (equivalent to ~/).

All files received by *uucp* will be owned by *uucp*.
The **−m** option will only work sending files or receiving a single file. Receiving multiple files specified by special shell characters **? * [...]** will not activate the **−m** option.

The forwarding of files through other systems may not be compatible with the previous version of *uucp*. If forwarding is used, all systems in the route must have the same version of *uucp*.

BUGS

Protected files and files that are in protected directories that are owned by the requestor can be sent by *uucp*. However, if the requestor is root, and the directory is not searchable by "other" or the file is not readable by "other", the request will fail.

NAME

uustat − uucp status inquiry and job control

SYNOPSIS

uustat [**−a**]
uustat [**−m**]
uustat [**−p**]
uustat [**−q**]
uustat [**−k***jobid*]
uustat [**−r***jobid*]
uustat [**−s***system*] [**−u***user*]

DESCRIPTION

uustat will display the status of, or cancel, previously specified *uucp* commands, or provide general status on *uucp* connections to other systems. Only one of the following options can be specified with *uustat* per command execution:

−a Output all jobs in queue.

−m Report the status of accessibility of all machines.

−p Execute a "ps −flp" for all the process-ids that are in the lock files.

−q List the jobs queued for each machine. If a status file exists for the machine, its date, time and status information are reported. In addition, if a number appears in () next to the number of **C** or **X** files, it is the age in days of the oldest **C./X.** file for that system. The Retry field represents the number of hours until the next possible call. The Count is the number of failure attempts. NOTE: for systems with a moderate number of outstanding jobs, this could take 30 seconds or more of real-time to execute. As an example of the output produced by the **−q** option:

```
eagle     3C   04/07-11:07   NO DEVICES AVAILABLE
mh3bs3    2C   07/07-10:42   SUCCESSFUL
```

The above output tells how many command files are waiting for each system. Each command file may have zero or more files to be sent (zero means to call the system and see if work is to be done). The date and time refer to the previous interaction with the system followed by the status of the interaction.

−k*jobid* Kill the *uucp* request whose job identification is *jobid*. The killed *uucp* request must belong to the person issuing the *uustat* command unless one is the super-user.

−r*jobid* Rejuvenate *jobid*. The files associated with *jobid* are touched so that their modification time is set to the current time. This prevents the cleanup daemon from deleting the job until the jobs modification time reaches the limit imposed by the deamon.

Either or both of the following options can be specified with *uustat*:

−s*sys* Report the status of all *uucp* requests for remote system *sys*.
−u*user* Report the status of all *uucp* requests issued by *user*.

Output for both the **−s** and **−u** options has the following format:

```
eaglen0000  4/07-11:01:03       (POLL)
eagleN1bd7  4/07-11:07          Seagledan522 /usr/dan/A
eagleC1bd8  4/07-11:07          Seagledan59 D.3b2al2ce4924
                 4/07-11:07     Seagledanrmail mike
```

With the above two options, the first field is the *jobid* of the job. This is followed by the date/time. The next field is either an 'S' or 'R' depending on whether the job is to send or request a file. This is followed by the user-id of the user who queued the job. The next field contains the size of the file, or in the case of a remote execution (*rmail* - the command used for remote mail), the name of the command. When the size appears in this field, the file name is also given. This can either be the name given by the user or an internal name (e.g., D.3b2alce4924) that is created for data files associated with remote executions (*rmail* in this example).

When no options are given, *uustat* outputs the status of all *uucp* requests issued by the current user.

FILES

/usr/spool/uucp/* spool directories

SEE ALSO

uucp(1C).

NAME

uuto, uupick – public UNIX-to-UNIX system file copy

SYNOPSIS

uuto [options] source-files destination
uupick [**–s** system]

DESCRIPTION

uuto sends *source-files* to *destination*. *uuto* uses the *uucp*(1C) facility to send files, while it allows the local system to control the file access. A source-file name is a path name on your machine. Destination has the form:

system!*user*

where *system* is taken from a list of system names that *uucp* knows about (see *uuname*). *User* is the login name of someone on the specified system.

Two *options* are available:

–p Copy the source file into the spool directory before transmission.
–m Send mail to the sender when the copy is complete.

The files (or sub-trees if directories are specified) are sent to PUBDIR on *system*, where PUBDIR is a public directory defined in the *uucp* source. By default this directory is /usr/spool/uucppublic. Specifically the files are sent to

PUBDIR/receive/*user*/*mysystem*/files.

The destined recipient is notified by *mail*(1) of the arrival of files.

Uupick accepts or rejects the files transmitted to the user. Specifically, *uupick* searches PUBDIR for files destined for the user. For each entry (file or directory) found, the following message is printed on the standard output:

from *system*: [file *file-name*] [dir *dirname*] **?**

Uupick then reads a line from the standard input to determine the disposition of the file:

<new-line> Go on to next entry.

d Delete the entry.

m [*dir*] Move the entry to named directory *dir*. If *dir* is not specified as a complete path name (in which $HOME is legitimate), a destination relative to the current directory is assumed. If no destination is given, the default is the current directory.

a [*dir*] Same as **m** except moving all the files sent from *system*.

p Print the content of the file.

q Stop.

EOT (control-d) Same as **q**.

!*command* Escape to the shell to do *command*.

* Print a command summary.

Uupick invoked with the **-s***system* option will only search the PUBDIR for files sent from *system*.

FILES

PUBDIR /usr/spool/uucppublic   public directory

SEE ALSO

mail(1), uucp(1C), uustat(1C), uux(1C).
uucleanup(1M) in the *System Administrator's Reference Manual.*

WARNINGS

In order to send files that begin with a dot (e.g., .profile) the files must by qualified with a dot. For example: .profile, .prof*, .profil? are correct; whereas *prof*, ?profile are incorrect.

NAME

uux − UNIX-to-UNIX system command execution

SYNOPSIS

uux [options] command-string

DESCRIPTION

uux will gather zero or more files from various systems, execute a command on a specified system and then send standard output to a file on a specified system.

NOTE: For security reasons, most installations limit the list of commands executable on behalf of an incoming request from *uux*, permiting only the receipt of mail (see *mail*(1)). (Remote execution permissions are defined in **/usr/lib/uucp/Permissions**.)

The *command-string* is made up of one or more arguments that look like a shell command line, except that the command and file names may be prefixed by *system-name***!**. A null *system-name* is interpreted as the local system.

File names may be one of

(1) a full path name;

(2) a path name preceded by ~*xxx* where *xxx* is a login name on the specified system and is replaced by that user's login directory;

(3) anything else is prefixed by the current directory.

As an example, the command

uux "!diff usg!/usr/dan/file1 pwba!/a4/dan/file2 > !~/dan/file.diff"

will get the *file1* and *file2* files from the "usg" and "pwba" machines, execute a *diff*(1) command and put the results in *file.diff* in the local PUBDIR/dan/ directory.

Any special shell characters such as **<>;|** should be quoted either by quoting the entire *command-string*, or quoting the special characters as individual arguments.

uux will attempt to get all files to the execution system. For files that are output files, the file name must be escaped using parentheses. For example, the command

uux a!cut -f1 b!/usr/file \(c!/usr/file\)

gets /usr/file from system "b" and sends it to system "a", performs a *cut* command on that file and sends the result of the *cut* command to system "c".

uux will notify you if the requested command on the remote system was disallowed. This notification can be turned off by the **−n** option. The response comes by remote mail from the remote machine.

The following *options* are interpreted by *uux*:

− The standard input to *uux* is made the standard input to the *command-string*.

−**a***name* Use *name* as the user identification replacing the initiator user-id. (Notification will be returned to the user.)

−b Return whatever standard input was provided to the *uux* command if the exit status is non-zero.

−c Do not copy local file to the spool directory for transfer to the remote machine (default).

−C Force the copy of local files to the spool directory for transfer.

−g*grade* *Grade* is a single letter/number; lower ASCII sequence characters will cause the job to be transmitted earlier during a particular conversation.

−j Output the jobid ASCII string on the standard output which is the job identification. This job identification can be used by *uustat* to obtain the status or terminate a job.

−n Do not notify the user if the command fails.

−p Same as −: The standard input to *uux* is made the standard input to the *command-string*.

−r Do not start the file transfer, just queue the job.

−s*file* Report status of the transfer in *file*.

−x*debug_level*
Produce debugging output on the standard output. The *debug_level* is a number between 0 and 9; higher numbers give more detailed information.

−z Send success notification to the user.

FILES

/usr/lib/uucp/spool spool directories
/usr/lib/uucp/Permissions
remote execution permissions
/usr/lib/uucp/* other data and programs

SEE ALSO

cut(1), mail(1), uucp(1C), uustat(1C).

WARNINGS

Only the first command of a shell pipeline may have a *system-name*!. All other commands are executed on the system of the first command.
The use of the shell metacharacter * will probably not do what you want it to do. The shell tokens << and >> are not implemented.

The execution of commands on remote systems takes place in an execution directory known to the *uucp* system. All files required for the execution will be put into this directory unless they already reside on that machine. Therefore, the simple file name (without path or machine reference) must be unique within the *uux* request. The following command will NOT work:

```
uux "a!diff b!/usr/dan/xyz c!/usr/dan/xyz > !xyz.diff"
```

but the command

```
uux "a!diff a!/usr/dan/xyz c!/usr/dan/xyz > !xyz.diff"
```

will work. (If *diff* is a permitted command.)

BUGS

Protected files and files that are in protected directories that are owned by the requestor can be sent in commands using *uux*. However, if the requestor is root, and the directory is not searchable by "other", the request will fail.

NAME

vi — screen-oriented (visual) display editor based on ex

SYNOPSIS

vi [**−t** *tag*] [**−r** *file*] [**−w***n*] [**−R**] [**−x**] [+*command*] *name* ...
view [**-t** *tag*] [**−r** *file*] [**−w***n*] [**−R**] [**−x**] [+*command*] *name*
vedit [**−t** *tag*] [**−r** *file*] [**−w***n*] [**−R**] [**−x**] [+*command*] *name*

DESCRIPTION

vi (visual) is a display-oriented text editor based on an underlying line editor *ex*(1). It is possible to use the command mode of *ex* from within *vi* and vice-versa.

When using *vi*, changes you make to the file are reflected in what you see on your terminal screen. The position of the cursor on the screen indicates the position within the file.

INVOCATION

The following invocation options are interpreted by *vi*:

−t *tag* — Edit the file containing the *tag* and position the editor at its definition.

−r*file* — Recover *file* after an editor or system crash. If *file* is not specified a list of all saved files will be printed.

−w*n* — Set the default window size to *n*. This is useful when using the editor over a slow speed line.

−R — Read only mode; the **readonly** flag is set, preventing accidental overwriting of the file.

+*command* — The specified *ex* command is interpreted before editing begins.

−x — Encryption option; when this option is used, the file will be encrypted as it is being written and will require an encryption key to be read (see *crypt*(1)). Also, see the **WARNING** section at the end of this manual page.

The *name* argument indicates files to be edited.

The *view* invocation is the same as *vi* except that the **readonly** flag is set.

The *vedit* invocation is intended for beginners. The **report** flag is set to 1, and the **showmode** and **novice** flags are set. These defaults make it easier to get started learning the editor.

VI MODES

Command — Normal and initial mode. Other modes return to command mode upon completion. ESC (escape) is used to cancel a partial command.

Input — Entered by the following options **a i A I o O c C s S R**. Arbitrary text may then be entered. Input mode is normally terminated with ESC character, or abnormally with interrupt.

Last line — Reading input for : / ? or !; terminate with CR to execute, interrupt to cancel.

COMMAND SUMMARY

Sample commands

← ↓ ↑ →	arrow keys move the cursor
h j k l	same as arrow keys
i*text*ESC	insert text *abc*
cw*new*ESC	change word to *new*
ea*s*ESC	pluralize word
x	delete a character
dw	delete a word
dd	delete a line
3dd	... 3 lines
u	undo previous change
ZZ	exit vi, saving changes
:q!CR	quit, discarding changes
/*text***CR**	search for *text*
^U ^D	scroll up or down
:*ex cmd***CR**	any ex or ed command

Counts before vi commands

Numbers may be typed as a prefix to some commands. They are interpreted in one of these ways.

line/column number	**z G |**
scroll amount	**^D ^U**
repeat effect	most of the rest

Interrupting, canceling

ESC	end insert or incomplete cmd
DEL	(delete or rubout) interrupts
^L	reprint screen if DEL scrambles it
^R	reprint screen if ^L is → key

File manipulation

:wCR	write back changes
:qCR	quit
:q!CR	quit, discard changes
:e *name***CR**	edit file *name*
:e!CR	reedit, discard changes
:e + *name***CR**	edit, starting at end
:e +*n***CR**	edit starting at line *n*
:e #CR	edit alternate file
	synonym for **:e #**

:w *name***CR**	write file *name*
:w! *name***CR**	overwrite file *name*
:shCR	run shell, then return
:!*cmd***CR**	run *cmd*, then return
:nCR	edit next file in arglist
:n *args***CR**	specify new arglist
^G	show current file and line
:ta *tag***CR**	to tag file entry *tag*
^]	**:ta**, following word is *tag*

In general, any *ex* or *ed* command (such as *substitute* or *global*) may be typed, preceded by a colon and followed by a **CR**.

Positioning within file

^F	forward screen
^B	backward screen
^D	scroll down half screen
^U	scroll up half screen
G	go to specified line (end default)
/*pat*	next line matching *pat*
?*pat*	prev line matching *pat*
n	repeat last / or **?**
N	reverse last / or **?**
/*pat*/+*n*	nth line after *pat*
?*pat*?−*n*	nth line before *pat*
]]	next section/function
[[	previous section/function
(	beginning of sentence
)	end of sentence
{	beginning of paragraph
}	end of paragraph
%	find matching **( )** { or }

Adjusting the screen

^L	clear and redraw
^R	retype, eliminate @ lines
zCR	redraw, current at window top
z−CR	... at bottom
z.CR	... at center
/*pat*/**z−CR**	*pat* line at bottom
z*n***.CR**	use *n* line window
^E	scroll window down 1 line
^Y	scroll window up 1 line

Marking and returning

``	move cursor to previous context
''	... at first non-white in line
m*x*	mark current position with letter *x*
`*x*	move cursor to mark *x*
'*x*	... at first non-white in line

Line positioning

H	top line on screen
L	last line on screen
M	middle line on screen
+	next line, at first non-white
–	previous line, at first non-white
CR	return, same as +
↓ or **j**	next line, same column
↑ or **k**	previous line, same column

Character positioning

^	first non white
0	beginning of line
$	end of line
h or →	forward
l or ←	backwards
^**H**	same as ←
space	same as →
f*x*	find *x* forward
F*x*	**f** backward
t*x*	upto *x* forward
T*x*	back upto *x*
;	repeat last **f F t** or **T**
,	inverse of ;
|	to specified column
%	find matching **(** { **)** or }

Words, sentences, paragraphs

w	word forward
b	back word
e	end of word
)	to next sentence
}	to next paragraph
(	back sentence
{	back paragraph
W	blank delimited word
B	back **W**
E	to end of **W**

Corrections during insert

^H	erase last character
^W	erase last word
erase	your erase, same as **^H**
kill	your kill, erase input this line
\	quotes **^H**, your erase and kill
ESC	ends insertion, back to command
DEL	interrupt, terminates insert
^D	backtab over *autoindent*
↑^D	kill *autoindent*, save for next
0^D	... but at margin next also
^V	quote non-printing character

Insert and replace

a	append after cursor
i	insert before cursor
A	append at end of line
I	insert before first non-blank
o	open line below
O	open above
r*x*	replace single char with *x*
R*text***ESC**	replace characters

Operators

Operators are followed by a cursor motion, and affect all text that would have been moved over. For example, since **w** moves over a word, **dw** deletes the word that would be moved over. Double the operator, e.g., **dd** to affect whole lines.

d	delete
c	change
y	yank lines to buffer
<	left shift
>	right shift
!	filter through command
=	indent for LISP

Miscellaneous Operations

C	change rest of line (**c$**)
D	delete rest of line (**d$**)
s	substitute chars (**cl**)
S	substitute lines (**cc**)
J	join lines
x	delete characters (**dl**)
X	... before cursor (**dh**)
Y	yank lines (**yy**)

Yank and Put

Put inserts the text most recently deleted or yanked. However, if a buffer is named, the text in that buffer is put instead.

p	put back text after cursor
P	put before cursor
"*x***p**	put from buffer *x*
"*x***y**	yank to buffer *x*
"*x***d**	delete into buffer *x*

Undo, Redo, Retrieve

u	undo last change
U	restore current line
.	repeat last change
"*d***p**	retrieve *d*'th last delete

AUTHOR

vi and *ex* were developed by The University of California, Berkeley California, Computer Science Division, Department of Electrical Engineering and Computer Science.

FILES

/usr/lib/terminfo/?/* compiled terminal description database
/usr/lib/.COREterm/?/* subset of compiled terminal description database, supplied on hard disk d

SEE ALSO

ed(1), edit(1), ex(1).
User's Guide.
Editing Guide.

WARNING

The **−x** option is provided with the Security Administration Utilities, which is available only in the United States.

Tampering with entries in */usr/lib/.COREterm/?/** or */usr/lib/terminfo/?/** (for example, changing or removing an entry) can affect programs such as *vi*(1) that expect the entry to be present and correct. In particular, removing the "dumb" terminal may cause unexpected problems.

BUGS

Software tabs using **^T** work only immediately after the *autoindent*.

Left and right shifts on intelligent terminals do not make use of insert and delete character operations in the terminal.

NAME

wait – await completion of process

SYNOPSIS

wait [*n*]

DESCRIPTION

Wait for your background process whose process id is *n* and report its termination status. If *n* is omitted, all your shell's currently active background processes are waited for and the return code will be zero.

The shell itself executes *wait*, without creating a new process.

SEE ALSO

sh(1).

CAVEAT

If you get the error message *cannot fork, too many processes*, try using the *wait*(1) command to clean up your background processes. If this doesn't help, the system process table is probably full or you have too many active foreground processes. (There is a limit to the number of process ids associated with your login, and to the number the system can keep track of.)

BUGS

Not all the processes of a 3- or more-stage pipeline are children of the shell, and thus cannot be waited for.

If *n* is not an active process id, all your shell's currently active background processes are waited for and the return code will be zero.

NAME

wall – write to all users

SYNOPSIS

/etc/wall

DESCRIPTION

wall reads its standard input until an end-of-file. It then sends this message to all currently logged-in users preceded by:

Broadcast Message from ...

It is used to warn all users, typically prior to shutting down the system.

The sender must be super-user to override any protections the users may have invoked (see *mesg*(1)).

FILES

/dev/tty*

SEE ALSO

mesg(1), write(1).

DIAGNOSTICS

"Cannot send to ..." when the open on a user's tty file fails.

NAME

wc − word count

SYNOPSIS

wc [**−lwc**] [names]

DESCRIPTION

wc counts lines, words, and characters in the named files, or in the standard input if no *names* appear. It also keeps a total count for all named files. A word is a maximal string of characters delimited by spaces, tabs, or new-lines.

The options **l**, **w**, and **c** may be used in any combination to specify that a subset of lines, words, and characters are to be reported. The default is **−lwc**.

When *names* are specified on the command line, they will be printed along with the counts.

NAME

who − who is on the system

SYNOPSIS

who [**−uTlHqpdbrtas**] [file]

who am i

who am I

DESCRIPTION

who can list the user's name, terminal line, login time, elapsed time since activity occurred on the line, and the process-ID of the command interpreter (shell) for each current UNIX system user. It examines the **/etc/utmp** file at login time to obtain its information. If *file* is given, that file (which must be in *utmp*[4] format) is examined. Usually, *file* will be **/etc/wtmp**, which contains a history of all the logins since the file was last created.

who with the **am i** or **am I** option identifies the invoking user.

The general format for output is:

name [state] line time [idle] [pid] [comment] [exit]

The *name, line,* and *time* information is produced by all options except **−q**; the *state* information is produced only by **−T**; the *idle* and *pid* information is produced only by **−u** and **−l**; and the *comment* and *exit* information is produced only by **−a**. The information produced for **−p**, **−d**, and **−r** is explained during the discussion of each option, below.

With options, *who* can list logins, logoffs, reboots, and changes to the system clock, as well as other processes spawned by the *init* process. These options are:

−u This option lists only those users who are currently logged in. The *name* is the user's login name. The *line* is the name of the line as found in the directory **/dev**. The *time* is the time that the user logged in. The *idle* column contains the number of hours and minutes since activity last occurred on that particular line. A dot (**.**) indicates that the terminal has seen activity in the last minute and is therefore "current". If more than twenty-four hours have elapsed or the line has not been used since boot time, the entry is marked **old**. This field is useful when trying to determine whether a person is working at the terminal or not. The *pid* is the process-ID of the user's shell. The *comment* is the comment field associated with this line as found in **/etc/inittab** (see *inittab*[4]). This can contain information about where the terminal is located, the telephone number of the dataset, type of terminal if hard-wired, etc.

−T This option is the same as the **−s** option, except that the *state* of the terminal line is printed. The *state* describes whether someone else can write to that terminal. A + appears if the terminal is writable by anyone; a − appears if it is not. **root** can write to all lines having a + or a − in the *state* field. If a bad line is encountered, a **?** is printed.

−l This option lists only those lines on which the system is waiting for someone to login. The *name* field is **LOGIN** in such cases. Other fields are the same as for user entries except that the *state* field does not exist.

−H This option will print column headings above the regular output.

−q This is a quick *who*, displaying only the names and the number of users currently logged on. When this option is used, all other options are ignored.

−p This option lists any other process which is currently active and has been previously spawned by *init*. The *name* field is the name of the program executed by *init* as found in **/etc/inittab**. The *state*, *line*, and *idle* fields have no meaning. The *comment* field shows the *id* field of the line from **/etc/inittab** that spawned this process. See *inittab*(4).

−d This option displays all processes that have expired and not been respawned by *init*. The *exit* field appears for dead processes and contains the termination and exit values (as returned by *wait*[2]), of the dead process. This can be useful in determining why a process terminated.

−b This option indicates the time and date of the last reboot.

−r This option indicates the current *run-level* of the *init* process. In addition, it produces the process termination status, process id, and process exit status (see *utmp*(4)) under the *idle*, *pid*, and *comment* headings, respectively.

−t This option indicates the last change to the system clock (via the *date*[1] command) by **root**. See *su*(1).

−a This option processes **/etc/utmp** or the named *file* with all options turned on.

−s This option is the default and lists only the *name*, *line*, and *time* fields.

Note to the super-user: after a shutdown to the single-user state, *who* returns a prompt; the reason is that since **/etc/utmp** is updated at login time and there is no login in single-user state, *who* cannot report accurately on this state. *who am i*, however, returns the correct information.

FILES

/etc/utmp
/etc/wtmp
/etc/inittab

SEE ALSO

date(1), login(1), mesg(1), su(1M).
init(1M) in the *System Administrator's Reference Manual*.
wait(2), inittab(4), utmp(4) in the *Programmer's Reference Manual*.

NAME

write – write to another user

SYNOPSIS

write user [line]

DESCRIPTION

write copies lines from your terminal to that of another user. When first called, it sends the message:

Message from *yourname* **(tty??)** [*date*]...

to the person you want to talk to. When it has successfully completed the connection, it also sends two bells to your own terminal to indicate that what you are typing is being sent.

The recipient of the message should write back at this point. Communication continues until an end of file is read from the terminal, an interrupt is sent, or the recipient has executed "mesg n". At that point *write* writes **EOT** on the other terminal and exits.

If you want to write to a user who is logged in more than once, the *line* argument may be used to indicate which line or terminal to send to (e.g., **tty00**); otherwise, the first writable instance of the user found in **/etc/utmp** is assumed and the following message posted:

user is logged on more than one place.
You are connected to "*terminal*".
Other locations are:
terminal

Permission to write may be denied or granted by use of the *mesg(1)* command. Writing to others is normally allowed by default. Certain commands, such as *pr*(1) disallow messages in order to prevent interference with their output. However, if the user has super-user permissions, messages can be forced onto a write-inhibited terminal.

If the character **!** is found at the beginning of a line, *write* calls the shell to execute the rest of the line as a command.

The following protocol is suggested for using *write*: when you first *write* to another user, wait for them to *write* back before starting to send. Each person should end a message with a distinctive signal (i.e., **(o)** for "over") so that the other person knows when to reply. The signal **(oo)** (for "over and out") is suggested when conversation is to be terminated.

FILES

/etc/utmp   to find user
/bin/sh   to execute **!**

SEE ALSO

mail(1), mesg(1), pr(1), sh(1), who(1).

DIAGNOSTICS

"user is not logged on" if the person you are trying to *write* to is not logged on.
"Permission denied" if the person you are trying to *write* to denies that permission (with *mesg*).

"Warning: cannot respond, set mesg -y" if your terminal is set to *mesg n* and the recipient cannot respond to you.

"Can no longer write to user" if the recipient has denied permission (*mesg n*) after you had started writing.

NAME

xargs − construct argument list(s) and execute command

SYNOPSIS

xargs [flags] [command [initial-arguments]]

DESCRIPTION

xargs combines the fixed *initial-arguments* with arguments read from standard input to execute the specified *command* one or more times. The number of arguments read for each *command* invocation and the manner in which they are combined are determined by the flags specified.

command, which may be a shell file, is searched for, using one's **$PATH**. If *command* is omitted, **/bin/echo** is used.

Arguments read in from standard input are defined to be contiguous strings of characters delimited by one or more blanks, tabs, or new-lines; empty lines are always discarded. Blanks and tabs may be embedded as part of an argument if escaped or quoted. Characters enclosed in quotes (single or double) are taken literally, and the delimiting quotes are removed. Outside of quoted strings a backslash (\) will escape the next character.

Each argument list is constructed starting with the *initial-arguments*, followed by some number of arguments read from standard input (Exception: see **−i** flag). Flags **−i**, **−l**, and **−n** determine how arguments are selected for each command invocation. When none of these flags are coded, the *initial-arguments* are followed by arguments read continuously from standard input until an internal buffer is full, and then *command* is executed with the accumulated args. This process is repeated until there are no more args. When there are flag conflicts (e.g., **−l** vs. **−n**), the last flag has precedence. *Flag* values are:

−l*number* *command* is executed for each non-empty *number* lines of arguments from standard input. The last invocation of *command* will be with fewer lines of arguments if fewer than *number* remain. A line is considered to end with the first new-line *unless* the last character of the line is a blank or a tab; a trailing blank/tab signals continuation through the next non-empty line. If *number* is omitted, 1 is assumed. Option **−x** is forced.

−i*replstr* Insert mode: *command* is executed for each line from standard input, taking the entire line as a single arg, inserting it in *initial-arguments* for each occurrence of *replstr*. A maximum of 5 arguments in *initial-arguments* may each contain one or more instances of *replstr*. Blanks and tabs at the beginning of each line are thrown away. Constructed arguments may not grow larger than 255 characters, and option **−x** is also forced. {} is assumed for *replstr* if not specified.

−n*number* Execute *command* using as many standard input arguments as possible, up to *number* arguments maximum. Fewer arguments will be used if their total size is greater than *size* characters, and for the last invocation if there are fewer than *number* arguments remaining. If option **−x** is also coded, each *number* arguments must fit in the *size* limitation, else *xargs* terminates execution.

−t Trace mode: The *command* and each constructed argument list are echoed to file descriptor 2 just prior to their execution.

−p Prompt mode: The user is asked whether to execute *command* each invocation. Trace mode (**−t**) is turned on to print the command instance to be executed, followed by a **?...** prompt. A reply of **y** (optionally followed by anything) will execute the command; anything else, including just a carriage return, skips that particular invocation of *command*.

−x Causes *xargs* to terminate if any argument list would be greater than *size* characters; **−x** is forced by the options **−i** and **−l**. When neither of the options **−i**, **−l**, or **−n** are coded, the total length of all arguments must be within the *size* limit.

−s*size* The maximum total size of each argument list is set to *size* characters; *size* must be a positive integer less than or equal to 470. If **−s** is not coded, 470 is taken as the default. Note that the character count for *size* includes one extra character for each argument and the count of characters in the command name.

−e*eofstr* *eofstr* is taken as the logical end-of-file string. Underbar (_) is assumed for the logical **EOF** string if **−e** is not coded. The value **−e** with no *eofstr* coded turns off the logical **EOF** string capability (underbar is taken literally). *xargs* reads standard input until either end-of-file or the logical **EOF** string is encountered.

xargs will terminate if either it receives a return code of **−1** from, or if it cannot execute, *command*. When *command* is a shell program, it should explicitly *exit* (see *sh*(1)) with an appropriate value to avoid accidentally returning with **−1**.

EXAMPLES

The following will move all files from directory $1 to directory $2, and echo each move command just before doing it:

```
ls $1 | xargs −i −t mv $1/{} $2/{}
```

The following will combine the output of the parenthesized commands onto one line, which is then echoed to the end of file *log*:

```
(logname; date; echo $0 $*) | xargs >>log
```

The user is asked which files in the current directory are to be archived and archives them into *arch* (1.) one at a time, or (2.) many at a time.

1. ls | xargs −p −l ar r arch
2. ls | xargs −p −l | xargs ar r arch

The following will execute *diff*(1) with successive pairs of arguments originally typed as shell arguments:

echo $* | xargs −n2 diff

SEE ALSO

sh(1).

Index to Utilities

■ Editing Utilities

■ Essential Utilities

■ Graphics Utilities

■ Help Utilities

■ Inter-process Communications Utilities

■ Line Printer Spooling Utilities

TEAR OUT THIS PAGE TO ORDER ADDITIONAL COPIES OF THIS TITLE AS WELL AS COPIES OF THE OTHER VOLUMES IN THE PRENTICE HALL/AT&T UNIX® SYSTEM V RELEASE 3.0 SERIES

QUANTITY	TITLE/AUTHOR	ISBN	PRICE	TOTAL
______	UNIX® System V Utilities Release Notes, AT&T	013–940552–6	$21.95	______
______	UNIX® System V Programmer's Reference Manual, AT&T	013–940479–1	$34.95	______
______	UNIX® System V Network Programmer's Guide, AT&T	013–940461–9	$24.95	______
______	UNIX® System V Streams Programmer's Guide, AT&T	013–940537–2	$24.95	______
______	UNIX® System V Streams Primer, AT&T	013–940529–1	$21.95	______
______	UNIX® System V User's Reference Manual, AT&T	013–940487–2	$34.95	______
______	UNIX® System V User's Guide, 2nd Ed., AT&T	013–940545–3	$24.95	______
______	UNIX® System V Programmer's Guide, AT&T	013–940438–4	$34.95	______

TOTAL $______
–DISCOUNT (IF APPROPRIATE) ______
NEW TOTAL $______

AND TAKE ADVANTAGE OF THESE SPECIAL OFFERS!

When ordering 3 or 4 copies (of the same or different titles) take 10% off the total list price.

When ordering 5 to 20 copies (of the same or different titles) take 15% off the total list price.

To receive a greater discount when ordering more than 20 copies, call or write: Special Sales Department, College Marketing, Prentice Hall, Englewood Cliffs, N.J. 07632 (201–592–2406).

SAVE!

If payment accompanies order, plus your state's sales tax where applicable, Prentice Hall pays postage and handling charges. Same return privilege refund guaranteed. Please do not mail in cash.

☐ **PAYMENT ENCLOSED**—shipping and handling to be paid by publisher (please include your state's tax where applicable).

☐ **SEND BOOKS ON 15-DAY TRIAL BASIS** & bill me (with small charge for shipping and handling).

Name ______

Address ______

City ______ State ______ Zip ______

I prefer to charge my ☐ Visa ☐ MasterCard

Card Number ______ Expiration Date ______

Signature ______

All prices listed are subject to change without notice.
OFFER NOT VALID OUTSIDE U.S.

MAIL YOUR ORDER TO: Prentice Hall Book Distribution Center, Route 59 at Brook Hill Drive, West Nyack, NY 10994

EPT. 1

D–JSAR–RO(3)